# Connections and Reflections on Culture and the Arts

## A Textbook for HUM2410— Arts and Humanities I

## Preliminary Edition

*North Carolina Central University*

**KENDALL/HUNT PUBLISHING COMPANY**
4050 Westmark Drive    Dubuque, Iowa  52002

Special thanks to . . .

The Arts and Humanities Committee

Stephanie Freeman, Editor
Janice Dargan
Ben DeVan
Dawn Formey
Timothy Holley
Chad Hughes
Sonya Joyner
Helen Othow
Michele Patterson
Brennetta Simpson
Kongite Wessene
Carlton Wilson
Grover Wilson

You helped to shape and develop this course into something dynamic and powerful.
All of you are stellar educators and inspirations. With your guidance, "The Arts and Humanities Program is soaring to new heights of excellence!"

Special thanks to these contributors:
Yvonne Ward and Rodney Dixon, who gave of their time, talent, and knowledge to develop the DVD for this course.

Antonio Wallace, whose excellent photography brought some of NCCU's artwork to life.
Chad Hughes, who shared some of his art and, therefore, some of his heart with us.
The faculty, staff, and students of North Carolina Central University.

Cover images of female, Monet painting, and "Drama" copyright © 2006 JupiterImages Corporation.

Cover images of man, horn, and background wave copyright © 2006 Digital Vision.

# Contents

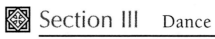 Section III   Dance                                     127

Section IV   Art Criticism                                  211

# SECTION 1

# Religion

# Introduction to World Religions: An Outline and Research Guide

*Carol Bartunek*

 Hinduism

### BEGINNING OF HINDUISM

#### *1800 B.C.E.*

- Aryan people—fair skinned
- Originally from central Eurasia—nomadic
- Migrated down into the Northwestern part of the Indian subcontinent
  - Migrations lasted for a thousand years
  - Some migrated west into Greece and Europe

### PRE-ARYAN

#### *The Indian sub-continent was populated by a dark-skinned people who are referred to as* **Dravidians.**

- Not nomadic
- Agricultural
- Advanced civilization
- Major cities
  - Mohenjo-Daro
  - Harappa
  - Language—Type of pictographic writing (as yet undeciphered)
- Religion of the Dravidians
  - various statues
  - buildings

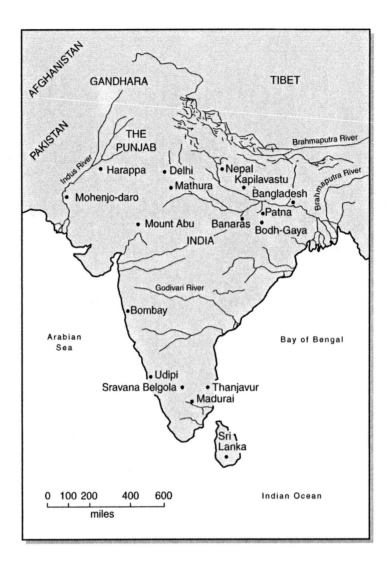

## Aryan Conquest

### Aryans = "Noble Ones"
- First to tame horses
- Fair-complected; related to *Hyskos*
- Related to the Celtic
- Middle East (6th–4th centuries)
- Settled in Persia—Euptus Valley. Later, lands west of Persia—named Iran, or, "The Land of the Aryans"

### 1800s migrated to India
When Aryans arrived—found Dravidian (Native Indian) culture deteriorating

Aryan chiefs or leaders called *Rajas*

By 6th century, Aryans settled in India

| CASTES in order of rank | The "Twice-Born" Aryan Castes | | | Non-Aryan excluded from "Twice-Born" religion | Excluded even by Shudras |
|---|---|---|---|---|---|
| | **BRAHMIN**<br>*Priests*<br>Teachers<br>Advisors to<br>rulers | **KSHATRIYA**<br>*Rulers*<br>Kings, princes<br>warriors | **VAISHYA**<br>*"The People"*<br>Agriculturalists<br>Merchants<br>Traders | **SHUDRA**<br>*Servants* of the<br>upper 3 castes<br>Gardeners<br>Musicians<br>Artisans<br>Barbers | **OUTCASTE**<br>Street-<br>sweepers,<br>leather-<br>workers |
| | Influenced by WORLD-AFFIRMING Vedic views | | | Influenced by WORLD-NEGATING Jain and Buddhist views | All non-Hindus are excluded also |
| **STAGES OF LIFE** | **STUDENT**<br>Clothing,<br>subjects, length of<br>schooling<br>differ for each<br>caste | **HOUSEHOLDER**<br>All are obligated<br>to marry and start<br>a household | **RETIRED PERSON**<br>"Forest Dweller"<br>Hermit | **ASCETIC**<br>Not a "stage"<br>Anyone at any time<br>may become<br>an ascetic | |
| **GOALS OF LIFE** | **DHARMA**<br>*Virtues*<br>Caste-related<br>duties, both<br>social and ritual,<br>morality | **ARTHA**<br>*Material Success*<br>The attaining of<br>wealth and power | **KAMA**<br>*Pleasure*<br>Aesthetic enjoy-<br>ment of art,<br>music, sex, dance,<br>poetry, drama | **MOKSHA**<br>*Release* through:<br>Knowledge,<br>Disciplines (yoga),<br>Devotion to gods,<br>Karma-yoga | |

## DEVELOPMENT OF CASTE SYSTEM

### *Word caste = "Varna" or color of skin*
Different types of castes determined one's life

- Religious
- Political
- Economic
- Social

### *Over a period of time, caste system organized into four large groups*
1. Brahmins
2. Kshatriyas
3. Vaishyas
4. Shudras

## ARYAN RELIGION

### Knowledge found in Vidic literature

### Polytheistic
- Gods personified forces of nature (fire, rain, etc.)

### Sacrifice chief manner of worship
- Some human
- Most animal (horse, bull)
- Use of drug called *soma*

## VIDIC ERA

### Vadas
- Sacred scripture of Hinduism
- means "to see" written in Vidic, a type of Sanskrit
- Developed between 1500 B.C.E.–400 B.C.E.
- Transmitted orally at first

### Four Basic Vedic books
1. Rig-Veda
2. Yajur-Veda
3. Sama-Veda
4. Atharva-Veda

### Each of the vedic books is made up of four parts:
1. Mantras
2. Brahmanas
3. Aranyakas
4. Upanishads

### Upanishads
- Concept of Karma
- Word means "To do or to alter"

### Concept of Samsara
- Word means "To wander across"

### Goal of life = Moksha
The code of *Manu*

- The place each group of people have in the circle of life
- Contains four stages of a man's life
- Moral ethics
- Woman's role
- Laws against murder, etc.

- Idea of time
  - Every thing in a state of change
  - Change all the time

### Bhagavad Gita
- Epic poem—great battle between two heroes and gods
- Basic teachings of the Gita

### Post-classical Hinduism
- Start of the division of thousands of gods into a system of gods
- The worship of a few major deities
- Individual devotion to certain gods
- Become devotees
- Temples built
- Gods take various forms—become involved in human affairs
- Given wives
- By devotion to one god, god shows favor

### Three Major Gods
- Divisions of Brahman
  1. Brahma—The Creator
  2. Shiva—The Destroyer
  3. Vishnu—The Preserver

### Another movement
- "Way to knowledge"

## LEVEL II
## LESSER GODS

Asvins—physicians to the gods
Ushas—Dawn Goddess—cows represent day of week
Surya—Sun God—7 horses—day of week
Agni—God of Fire
Indra—God of Firmament (thousand eyes all seeing God)
Chandra—God of the Moon
Vayu—Wind
The Maruts—in charge of storm clouds

## LEVEL III
## LESSER GODS

Yakshinis/Yakshas—demon followers of Kubera—God of Wealth
Ravana—demon king
Rakshasas—followers of Ravana
Manu—old God who survived a flood

**Hindu Divinities**

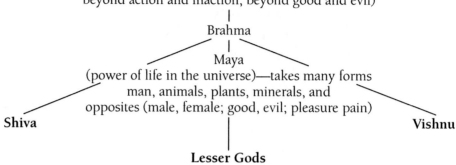

**BRAHMAN**
Referred to as "It" or "That"
(absolute, one, indivisible, unchangeable,
beyond action and inaction, beyond good and evil)

Brahma

Maya
(power of life in the universe)—takes many forms
man, animals, plants, minerals, and
opposites (male, female; good, evil; pleasure pain)

**Shiva**                                                                 **Vishnu**

**Lesser Gods**

**LEVEL I**
MAJOR GODS

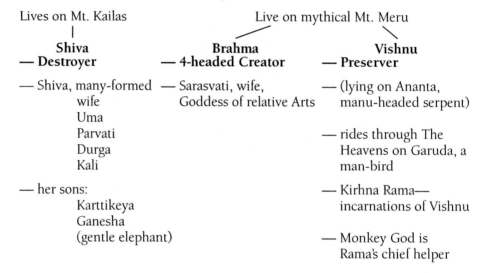

Lives on Mt. Kailas                        Live on mythical Mt. Meru

**Shiva**                    **Brahma**                    **Vishnu**
**— Destroyer**          **— 4-headed Creator**        **— Preserver**

— Shiva, many-formed     — Sarasvati, wife,          — (lying on Ananta,
    wife                     Goddess of relative Arts         manu-headed serpent)
    Uma
    Parvati                                                  — rides through The
    Durga                                                        Heavens on Garuda, a
    Kali                                                         man-bird

— her sons:                                              — Kirhna Rama—
    Karttikeya                                                   incarnations of Vishnu
    Ganesha
    (gentle elephant)                                        — Monkey God is
                                  Rama's chief helper

Soma—God who is the intoxicating juice of the sacred soma plant

Varuna—and the monster fish Makara

Vritra—enemy of the Gods (snake)

Yama—King of Death

Kinnaras—heavenly musicians

Apsarases—water nymphs who tempt ascetics

Nagas—Snake Gods

Vrikshadevatas—kick trees to show that nature has to be stimulated
    before procreation

• Way the wealthy chose to demonstrate their faith

• The study of six systems of philosophy all based on vedas

    1. The Sahkhya system

    2. The Yoga system

    3. The Mimansa system

    4. The Vaisheshika system

## The Hindu Gods

### The gods of the Vedic period

**AGNI**
The life-force of nature. The god of fire and sacrifice.

**INDRA**
The sky-god and god of war.

**VARUNA**
The upholder of the cosmic order, with power to punish and reward.

### The later gods

**BRAHMA-THE CREATOR**
The lord of all creatures. He is above and beyond worship, and there are hardly any temples dedicated to him.

**VISHNU-THE PRESERVER**
The controller of human fate. He draws near to mankind in ten incarnations *(avatars)*. He is generally kindly.

**SHIVA-THE DESTROYER**
The source of both good and evil. The destroyer of life and also the one who recreates new life.

**SARASVATI**
Consort of Brahma. The goddess of knowledge, learning and truth.

**LAKSHMI**
Wife of Vishnu. The goddess of fortune and beauty.

**KALI/DURGA**
Consort of Shiva. The 'great mother'. She is the symbol of judgement and death.

### The ten avatars of Vishnu

**1. MATSYA**
The fish. He appeared at the time of the great flood, to warn mankind.
**2. KURMA**
The tortoise. He rescued treasures from the flood.

**3. VARAHA**
The boar. He raised the earth from the flood.

**4. NARA-SIMHA**
The man-lion. He defeated evil demons.

**5. VAMANA**
The dwarf. He defeated evil demons.

**6. PARUSHA-RAMA**
'Rama with an axe'. He destroyed the members of the Kshatriya warrior-castle who threatened to dominate the world.

**7. RAMA-CHANDRA**
The hero of the Ramayana epic. He was a noble hero who combatted the evil in the world. He is the epitome of virtue.

**8. KRISHNA**
As well as being an avatar of Vishnu, Krishna is a god in his own right, the most popular of all the gods. He is also the hero of many myths, depicted as a lover, a warrior and a king.

**9. BUDDHA**
'The enlightened one'. The ninth avatar is Gautama the Buddha, founder of Buddhism.

**10. KALKI**
The tenth avatar is yet to come.

5. The Nyaya system
6. The Vendata system

## *Major Hinduism*
- Reform movements
  - Suttee
  - Betrothal of children
  - Gandhi
  - Caste system
- Holidays

**The Festivals of Hinduism**

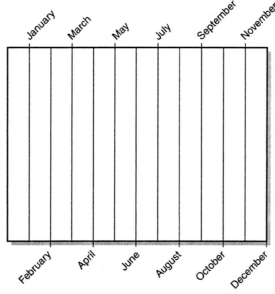

**DIVALI/NEW YEAR**

A festival of lights, when presents are given.
Lakshmi, the goddess of good fortune, visits every house which is lit by a lamp.

**Holi**

A joyful spring festival dedicated to Krishna. Originally a fertility ceremony. It is celebrated with street dancing, processions and bonfires.

**DASARA**

Ten days of celebration in honour of Kali. There are processions, dances and presents are given.

**Local festivals**

There are many festivals specific to certain areas or towns. Some of these are held in honour of the great gods such as Shiva and Sarasvati. Others are the annual festivals of local gods. Relogious pilgrimages often take place at specific times of the year, accompanied by festivities.

 Buddhism

### Beginning of Buddhism
- India—6th century B.C.E.

### Life of Buddha (Gautama)
- Lived 560–480 B.C.E.
- Born in a wealthy family
- Gautama a special baby
  - Legend told about his future
  - Four sights
- Grew up surrounded by beauty
- Well-educated
- Age 30 he became aware of the real world
- Leaves his family is search of the answers to life's misery

### Sought answers
- First through philosophy
- Second through asceticism

### He participated in all kinds of strenuous severe ascetic practices:
- Fasting
- Sitting in painful positions

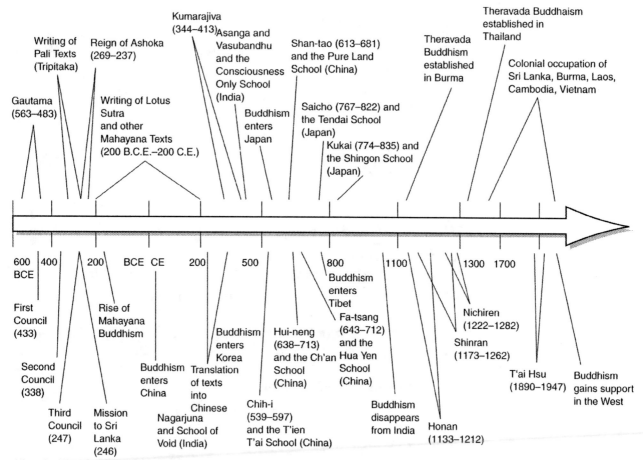

**Historical Developments in Buddhism**

Within the timeline:

Gautama (563–483)

Writing of Pali Texts (Tripitaka)

Reign of Ashoka (269–237)

Writing of Lotus Sutra and other Mahayana Texts (200 B.C.E.–200 C.E.)

Kumarajiva (344–413)

Asanga and Vasubandhu and the Consciousness Only School (India)

Buddhism enters Japan

Shan-tao (613–681) and the Pure Land School (China)

Saicho (767–822) and the Tendai School (Japan)

Kukai (774–835) and the Shingon School (Japan)

Theravada Buddhism established in Burma

Theravada Buddhaism established in Thailand

Colonial occupation of Sri Lanka, Burma, Laos, Cambodia, Vietnam

600 BCE    400    200    BCE    CE    200    500    800    1100    1300    1700

First Council (433)

Second Council (338)

Third Council (247)

Rise of Mahayana Buddhism

Mission to Sri Lanka (246)

Buddhism enters China

Translation of texts into Chinese

Nagarjuna and School of Void (India)

Buddhism enters Korea

Chih-i (539–597) and the T'ien T'ai School (China)

Hui-neng (638–713) and the Ch'an School (China)

Buddhism enters Tibet

Fa-tsang (643–712) and the Hua Yen School (China)

Buddhism disappears from India

Honan (1133–1212)

Shinran (1173–1262)

Nichiren (1222–1282)

T'ai Hsu (1890–1947)

Buddhism gains support in the West

### All in hopes of finding enlightenment

Turning point in his search

- Gives up all the extreme practices
- Turns to meditation

### Upon achieving enlightenment, is called "Buddha" or Enlightened One; he was age 35

### During his meditation he had a vision:

- Cycle of birth and death
- Humans caught in this cycle "Tanha"

### First things Buddha did after enlightenment:

- Return to city; gain followers
- Sangha—monastic order
- Requirements of followers
- Creed

### Teachings of Buddha
- Type of reformed Hinduism
- Rejected vedas
- Animal sacrifice

### Unique teachings
- Anatman
- 4 Noble truths
- Eight-fold path
- Nirvana (arhat)

## DEVELOPMENT OF BUDDHISM

### Shared Hindu belief:
- Goal of life is to be released from the cycle of birth and death
- Release depends upon the works of the individual

### *Today, Buddhism is much different than its earliest beginnings—has become a major world religion*

### *Major changes started less than a year after Buddha's death*
- Fighting over the *real* meaning of his teachings

### Two major councils called
- First one failed
- Second one—390 B.C.E.
- Development of two major groups
  1. Theravada
  2. Mahayana

### Theravada
- More conservative
- Closer to original
- More for priests/monks
- Relics important
- Living quarters of monks

### Mahayana
- Secret teachings
- Gautama more than just a man—he was divine
- Other divine beings
- Development of worship services
- Bodhisaitvas

## The Main Streams
## of Buddhism

The Main Streams
of Buddhism

THERAVADA
The strict "doctrine of the elders"

MAHAYANA
The "large vehicle," accommodating many
different beliefs.

Shinto

Ch'an/Zen

Chinese meditative practice

Vajrayana/Lamaism/Tibetan Buddhism

Tantrism, occult, Tibetan Bon

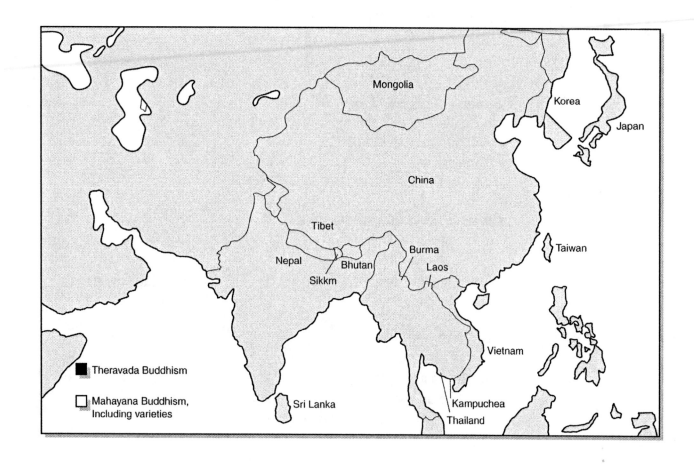

Mongolia

Korea

Japan

China

Tibet

Burma

Taiwan

Nepal

Bhutan

Laos

Sikkm

Vietnam

Theravada Buddhism

Mahayana Buddhism,
Including varieties

Sri Lanka

Kampuchea

Thailand

### The spread of Mahayana Buddhism
- China—1st century C.E.
- Japan—6th century C.E.
- Mongolia/Tibet—end of 6th century (remote development of slightly different traditions)
- India—Buddhism dies out during 11th–13th centuries

## DIFFERENT GROUPS OF BUDDHISM

### Today there are four major groups:
1. Pure—land: (ching-T; U, Jodo)
2. Intuitive: Ch'an/Zen
3. Rationalist: T'ien-T'ai (Tendai)
4. Sociopolitical: Nichiren

### Still another type of Buddhism is Tibetan Buddhism
- Uses recitation of certain phrases, names or magical words

### Tibet—7th century C.E.
- Use of magic as a means of coping with problems of life
- Referred to as *Tantric* (because of manuals they use called *tantras*).
- Use of the word "om"
- Prayer wheel

## LEADERS OR CLERGY

### Lamas—"Superior One"
9th Century B.C.E.
- Development of monasteries
- Land grants
- Monks became rulers of Tibet

### Lamas divided into two orders
1. Yellow hats—largest
   Dalai Lama—Head leader
2. Red hats—Developed scripture: "The Book of the Dead," written in 8th century B.C.E.

### Twentieth Century
- China invades Tibet
- Dalai Lama flees to India
- Still in exile today

## Characteristic of Chinese religion:

- Acceptable to believe in more than one system

## History of religion falls into several broad categories:

1. Polytheistic/Ancestor worship
2. Aware of one supreme god—Chou Dynasty—era of Lao-Tzu
3. Development of Taoism
4. Synthesis among Buddhism, Taoism and Confucianism

## Basic Chinese religious concepts

1. Many gods and spirits with major gods of earth and universe
2. Yin and Yang
3. Ancestor worship
4. Divination

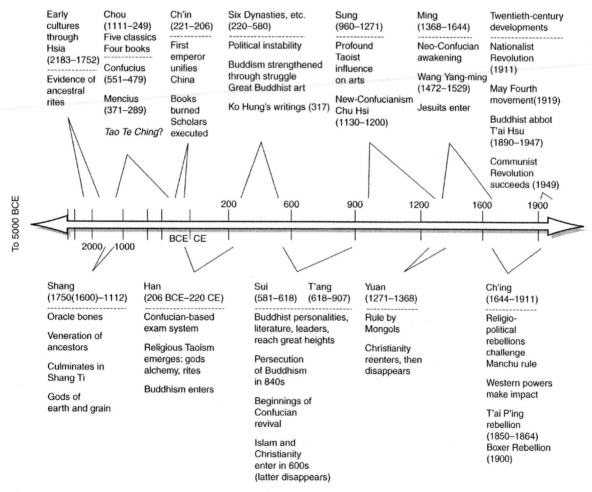

**Early cultures through Hsia (2183–1752)**
Evidence of ancestral rites

**Chou (1111–249)**
Five classics
Four books
Confucius (551–479)
Mencius (371–289)
Tao Te Ching?

**Ch'in (221–206)**
First emperor unifies China
Books burned
Scholars executed

**Six Dynasties, etc. (220–580)**
Political instability
Buddism strengthened through struggle
Great Buddhist art
Ko Hung's writings (317)

**Sung (960–1271)**
Profound Taoist influence on arts
New-Confucianism
Chu Hsi (1130–1200)

**Ming (1368–1644)**
Neo-Confucian awakening
Wang Yang-ming (1472–1529)
Jesuits enter

**Twentieth-century developments**
Nationalist Revolution (1911)
May Fourth movement(1919)
Buddhist abbot T'ai Hsu (1890–1947)
Communist Revolution succeeds (1949)

To 5000 BCE — 2000 / 1000 — BCE : CE — 200 — 600 — 900 — 1200 — 1600 — 1900

**Shang (1750(1600)–1112)**
Oracle bones
Veneration of ancestors
Culminates in Shang Ti
Gods of earth and grain

**Han (206 BCE–220 CE)**
Confucian-based exam system
Religious Taoism emerges: gods alchemy, rites
Buddhism enters

**Sui (581–618)    T'ang (618–907)**
Buddhist personalities, literature, leaders, reach great heights
Persecution of Buddhism in 840s
Beginnings of Confucian revival
Islam and Christianity enter in 600s (latter disappears)

**Yuan (1271–1368)**
Rule by Mongols
Christianity reenters, then disappears

**Ch'ing (1644–1911)**
Religio-political rebellions challenge Manchu rule
Western powers make impact
T'ai P'ing rebellion (1850–1864)
Boxer Rebellion (1900)

*Religion During the Chinese Dynasties*

### Decline of Feudal System—Chou Dynasty

TAOISM

#### Life of Lao-Tzu
Tao Tê Ching
Early Taoist philosopher: Chuang-Tzu—4th century B.C.E.

1. Compiled book called the "Tao" (Way of Universe)
   - Beyond being named
   - Moving body of water
   - Struggle against Tao
   - Everything destroyed
   - Go with the flow: live quiet, simple lives
2. Life is the greatest of all possessions
3. Life is to be lived simply
4. Pomp and glory are to be despised

#### Major schools of thought 3rd and 4th Centuries
- Confucians
- Legalists
- Mohists

CONFUCIANISM

#### As a religion—very different
Despite differences—deeply affected by the Chinese character

#### Life of Confucius
- Earliest material about Confucius: "Analects of Confucius"
- Born 551 B.C.E.
- Educated—interested in government and society
- Teacher
- Became government employee
- Compiled his teachings

#### Teachings of Confucius
- Developed: a system of ethics
  - theory of government
  - set of personal and social goals
- Teachings based on certain central themes:
  1. Idea of "Li"
  2. Five basic relationships
     - Father to son
     - Elder brother to younger brother
     - Husband to wife

- Elder to junior
- Ruler to subject

- Inward expression of Confucian ideals—called *Jen* = Love, Goodness
- Goal = to have balance of *Li* and *Jen,* which leads to a "Superior Human Being"
- Concept of original sin

## DEVELOPMENT OF CONFUCIANISM

- Confucius died—small group of disciples
- 500 years after death becomes integral part of Chinese culture

## CHINESE HOLIDAYS

- New Year
- Dragon Boat Festival
- All Souls Day

# 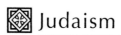 Judaism

History of Human Relationship to a
Transcendent Being: Referred To in
the Jewish Faith as God, Lord, Elohim,
Yaweh, Father

2000 years of Egyptian, Mesopotamian History
before the beginning of Hebrew or Jewish history

| | |
|---|---|
| *Pre-Exodus History* <br> *Book of Genesis*—1950 B.C.E. <br> (a verbal history) | Nomadic tribes roaming Egypt, Syria, and Mesopotamia <br> *Patriarchs:*  Abraham <br>               Isaac <br>               Jacob <br>               Joseph |
| *Book of Exodus*—the beginning of Hebrew history—1290 B.C.E. | Moses: stories of his life and birth <br> — Found in a basket <br> — Son of the Pharoah's daughter <br> — Born a Jew, raised an Egyptian <br> — Burning bush <br> — The Plague (Passover) <br> — The Exodus <br> — Parting of the Red Sea <br> — Ten Commandments <br>     The Book of the Covenant = <br>         Exodus, Chapters 20 through 23 |
| *Book of Leviticus* | Golden Rule—Love your neighbor as yourself |
| *Book of Numbers* | Israel's wandering for 40 years |
| *Book of Deuteronomy* | Israel's earliest code of social and agricultural laws |

**\*End of the Torah = First five books of the Bible**

| | |
|---|---|
| Book of Joshua | Military invasion into Canaan (Palestine) |
| Book of Judges | Establishment of the city of Jerusalem and a government with the selection of monarchial leadership: Saul and David |
| | Establishment of the Temple Mound |
| | Called *"Israel's Golden Age"* |
| Saul's reign—1020–1000 B.C.E. | Took his own life |
| David's reign—999–993 B.C.E. | Established the boundaries of the Israelite Nation |
| | Produced a stable government and economy |
| Solomon's reign—961–922 B.C.E. | He built many palaces and used taxpayers' money . . . He was not a beloved king |
| | Upon Solomon's death, ten of the northern tribes seceded from the Kingdom of Judea* |

**\*This division split the Nation of Israel for all time**

| | |
|---|---|
| 800 B.C.E.—First written history recorded | Southern tribes stayed in Jerusalem and remained true to the Davidic Dynasty |
| | Known as the Kingdom of Judah |
| | Northern tribes continued a half-century of instability until King Omri seized the throne and built the city of Samaria |
| | Northern tribes became known as the Kingdom of Israel |
| | Omri's son Ahab married Jezebel (a Phoenician princess) |
| 869 B.C.E. | Ahab became King |
| | Jezebel wanted to introduce the worship of Baal to Israel |
| | A struggle broke out under the leadership of Elijah |
| | Elijah won and became a hero . . . later became known as a symbol of prophecy . . . |

This was the beginning of the foundation for the
works of the great prophets of the 8th and 9th
centuries . . . or as it is called *"The Great Age of Prophets"*

| | |
|---|---|
| 721 B.C.E. | After Elijah the *Northern Kingdom* continued for another century then fell to *Assyrian invasion* |
| | At this point the Northern tribes disappeared from records of history . . . The people were carried off never to return . . . becoming *"The Ten Lost Tribes of Israel"* |
| 586 B.C.E. | *The Babylonians* under Nebuchadnezzar conquered the *Southern Kingdom of Judah* capturing the city of Jerusalem |
| | The great temple was destroyed and the Jews carried off into Babylonian captivity |

**\*The end of ancient Israelite people**

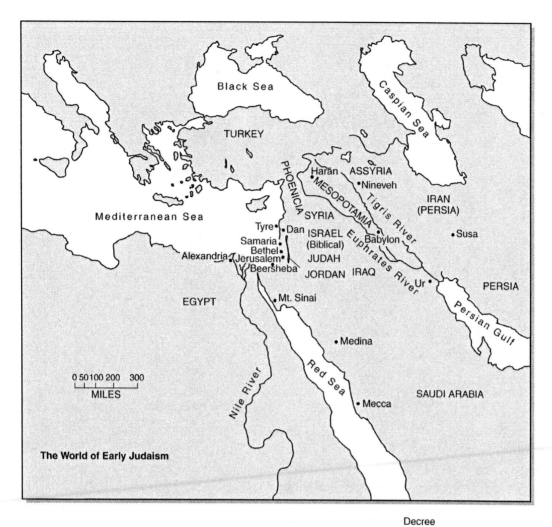

The World of Early Judaism

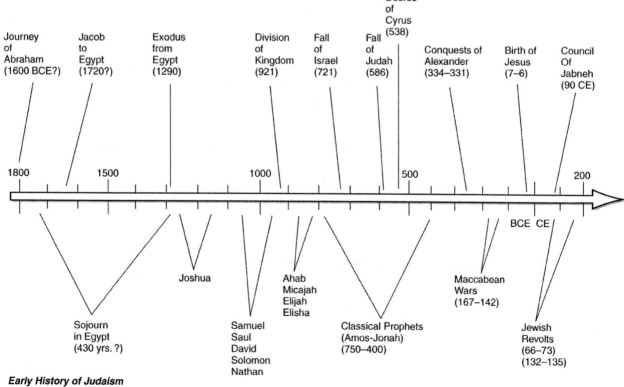

*Early History of Judaism*

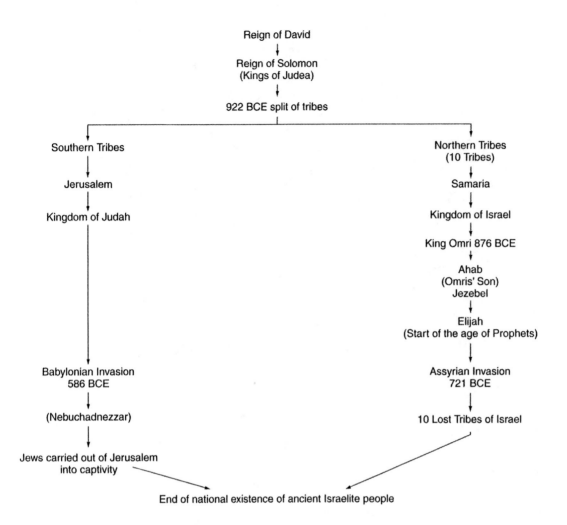

Reign of David
↓
Reign of Solomon
(Kings of Judea)
↓
922 BCE split of tribes

Southern Tribes
↓
Jerusalem
↓
Kingdom of Judah
↓
Babylonian Invasion
586 BCE
↓
(Nebuchadnezzar)
↓
Jews carried out of Jerusalem
into captivity

Northern Tribes
(10 Tribes)
↓
Samaria
↓
Kingdom of Israel
↓
King Omri 876 BCE
↓
Ahab
(Omris' Son)
Jezebel
↓
Elijah
(Start of the age of Prophets)
↓
Assyrian Invasion
721 BCE
↓
10 Lost Tribes of Israel

End of national existence of ancient Israelite people

During the 8th through 6th centuries B.C.E., the "Age of Prophets" emerged

Prophetic Religion—783–742 B.C.E.

Hebrew word for prophet meant to "speak for" (Greek = foretelling)

Prophets perceived as being able to *speak for God* (start of the clerical vocations, i.e., ministers, priests, clergy)

The Early Prophets: Moses, David, Elijah

Writing Prophets: 12

Reminded the people of their history: proclaimed "God was still ruling the world and was going to vindicate the people of Israel"

Start of the concept of looking forward to the future (Messianic foretelling)

This concept literally transformed the Hebrew religion

### The Great Prophets—700–500 B.C.E.

- Amos—750 B.C.E.
- Hosea—740 B.C.E.
- Isaiah—742–690 B.C.E.
- Micah—725–700 B.C.E.
- Jeremiah—650–580 B.C.E.
- Ezekiel—625–570 B.C.E.

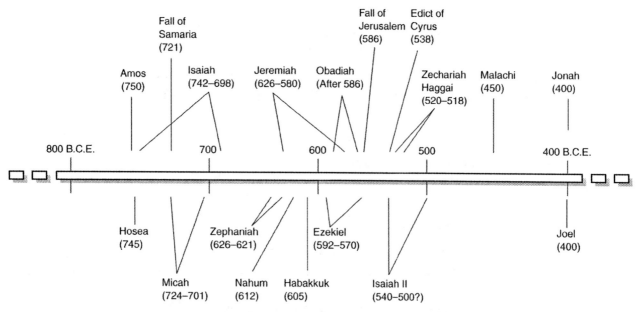

**The Classical Hebrew Prophets**

### *Deutero–Isaiah—550 B.C.E. (Suffering Servant); 539 B.C.E.—Persia conquered Babylon*

- Cyrus—Persian Monarch
- Jews allowed to return to Jerusalem. End of exile
- Small group returned to rebuild Jerusalem

### *During this time Israel's religious life became the central fact of its existence.*

Four main patterns of religious life emerged:

1. Priestly and legal Judaism
2. Devotional Judaism
3. Wisdom, literature and piety
4. Apocalypse

## DISPERSION

Dispersion/Diaspora: The scattering or migrating of a group.

Began in 586 B.C.E. with the fall of Jerusalem and Babylonian exile.

Further scattering took place two centuries later with Alexander's conquest of Judea in 332 B.C.E.

Death of Alexander (323 B.C.E.) found Judea right in the middle of political and military activity—between two kingdoms:

Syria and Egypt (capital for both in Alexandria)

Series of wars—Jews move to Antioch, Rome, other cities

Jews lived among Gentiles

Were affected by new environment

Never lost loyalty to Judaism:
    Support:     Temple
                Sanhedrin
This caused hostility among non-Jews (anti-Semitic attitudes)
Jews remained under Roman rule until 70 C.E. (the fall of Jerusalem)

## SECOND FALL OF JERUSALEM

Roman army under Titus

Three more wars

## GREAT DISPERSION

70 C.E. through modern founding of Israel 1948

Destruction of temple produced changes in Judaism—synagogue, rabbis

### *The dispersion resulted in two achievements:*
    1. The Septuagint
    2. The writings or philosophy of Philo Judaeus
Judaism seeking converts
        (20–50 C.E.)—Gentile
        "God Fearers"

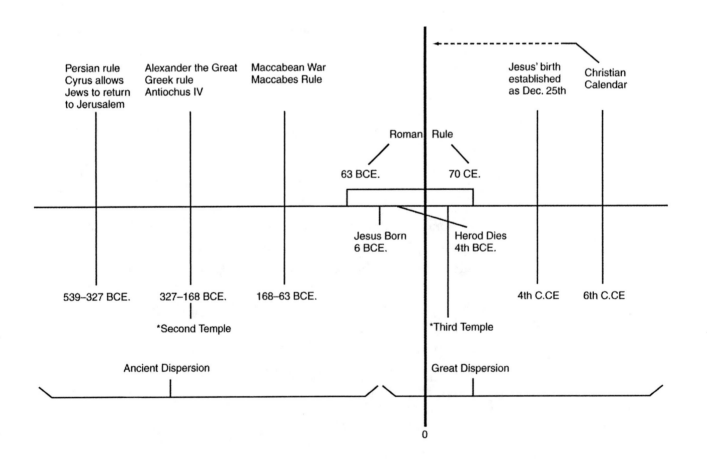

### *Individual differences fostered the development of various groups*
Sadducees

- Liberals (literalism)
- Tolerant toward Rome
- Wealthy
- Rejected ideas of angels, apocalypse, resurrection

### *Pharisees (means Separatist)*
- Pious
- Rigid in faith
- Believed in angels, apocalypse, resurrection
- more mystical

### *Zealots*
- Largest group
- Refused to collaborate with Rome
- Caused many revolts against Rome
- Believed Heaven sent General, King was coming any time

### *Essenes (Second century B.C.E.–68 C.E.)*
- Rejected military (pacifism)
- Established monastic society, escape the evil world
- Lived strict religious discipline
- Community property

### *Qumran*
Dead Sea Scrolls

- First scrolls found in 1947
- Community disappeared
- Hymns, Psalms, records of religious discipline
- Narratives about mysterious "Righteous Teacher" and an "Evil Priest"

Messianic expectation

Battle between good and evil

## MEDIEVAL PERIOD

Rise of Christianity
- Jews would not convert; this caused hostility
- Christianity from first century became primarily Gentile

Constantine—312 C.E.
- Christianity official religion of his empire (Roman Empire)
- Anti-Semitism was at its highest

4th and 5th centuries
- Jews moved to Babylon again
- Babylon became the center for Judaism

6th and 7th centuries
- Islam burst upon the world (Christian Europe, Middle East, Central Asia)

8th and 9th centuries
- Islam became established
- Start of the Judeo-Islamic Age

10th and 11th centuries: Christian Crusades
- Lasted 200 years
- Launched to push back the Moslem armies
- Most failed, except the first one; recaptured Jerusalem
- Crusades became an excuse to pillage
    Sacked fellow Christians
    Constantinople never recovered and fell to the Turks (1453)

Two types of Judaism developed

1. Sephardic
   - Spain
   - Ladino
2. Ashkenazi
   - Germany
   - Yiddish

Maimonides
- Developed a philosophy that justified Jewish beliefs, rational thinking
  Many did not agree with this rational approach to their faith.

Seekers
- Developed the Kabbala
  - Means "tradition" but in this case "mystic tradition"
- Belief that the Torah and the Bible have an inner meaning
- Most famous book of Kabbala is the Zohar
  - Mysterious meanings
    Names, letters, numbers, locations (pesher) encouraged magical superstitions

### 16th and 17th centuries
Kabbalism very popular
- Group called Hasidics
- Revolt against the authority of the Talmud
- Opposition to orthodoxy
Hasidism grew (Poland, Russia, Israel, United States—like the Quakers)

### Jews remained objects of hostility and persecution throughout the Middle Ages.

Forbidden to hold real property

- All kinds of accusations against them

Forced to live in a prescribed section of the cities.

- Crowded, unclean, poor drainage
- Could not leave before daylight, must return before nightfall
- Birth of the ghetto

Because of this type of imprisonment, they developed some strong community traits.

- They became inward; skills of the mind
- Strong family traditions
- Had to go into trades and occupations that did not include property
  - Money changers
  - Lending or banking

### 18th century

- Age of Enlightenment
  Moses Mendelssohn
  - Translated the Torah into German
  - Wrote book "Jerusalem"
- This started a movement by the Jews toward emancipation
- Greatest in Great Britain and North America

### New forms of Jewish worship

| | | |
|---|---|---|
| 1. Orthodoxy | 40% | |
| 2. Conservatives | 30% | |
| 3. Reform | 30% | |

### Zionism

- Jewish nationalism
- Anti-Semitism, dream of returning to homeland
- A tremendous immigration back to Palestine
- Opposition of Arab states
- Arabs refused to cooperate with United Nations recommendation to divide Arabs and Jews
- Six-Day War
  Israel claimed:
  - Golan Heights from Syria
  - West Bank from Jordan
  - Gaza Strip from Egypt

Today Israel is supported by American-Jewish community but Arab nations (Islamic) are still warring.

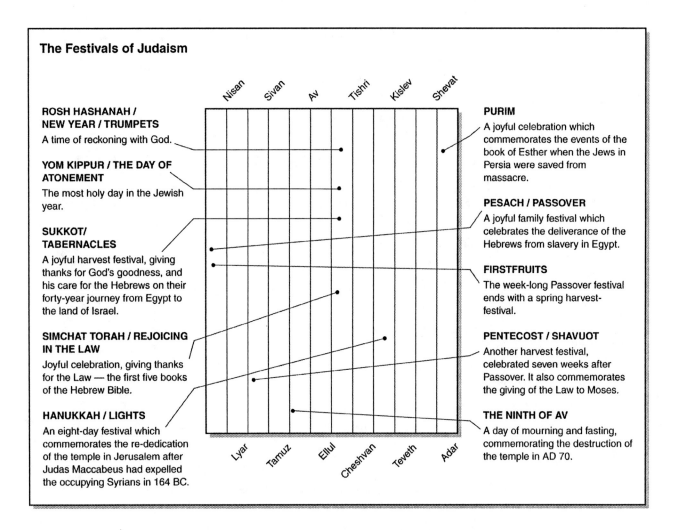

**The Festivals of Judaism**

**ROSH HASHANAH / NEW YEAR / TRUMPETS**
A time of reckoning with God.

**YOM KIPPUR / THE DAY OF ATONEMENT**
The most holy day in the Jewish year.

**SUKKOT/ TABERNACLES**
A joyful harvest festival, giving thanks for God's goodness, and his care for the Hebrews on their forty-year journey from Egypt to the land of Israel.

**SIMCHAT TORAH / REJOICING IN THE LAW**
Joyful celebration, giving thanks for the Law — the first five books of the Hebrew Bible.

**HANUKKAH / LIGHTS**
An eight-day festival which commemorates the re-dedication of the temple in Jerusalem after Judas Maccabeus had expelled the occupying Syrians in 164 BC.

**PURIM**
A joyful celebration which commemorates the events of the book of Esther when the Jews in Persia were saved from massacre.

**PESACH / PASSOVER**
A joyful family festival which celebrates the deliverance of the Hebrews from slavery in Egypt.

**FIRSTFRUITS**
The week-long Passover festival ends with a spring harvest-festival.

**PENTECOST / SHAVUOT**
Another harvest festival, celebrated seven weeks after Passover. It also commemorates the giving of the Law to Moses.

**THE NINTH OF AV**
A day of mourning and fasting, commemorating the destruction of the temple in AD 70.

Months around chart: Nisan, Sivan, Av, Tishri, Kislev, Shevat, Lyar, Tamuz, Ellul, Cheshvan, Teveth, Adar

 Christianity

### FIRST CENTURY B.C.E—JUDAISM

- Roman rule
- Herod the Great
  - Herod Antipus
  - Philip
  - Archelaus
  - Jesus born 4 B.C.E. (reign of Herod the Great)

### *Christianity vs. Judaism*

- Belief in Jesus as the Christ
- Primarily Gentile
- Greco-Roman origin
- Use of Greek and Latin language

### *Humanism*

- People of worth to God

### Jesus' Life and Teachings

- New Testament
  - Four Gospels
  - Matthew
  - Mark     ┤ Synoptic
  - Luke
  - John—differs in order and accounts

### Gospel—Good News or Proclamation

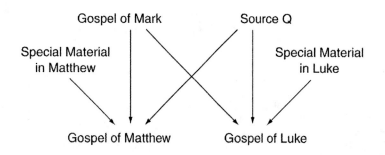

### The "Q" Source

Oral accounts put in writing about 40–50 C.E. (Jesus' teachings)

### Mark

- Oldest—70 C.E.
- Symbol: Lion

### Matthew

- 95 C.E.
- Symbol: Man (Humankind)
- Combines Q with Mark
- Written in Greek

### Luke

- 95 C.E.
- Symbol: Ox
- Combines Q with Mark

### John

- End of 2nd century
- Symbol: Eagle
- Son of Zebedee
- The favored Disciple (brother of Jesus?)

- Differs
  - Portrait of Jesus
  - Order of events

### Christian Movement
- Started in Jerusalem
  - Messiah had come
  - Raised from the dead
  - Spiritually present
  - Would return to rule over God's kingdom
- Love feast, Holy Communion (in memory)

New Christian community met in homes—members: Jews accused of being disloyal to the Torah, conflicts

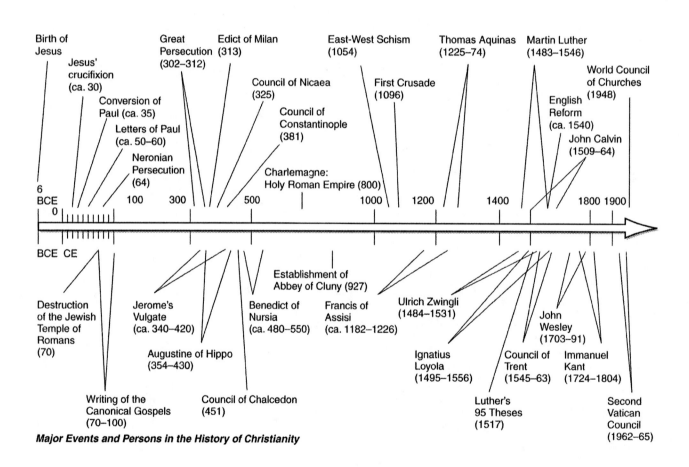

*Major Events and Persons in the History of Christianity*

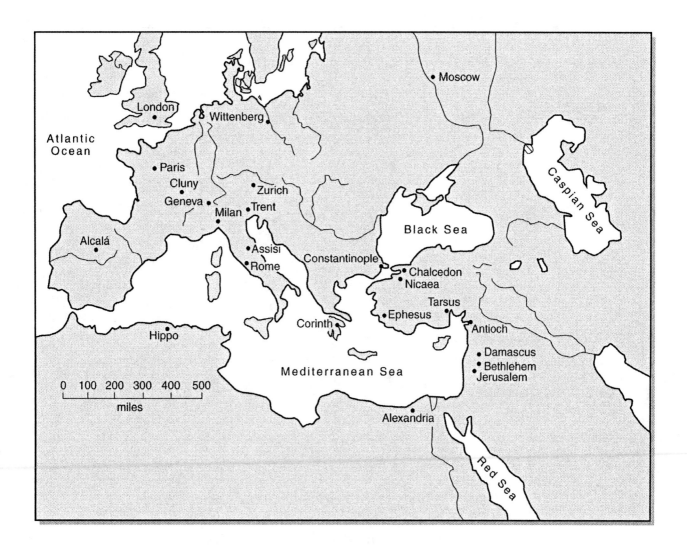

### First century C.E.

### Paul: Missionary (spread the "Good News")
- Gentile Christianity
- Conversion experience; blinded
- Established churches throughout the known Roman Empire, Greece, and Asia Minor

Christ pre-existent (before time)

Divine figure in human form

In Christ: Victory over sin and death

Paul died during Nero's persecution of Christians (60–64 C.E.)

### John
- Also believed Jesus was a pre-existent divine figure "Incarnate Word"
- Foundation of Christian Orthodoxy (Creed and Theology)

During the persecutions of the 1st century belief in the second coming was very strong. The writing of "The Book of Revelation" dates 95–96 C.E. Great deal of mysticism

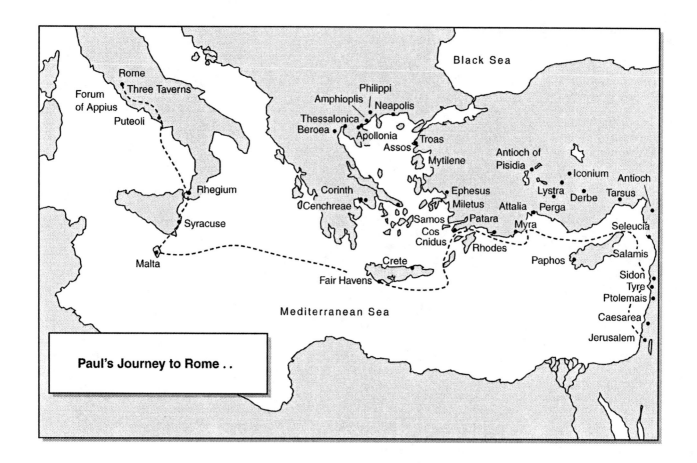

The map shows the following labels:

Black Sea

Rome
Three Taverns
Forum of Appius
Puteoli

Philippi
Amphiopolis
Neapolis
Thessalonica
Beroea
Apollonia
Assos
Troas
Mytilene

Antioch of Pisidia
Iconium
Antioch
Lystra
Derbe
Tarsus

Rhegium

Corinth
Cenchreae
Ephesus
Miletus
Attalia
Perga

Syracuse

Samos
Cos
Cnidus
Patara
Myra
Seleucia

Malta

Rhodes
Paphos
Salamis

Crete

Fair Havens

Sidon
Tyre
Ptolemais

Caesarea

Jerusalem

Mediterranean Sea

**Paul's Journey to Rome . .**

## Second century C.E.: Christianity in the Ancient World
- Christianity spread throughout Greco-Roman world
- Christians worshipped a King other than Caesar
- Conflicts for three centuries until Constantine (312 C.E.)

## Early Christian Theologies
- 100–500 C.E.—Two main issues
    1. What was the relation of Christian faith to other faiths?
    2. What was the nature of the Christian faith?

Early church forced to define its beliefs.

## Four persons emerged who established major theological concepts:
1. Justin
2. Clement
3. Origen
4. Tertullian

Third century—still conflict over Christ: divine or human. Finally, Constantine convened a general council—the Council of Nicaea, 325 C.E.
- Christ both God and man, divine and human
- Nicene Creed

### Jesus' Life, early years
- Birth (Nativity)
  - Gospels
  - Yeshua
  - December 25th (Saturnalia)
- Baptism
  - Gospels
  - John the Baptist
  - Temptation in the wilderness

### Ministry—Capernaum
- Disciples—7 (student followers)
- Sermon on the Mount (Matthew and Luke)
  - Beatitudes—9 (blessed ones)
- Apostles—12 (to send)
- Peter—The Rock (Messiah)
- Transfiguration
- Lazarus

### Final Days
- Jerusalem
  - Reason for going to Jerusalem
  - Money changers
- Last Supper
  - Bread and wine
  - Judas
- Arrest
  - Garden of Gethsemane
  - Blasphemy
  - Temple incident

### Trial
- High priest—Caiaphas
  Illegal trial (King of Jews?)
- Pontius Pilate washed his hands
- Turned over to the Jews (Barabbas)

### Crucified
- Golgotha (Place of the Skull)
- Two thieves
- Last words

- Burial and resurrection
  - Third day, Easter
- Appearances to disciples
  - Pentecost: Holy Spirit
- Start of Christian community

### Jesus' Teachings
- Repent of sins
- Moral and ethical standards to enter Heaven
- Taught through parables

### Development of authority
- Set liturgies: prayers, hymns, baptism, the Eucharist, reading of Scripture, giving of monetary offerings
- Apostles appointed persons to carry teachings abroad

**Events in the Life of Jesus as Recorded in the Gospels**

| | | Matthew | Mark | Luke | John |
|---|---|---|---|---|---|
| **Early Years** | Birth | 1:18–25 | | 2:1–7 | |
| | Visit of the Wise Men | 2:1–12 | | | |
| | Flight into Egypt | 2:13–21 | | | |
| | Teaching in the Temple | | | 2:41–51 | |
| | Jesus' baptism | 3:13–17 | 1:9–11 | 3:21–22 | |
| | Changing water into wine | | | | 2:1–11 |
| | Temptation in the Wilderness | 4:1–11 | 1:12–13 | 4:1–13 | |
| **Jesus Ministry** | Start of the Galilean ministry | 4:12–17 | 1:14–15 | 4:14–15 | |
| | Summoning the first disciples | 4:18–22 | 1:16–20 | 5:1–11 | 1:35–51 |
| | Sermon on the Mount | 5:1–7:29 | | 6:20–49 | |
| | Naming the Apostles | 10:1–42 | 3:13–19;6:7–19 | 9:1–6 | |
| | Feeding 5,000 | 14:13–21 | 6:32–44 | 9:10–17 | 6:1–14 |
| | Walking on water | 14:22–33 | 6:45–52 | | 6:16–21 |
| | Peter declares Jesus to be the Christ | 16:16 | 8:29 | 9:20 | |
| | Transfiguration of Jesus | 17:1–13 | 9:2–8 | 9:28–36 | |
| | Raising of Lazarus | | | | 11:1–44 |
| **Final Days** | Entry into Jerusalem | 2:1–11 | 11:1–10 | 19:28–44 | 12:12–19 |
| | Cleansing of the Temple | 21:12–13 | 11:15–17 | 19:45–46 | 2:13–17 |
| | Judas betrays Jesus | 26:14–16 | 14:10–11 | 22:3–6 | |
| | Preparations for Passover | 26:17–19 | 14:12–16 | 22:7–13 | |
| | Last Supper | 26:20–29 | 14:17–25 | 22:14–18 | 13:1–30 |
| | Arrest | 26:47–56 | 14:43–52 | 22:47–53 | 18:2–12 |
| | Trial | 26:57–27:26 | 14:53–15:15 | 22:54–23:25 | 18:13–19:16 |
| | Crucifixion and death | 27:33–54 | 15:22–39 | 23:33–47 | 19:17–37 |
| | Burial | 27:57–61 | 15:42–47 | 23:50–56 | 19:38–42 |
| | Resurrection | 28:1–10 | 16:1–8 | 24:1–11 | 20:1–18 |
| | Appearances to disciples | 28:16–20 | 16:12–18 | 24:13–49 | 20:19–21:23 |
| | Ascension | | 16:19 | 24:50–51 | |

## APOSTOLIC SUCCESSION
- Bishops—overseers (presbyters), elders
- Deacons, ministers

Middle of 3rd century
Titles of church leaders finalized along with the duties of each

### Bishops
- above reproach
- Many leaders within each city
- Start of a vocation (ordination)

Start of the hierarchical structure of the church

### Beginning of 2nd century
A movement to identify *one* presiding bishop with supreme authority

### 3rd and 4th centuries
- Pope = papa
- Rome
- 382 C.E., Pope Damascus
- Rome as center of authority

### Monasticism
- Medieval Christianity

Saw the development of Catholic *Orders* in England, Germany, France

### Benedictines: Founded by Benedict in 470 C.E.
- Threefold rule for daily life: "Work, Study, Prayer"
- Cloistered monks
  - Renounce the evil world

### Friars: Development of an order that went out into the world
Two major groups of friars
1. Dominicans: founded by Dominic—Spaniard
   - Intellectual, philosophers
   - Inquisitors
2. Franciscans: founded by Francis of Assisi
   - Vow of service to humanity
   - Roamed the countryside caring for the poor and sick
   - Concern for nature and all God's creatures

Middle Ages: absolute spiritual authority of the Roman pontiff was established

### Two aspects of Medieval church power:
1. Inquisition: secret court. Tortured for crimes they did not commit
2. The Crusaders: bloodbaths, indulgences

## WORSHIP AND SACRAMENTS

### In the Catholic Church
### The Seven Sacraments:
1. Baptism
2. Confirmation
3. Penance
4. Marriage
5. Ordination (Holy Orders)
6. Last Anointing
7. Eucharist (Mass—giving thanks)

### Seasons of the Christian Year
1. Pentecost—red
2. Epiphany—green
3. Lent and Advent—purple
4. High Holidays—white

## THE CHRISTIAN CALENDAR YEAR

### Advent (purple or blue)
First Sunday of Advent to the fourth Sunday of Advent

### Christmas season (white or gold)
Nativity of the Lord (Christmas Eve, Christmas Day)
First Sunday after Christmas Day
New Year's Eve or New Year's Day
Epiphany of the Lord

### Season after the Epiphany (Ordinary Time; green)
First Sunday after the Epiphany (Baptism of the Lord; white)
Second Sunday after the Epiphany to the eighth Sunday after the Epiphany
Last Sunday after the Epiphany (Transfiguration Sunday; white)

### Lent (purple; red as an alternative for Holy Week)
Ash Wednesday
First Sunday in Lent to the fifth Sunday in Lent
Sixth Sunday in Lent (Passion/Palm Sunday)
Monday of Holy Week
Tuesday of Holy Week
Wednesday of Holy Week

Holy Thursday*

Good Friday* (no color)

Holy Saturday* (no color)

### Easter season (white or gold)

Resurrection of the Lord (Easter Eve, Easter Day, Easter Evening)*

Second Sunday of Easter to the sixth Sunday of Easter

Ascension of the Lord

Seventh Sunday of Easter

Day of Pentecost (red)

### Season after Pentecost (Ordinary Time or Kingdomtide; green)

First Sunday after Pentecost (Trinity Sunday; white)

Second Sunday after Pentecost to the twenty-sixth Sunday after Pentecost

All Saints (white)

Thanksgiving (red or white)

Last Sunday after Pentecost (Christ the King/Reign of Christ Sunday; white)

*The Great Three Days from sunset Holy Thursday to sunset Easter Day are a Unity—the climax of the Christian Year*

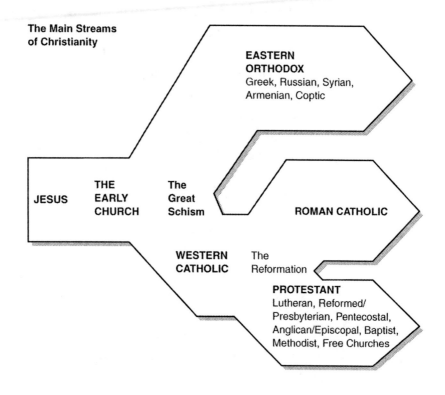

**The Main Streams of Christianity**

EASTERN ORTHODOX
Greek, Russian, Syrian, Armenian, Coptic

JESUS

THE EARLY CHURCH

The Great Schism

ROMAN CATHOLIC

WESTERN CATHOLIC

The Reformation

PROTESTANT
Lutheran, Reformed/Presbyterian, Pentecostal, Anglican/Episcopal, Baptist, Methodist, Free Churches

### Eastern Orthodox
- Contemplative, mystical and passive
- Resisted Rome's spiritual authority
- Close tie between church and state
  Byzantine emperors of Constantinople
  (Justinian—second Rome)
- Fall of Constantinople in 1453 C.E. (Muslims)
  Moscow = spiritual center

### Four main differences
1. Bound to government
2. No pope or supreme ruler (14 national churches)
3. No tradition of theological thinking
4. Monasticism more individualistic, contemplative, other-worldly nature, compared to Western tradition that works for and with society

Scholasticism—the use of philosophy to explain or defend religious faith

### St. Thomas Aquinas (1225–1274)
1. Presupposes an unmoved mover (God); world moving toward fulfillment
2. Believed also (Anselm of Canterbury; first archbishop of Canterbury) that God is a being greater than that which is inconceivable to humans
   - Common human experience of good/striving for absolute best is part of what people mean when they say "God"
   - Divine Designer: the world and universe are ordered

Thomas believed it was possible to prove logically the existence of "God" (path of the mind that leads to God)

With all this logical thinking about God, people started losing allegiance to the church

### Dissenting Groups
- John Wycliffe (1328–1384)
  - Against papal authority
  - Corruption of the church
  - Translated the Bible into English so common people could read it (Wycliffe lived in England)
- John Huss (1373–1415)
  - Took up Wycliffe's anti-papal cause
- People generally rebelled against the authority the church held over their lives
- Break-up of the medieval system

### Human interest shifts—start of the Renaissance period (late 1300s)

- Arts, music, nature
- Christian tradition still active, but human quality of life now becomes more important

### Age of Reformation (1500s)

- Begins with Martin Luther
- Ends with Glorious Revolution (1688)

### Five Main Traditions of Christianity:

1. Lutheranism
2. Calvinism
3. Anglicanism
4. Sectarianism
5. Modern Roman Catholicism

### Later, three additional movements:

1. 18th-century Enlightenment
2. Protestant Pietism
3. American Religious Experience

### Luther and Lutheranism

- Catholic monk
- Questioned Catholic policies and piety
  - 95 theses
- Excommunicated, went into hiding, translated N.T. into German (the Gutenberg Bible)
- Priesthood of all believers
- Luther's followers identified as the "League of Protestant" at the Diet of Speier in 1529 (conference; name "Protestant" fixed on those rebelling against Catholic church)

### Calvin and Calvinism

- Switzerland
  German-speaking
      Zurich—Zwingli
      Authority lay with the Christian congregations
  French-speaking
      Geneva—Farel

In 1536, Farel was visited by a follower by the name of John Calvin

- Became a lecturer on the Bible
- Ideal Christian Commonwealth
  All affairs of life/society conducted according to his interpretation of Christianity
  - Speech, clothes, manners
- Choice of pastors and elders by vote of congregations
- Founded the University of Geneva
- Protestants from all over Europe studied under Calvin
  - Bible—God's unerring guide

  Calvinism taken to Scotland by John Knox

### Calvinist Worship
- Open Bible at pulpit; Bible center of worship
- Preaching and singing
- Two sacraments only
  - Baptism
  - Lord's Supper (Communion)

### 1500s—Rising Middle Class joining the Calvinist Movement
God's favor found in:
- Hard work
- Thrift
- Industriousness
  Close relationship between Calvinism and Western capitalism

  Calvinism—seed bed of constitutional government and modern democracy

### Anglicanism—English Reformation
- No one leader
  - King Henry VIII
    Break with Rome
      Edward VI
- Book of Common Prayer
  - Changed "Eucharist" to Holy Communion
  - Denied "transubstantiation"
  - Affirmed Anglican clergy in the Apostolic Succession

  Queen Mary—Catholic; persecuted the Protestants

Queen Elizabeth—tolerated both Protestants and Catholics
- Act of Supremacy (1559)
  - Declared Church of England under the crown
  - Book of Common Prayer the standard for worship

  Became the Episcopal church in the United States

## Sectarianism
- Radical Reformation

  Small sects

  Sect is:
  1. Rigorous discipline
  2. Renounce society (pacifist)
  3. Reject private property and institution of government
  4. Renounce family and friends

  Most rejected baptism of infants—Anabaptists (Germany and Switzerland)

## Separatists—England
Separation from Church of England and government control of religion
- Baptists (1612)

  John Smyth, Roger Williams

  Rhode Island
- Congregationalists (1581)

  Robert Brown

  Pilgrims
- Methodists (1738)

  John Wesley, Charles Wesley
- Mennonites

  Menno Simmons
- Quakers (1648)

  Society of Friends

  George Fox
- Moravians (1760)

  Count Zinzendorf
- Unitarians (1604)

  Michael Servetus

## Revival of Roman Catholic Church
Reformation and Counter-Reformation
- Win back people
- New order—most famous: The Jesuits

### Council of Trent
- Meant to restore unity
- Stance against Protestant thought
- Vatican I
- Second Vatican Council (Vatican II)
  1963–1965
  Pope John the 23rd

### Protestants
- Remained in touch with society and social issues
- Emphasis on freedom as part of faith
- Some groups rejected society (sin, the devil)
- Literal interpretation of Bible
- Became known as *Fundamentalism*

### United States
- Founded by
  - Protestant Calvinists
    Religious freedom
  - Development of new forms of religion
    New England—theocracy
    Puritans—strict rules for every aspect of life (church, state, private lives)

Example of this control:

### Mathers: Massachusetts
- Richard Mather
- Increase Mather
- Cotton Mather
  - Salem witchcraft trials 1692

    Puritanism gradually replaced by a type of secularizing

### Jonathan Edwards
- Attacked growing self-sufficiency

  Colonies' first religious revival

### Other preachers echoed Edwards' ideas
- George Whitefield from England; "Great Awakening"
- Establishment of colleges
- Organizations for humanitarian causes; "Second Great Awakening"
- Frontier—Wild West

### Circuit Riders
- Height of religious revivals or camp meetings

*Puritans—intolerant*

*New religious freedom—toleration of differences*

## 19th century

- Urbanization
- Industrialization

Social problems started springing up
Social Gospel
Christians helping to solve the ills of society

- Settlement houses
- YMCA/YWCA

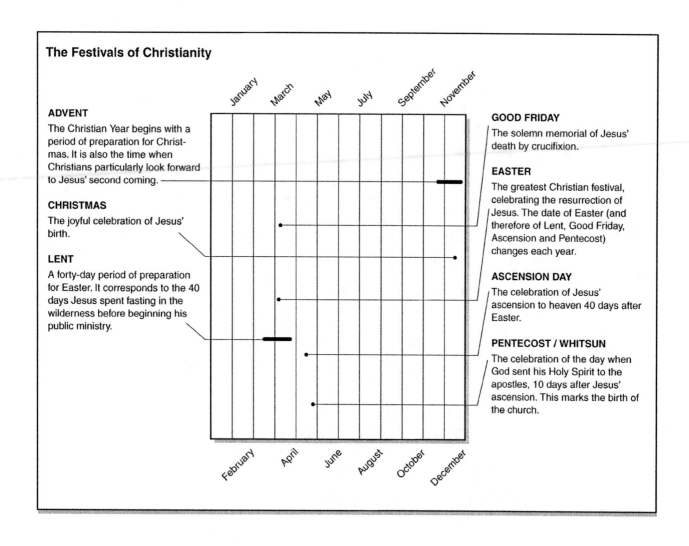

**The Festivals of Christianity**

**ADVENT**
The Christian Year begins with a period of preparation for Christmas. It is also the time when Christians particularly look forward to Jesus' second coming.

**CHRISTMAS**
The joyful celebration of Jesus' birth.

**LENT**
A forty-day period of preparation for Easter. It corresponds to the 40 days Jesus spent fasting in the wilderness before beginning his public ministry.

**GOOD FRIDAY**
The solemn memorial of Jesus' death by crucifixion.

**EASTER**
The greatest Christian festival, celebrating the resurrection of Jesus. The date of Easter (and therefore of Lent, Good Friday, Ascension and Pentecost) changes each year.

**ASCENSION DAY**
The celebration of Jesus' ascension to heaven 40 days after Easter.

**PENTECOST / WHITSUN**
The celebration of the day when God sent his Holy Spirit to the apostles, 10 days after Jesus' ascension. This marks the birth of the church.

## ISLAM

### *Background before birth of Muhammad*

- Islam began in Mecca
- Religion at the time (610 C.E.) was involved with multi-gods, goddesses, and shrines
- Also a belief in a high god: Allah
- People aware of Christianity and Judaism
- City dwellers
- Kaba: a sacred sanctuary in Mecca
- Mecca—hub of trade
    - Social tensions started to develop between the poor and the rich

### *Muhammad*

- Born in Mecca, 571 C.E.
- Age 25—ran trade caravans for wealthy businesswoman, Khadija
- Turned from the world of idolatry
  Became more contemplative
- Went out into the desert for months at a time

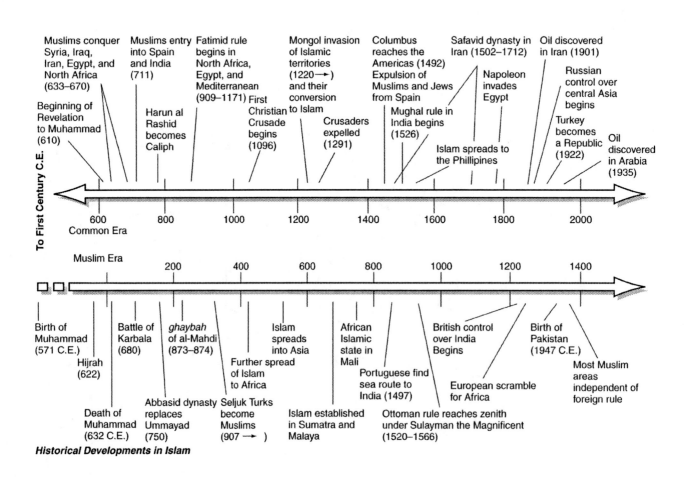

**Historical Developments in Islam**

### *"The Night of Power and Glory"*
- Vision of Gabriel
- Becomes the "Messenger of Allah"
- Last prophet through whom God spoke
- Returned to Mecca
  - Started preaching
  - Gained followers
  - Continued receiving revelations from God

### *Qur'an (Koran)*
- Mentions 28 prophets
- In Qur'an (God) Allah has spoken completely for the last time

### *Muhammad continued to preach. Merchants of Mecca became hostile*
- Persecution; forced to live and work in a single section of the city
  - Followers called Hashemites
- Revelations
  - Dealt with social justice and foretelling of doom and judgment

  Suras: Chapters of the Qur'an

## THE 99 NAMES: THE ATTRIBUTES OF ALLAH THE EXALTED

|    |              |                       |
|----|--------------|-----------------------|
| 1  | Ar-Rahman    | The Compassionate     |
| 2  | Ar-Rahim     | The Merciful          |
| 3  | Al-Malik     | King of Kings         |
| 4  | Al-Quddus    | The Holy              |
| 5  | As-Salam     | The Peace             |
| 6  | Al-Mu'min    | The Securer of Faith  |
| 7  | Al-Muhaymin  | The Protector         |
| 8  | Al-'Aziz     | The Mighty            |
| 9  | Al-Jabbar    | The Compeller         |
| 10 | Al-Muktakabbir | The Majestic        |
| 11 | Al-Kaliq     | The Creator           |
| 12 | Al-Bari      | The Maker from Naught |
| 13 | Al-Musawwir  | The Fashioner         |
| 14 | Al-Ghaffur   | The Forgiver          |
| 15 | Al-Qahhar    | The Subduer           |
| 16 | Al-Wahhab    | The Bestower          |
| 17 | Ar-Razzaq    | The Provider          |
| 18 | Al-Fattah    | The Opener of the Way |
| 19 | Al-'Alim     | The Omniscient        |
| 20 | Al-Qabid     | The Restrainer        |
| 21 | Al-Basit     | The Extender, Enlarger |

| 22 | Al-Khafid | The Abaser |
| 23 | Ar-Rafi' | The Exalter |
| 24 | Al-Mu'izz | The Strengthener |
| 25 | Al-Mudhill | The Humiliator |
| 26 | As-Sami | The All-Hearing |
| 27 | Al-Basir | The All-Seeing |
| 28 | Al-Hakam | The Judge |
| 29 | Al-'adl | The Just |
| 30 | Al-Latif | The Subtle |
| 31 | Al-Khabir | The Aware |
| 32 | Al-Halim | The Forebearing |
| 33 | Al-Azim | The Magnificent |
| 34 | Al-Jamil | The Beautiful |
| 35 | Ash-Shakur | The Grateful |
| 36 | Al-Aliyy | The High; Sublime |
| 37 | Al-Kabir | The Great |
| 38 | Al-Hafiz | The Guardian |
| 39 | Al-Muqit | The Sustainer |
| 40 | Al-Hasib | The Reckoner |
| 41 | An-Nur | The Light |
| 42 | Al-Karim | The Bountiful |
| 43 | Al-Raqib | The Watchful |
| 44 | Al-Mujib | The Hearkener of Prayer |
| 45 | Al-Wasi | The All-Embracing |
| 46 | Al-Hakim | The Wise |
| 47 | Al-Wadud | The Loving |
| 48 | Al-Majid | The All Perceiving |
| 49 | Al-Ba'ith | The Raiser from Death |
| 50 | Ash-Shahid | The Witness |
| 51 | Al-Hakk | The Truth |
| 52 | Al-Wakil | The Advocate |
| 53 | Al-Qawiyy | The Strong |
| 54 | Al-Matin | The Firm, Steady |
| 55 | Al-Waliyy | The Protecting Friend |
| 56 | Al-Hamid | The Praiseworthy |
| 57 | Al-Musiy | The Accountant |
| 58 | Al-Mubdi | The Producer |
| 59 | Al-Mu'id | The Restorer |
| 60 | Al-Muhyi | The Quickener |
| 61 | Al-Mumit | The Destroyer |
| 62 | Al-Mayy | The Alive |
| 63 | Al-Qayyum | The Eternal |

| 64 | Al-Shafi | The Healer |
|----|----------|-----------|
| 65 | Al-Khafi | The Remedy |
| 66 | Al-Wajid | The Finder |
| 67 | Al-Wahid | The Unique |
| 68 | Al-Samad | The Eternal Support of Creation |
| 69 | Al-Muqtadir | The Prevailing |
| 70 | Al-Muqaddim | The Expeditor |
| 71 | Al-Mu'akhkhir | The Retarder |
| 72 | Al-Awwal | The First |
| 73 | Al-Akhir | The Last |
| 74 | Al-Zahir | The Manifest |
| 75 | Al-Batin | The Hidden |
| 76 | Al-Wali | The Governor |
| 77 | Al-Muta'ali | The High Exalted |
| 78 | Al-Barr | The Righteous |
| 79 | At-Tawwab | The Relenting |
| 80 | Al-Muntaqim | The Avenger |
| 81 | Al-'afuww | The Pardoner, Mild |
| 82 | Al-Fazul | The Blessing |
| 83 | Al-Muqsit | The Equitable |
| 84 | Al-Jami | The Gatherer |
| 85 | Al-Ghani | The Self-Sufficient |
| 86 | Al-Mughni | The Enricher |
| 87 | Al-Mu'ti | The Giver |
| 88 | Al-Munawer | The Perfect |
| 89 | Al-Mani' | The Withholder |
| 90 | Ad-dar | The Distresser |
| 91 | An-Nafi | The Profiter |
| 92 | Al-Hadi | The Guide |
| 93 | Al-Badi | The Originator |
| 94 | Al-Baqi | The Everlasting |
| 95 | Al-Warith | The Inheritor |
| 96 | Ar-Rashid | The Unerring |
| 97 | Dhul-Jalal-Wal-Ikram | The Lord of Majesty and Bounty |
| 98 | Allaho-Akbar | Peace is Power |
| 99 | As-Sabur | The Patient |

Please note that these wazifas should not be practiced without the guidance of a teacher.

## THE FIVE PILLARS

1. Unity of God as expressed in the creed: "There is no God but Allah; Muhammad is the messenger of Allah"
2. Prayer five times a day
   - Friday in mosque

3. Alms giving—personal and private obligation
4. Fast of Ramadan
   - Calendar year of Islam

5. Pilgrimage to Mecca—Hajj
   a. Kaba, seven times
   b. Walk across valley; visit well called Zemzem
   c. Climb Mt. Arafat

At first the direction to face for prayer was Jerusalem. Then when Jews did not accept Muhammad, the direction became Mecca.

Followers became Muslims—one who surrenders
War between Mecca and Medina
630 C.E. fighting ended; Muhammad returns to Mecca
Muhammad becomes head of state; dies in 632 C.E.
- Successor: Abu Bakr
Established religion and state
State—federation of tribes

### First Caliphs

### Raiding parties
- Syria and Iraq
- Byzantine and Persian Empires
- Egypt Syria, Iraq

### 632–700 C.E.: Expansion continued
- Westward: North Africa to the Atlantic
- North: Constantinople
- East: All of Persia and Afghanistan; Central Asia and Pakistan

### 750 C.E.
- Large area remained a single state

After 750 C.E., military expansion slowed down; India the last to be occupied by force

After—Islam spread by trade: Malaysia, Indonesia, the Philippines and eastern China

### Islamic doctrine
Fundamental beliefs

### Two major pieces of literature:
- Qur'an (Koran; recite, read)
  - Sacred book
  - Written in Arabic

### Koran divided into chapters—Suras
- 114 Suras
- Suras divided into verses called ayats

### Hadith = traditions
- Religious methodology
- development of the law
- account of last judgment

  Moral and legal ordinances are most important

### After Muhammad's death
- Development of different views and interpretations

### Establishment of the Sharia: Sacred law of Islam
- "The Path of God's Commandments"
- Five major categories

### The Caliph's influence on organizational structure of Islam

### First four Caliphs most important
- Muhammad's son-in-law and cousin Ali was the first blood relative of Muhammad to become a caliph

### Shia (Shiites)
- Ten percent of Muslim population
- Rejected first three caliphs
- Believed in imams
- 12 imams before Judgment Day
- Ali was first imam
- Ayatollahs
  Ayatollah Khomeni

### Muslim mysticism—Sufism

### The Sunna/Sunnis
- Ninety percent of Muslim population
- No one could succeed Muhammad
- Successor only a guardian
- Can be any caliph from Quraish tribe
  1st—Abu Bakr, 632 C.E.
  2nd—Umar, 634 C.E.

3rd—Uthman, 644 c.e.

4th—Ali, 656 c.e. (Shia group)

### *Mystics and Philosophers*

- 1st century, monk types
  - Ninety-nine names of Allah
- Called Sufis, "wool wearers"
- Meditative, searching for illumination

### *Dervishes*

1. Kadirites
2. Rifaites
3. Maulawites

**The Mainstreams of Islam**

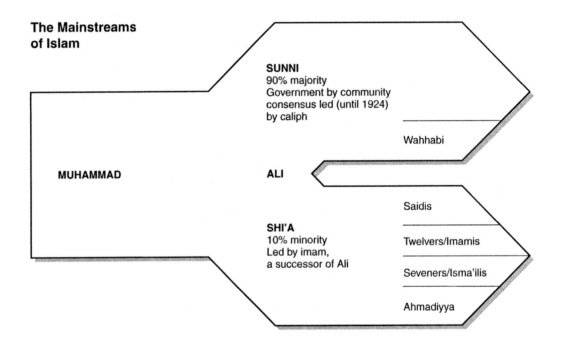

SUNNI
90% majority
Government by community
consensus led (until 1924)
by caliph

Wahhabi

MUHAMMAD

ALI

Saidis

SHI'A
10% minority
Led by imam,
a successor of Ali

Twelvers/Imamis

Seveners/Isma'ilis

Ahmadiyya

### MAJOR ACHIEVEMENTS

### *Mahmun—Caliph of (813–833 c.e.) Baghdad*

- House of Wisdom
- Books from Persia
  - India, Greek philosophers
- Believed in
- Basic order in the world
  - General laws

### *The merging of science and philosophy to produce the concept of "basic laws"*

- Laid the foundations of modern science and philosophical thought

### Muslim doctors
- Discovered blood circulation principle
- Treatment for smallpox
- Operations using anesthetics
- Methods used throughout Europe up to the 17th century

### In mathematics: Learned from India
- Adopted decimal system and use of zero
- Arab Muslims developed the subject of algebra
- Scientific study of the sky:
  Star names and astronomical terms
- First atlases and travel guides
- Earth measurements

### Tenth-century Spain
- City of Cordoba

### In the fine arts
- Islam took from the culture it found itself in
  - This created a unique style
    Decorative
    Abstract
  - Teachings of the Qur'an

### The future of Islam: Major issues
- Practices that violate human rights in many countries
- Varied degrees of differences (tribal, economic, political)
  - No united front

# The Festivals of Islam

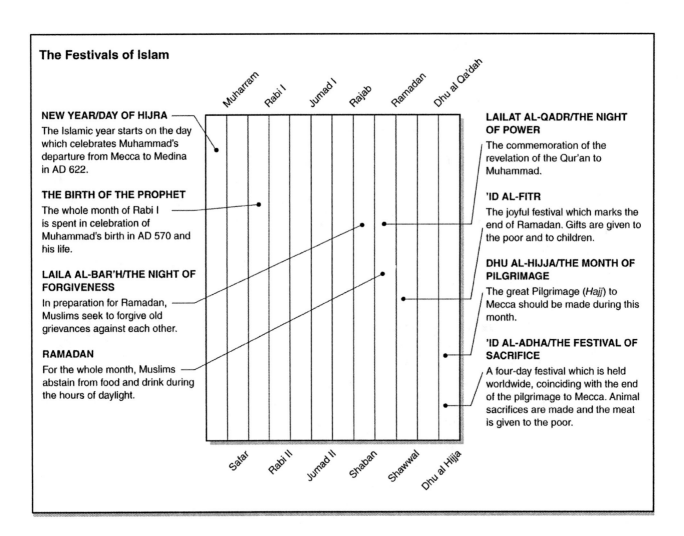

**NEW YEAR/DAY OF HIJRA**

The Islamic year starts on the day which celebrates Muhammad's departure from Mecca to Medina in AD 622.

**THE BIRTH OF THE PROPHET**

The whole month of Rabi I is spent in celebration of Muhammad's birth in AD 570 and his life.

**LAILA AL-BAR'H/THE NIGHT OF FORGIVENESS**

In preparation for Ramadan, Muslims seek to forgive old grievances against each other.

**RAMADAN**

For the whole month, Muslims abstain from food and drink during the hours of daylight.

**LAILAT AL-QADR/THE NIGHT OF POWER**

The commemoration of the revelation of the Qur'an to Muhammad.

**'ID AL-FITR**

The joyful festival which marks the end of Ramadan. Gifts are given to the poor and to children.

**DHU AL-HIJJA/THE MONTH OF PILGRIMAGE**

The great Pilgrimage (*Hajj*) to Mecca should be made during this month.

**'ID AL-ADHA/THE FESTIVAL OF SACRIFICE**

A four-day festival which is held worldwide, coinciding with the end of the pilgrimage to Mecca. Animal sacrifices are made and the meat is given to the poor.

Muharram · Rabi I · Jumad I · Rajab · Ramadan · Dhu al Qa'dah

Safar · Rabi II · Jumad II · Shaban · Shawwal · Dhu al Hijja

# SECTION II

# Music

# Ethnomusicology: Definitions, Directions, and Problems

*Bruno Nettl*

 ## Definitions

***Purpose*** To introduce the varied meanings of the term "ethnomusicology" and the various ways that ethnomusicologists think about what it is they do.

***Guidance*** There are probably about as many definitions of ethnomusicology as there are ethnomusicologists. Basically, the prefix "ethno" refers to "race" or "culture," and several other uses of that prefix are understood in the words ethnology, ethnobotony, and ethnohistory. The term "ethnic" is derived from the same word root, but it has a slightly different meaning than the prefix "ethno." The middle part of the word ethnomusicology, "music," can be defined as humanly organized sound other than speech sound that is capable of some form of communication. The suffix "ology" simply means the study of, or the science of. Thus, ethnomusicology literally means the cultural study of music. Another useful definition, not given in your text, is by Mantle Hood in the second edition of the *Harvard Dictionary of Music* (1972:298): "Ethnomusicology is an approach to the study of *any* music, not only in terms of itself but also in relation to its cultural context." One can also effectively think of ethnomusicology as the anthropology of music. Another field defined as the study of music is musicology, which should also mean the study of any or all music, but is not used in that manner today (although it was at one time). The term "musicology," by itself, usually means historical musicology, which places a greater emphasis upon music in its historical context than as a cultural phenomenon. Also, the most common application of the discipline of historical musicology is to European civilization.

*Terms*   Define or identify the following terms, based on readings from the text and/or other sources.

**ethnomusicology**

**musicology**

**historical musicology**

**anthropology**

**ethnology**

*Reading Comprehension*   Answer the following questions.

1. Write out the four definitions of ethnomusicology presented by the author:

   a. _____

   b. _____

   c. _____

   d. _____

2. Many ethnomusicologists began as _____, as students of _____, or as _____.

3. The term "ethnomusicology" has been in existence for several hundred years. True or False.

4. Two English terms for what preceded the term "ethnomusicology" are _____ and _____.

#  Directions

*Purpose*   To identify five concepts which ethnomusicologists hold to be important to their discipline, and which explain the various directions that the field has taken.

*Guidance*   The first concept concerns the idea that one of the identifying characteristics of mankind is that it makes music, and that these musics are as varied as are the languages and dialects spoken throughout the earth. Nevertheless, there may be some musical characteristics that are universal, and this possibility is of interest to ethnomusicologists. Still, because the ethnomusicologist is trained to hear minute differences as well as similarities between the innumerable types of music found in the world, figuring out how to describe and analyze the varieties of music is an important goal. The second concept points out the necessity for doing fieldwork. Every ethnomusicologist needs to be trained in the techniques of documenting musical events where they are found in their natural environment. This is often one of the most enjoyable aspects of being an ethnomusicologist, because of the experiences of living with different cultural groups. There are many ways of doing research in the field, and the method chosen is often determined by the research plan. Some ethnomusicologists learn how to perform the music of other cultures while living with them. This technique is similar to learning the language of the group with which you are studying. As one can attempt to become bilingual with the spoken or written language of a foreign culture, one can also attempt to become bimusical, although to do so would probably be secondary to the goals of the research. Nevertheless, one can enjoy the communication between teacher and student, and the depths of human understanding to be gained via learning some of a culture's music while in the field are great. The third concept is about notation, and this is perhaps the most difficult with which to deal. Western notation often does not work for non-Western musics, and much experimentation is constantly taking place to develop a visual notation that actually does describe the subtleties of a culture's music. The fourth concept is one of the most important in ethnomusicology, and the prefix of the name for the discipline, "ethno," directly refers to culture. Since every culture has music, it is important to realize that music can tell us something about a culture that other activities cannot tell us. Music may be like a key towards understanding a culture. Finally, the fifth concept is about the study of music in time, and how music grows, changes, stays the same, or even disappears. What are the processes that cause these developments through time? This concept is related to history, except that it is not written history. The ethnomusicologist often relies on oral history (conducting interviews) in his or her quest to understand what has happened and why.

*Terms*  Define or identify the following terms, based on readings from the text and/or other sources.

**fieldwork**

**notation or transcription of music**

**Seeger solution**

**Hipkins solution**

**Laban solution**

**acculturation**

*Reading Comprehension*  Answer the following questions.

5. List, in summary form, the five characteristics of the field of ethnomusicology:

  a. _____

  b. _____

c. _____

d. _____

e. _____

6. Westernization, modernization, urbanization are types of culture contact included under the term _____.

## Problems

*Purpose*   To consider the difficulties and problems that confront ethnomusicology as a discipline, while suggesting how ethnomusicologists are scholars who have great respect for and love of the music and people they study.

*Guidance*   Perhaps because of the youthfulness of ethnomusicology as a scientific discipline, it is still lacking in basic theory. This is because of the tremendous diversity of the musics and cultures in the world, because of the variety of approaches of ethnomusicologists themselves, and because of the abstract nature of music and what it means, what it does, and how it does it.

*Reading Comprehension*   Answer the following questions.

7. Ethnomusicologists have data on all the world's music. True or False.

8. A constant problem in ethnomusicology is the difficulty in achieving a proper balance between the observations of the _____ with the understanding of the _____ who has grown up in the culture.

9. Ethnomusicologists have not yet figured out an effective way to study music as a part of culture. True or False.

10. Ethnomusicologists have called the attention of _____ to the multitude of phenomena around the world on which they might draw for inspiration.

## Sample Test Questions

Multiple choice questions. Only one answer is correct.

1. Mantle Hood has formulated three solutions to the problem of transcribing or notating non-Western music. Which is *not* one of them: a. Hood Solution, b. Seeger Solution, c. Laban Solution, d. Hipkins Solution.

2. Which term means something quite different from what ethnomusicology is actually about: a. comparative musicology, b. musical ethnology, c. historical musicology, d. anthropology of music.

3. Which of the following best describes how an ethnomusicologist obtains his or her materials for research: a. through fieldwork, b. from recordings, c. out of books, d. by bringing an informant to the home, office, or studio for an interview and recording session.

4. Ethnomusicologists seem to be torn between which two ideals: a. unity of mankind and variety of musical phenomena, b. music as a universal language and mankind as a universal species, c. the unity of music and the diversity of mankind, d. music as language and language as music.
5. Ethnomusicologists are always interested in music as a phenomenon produced by a(n) a. composer, b. artist, c. musician, d. culture.

## ANSWERS TO READING COMPREHENSION QUESTIONS

1. a. The study of a music foreign to one's own; b. The study of contemporary musical systems; c. The study of music *in* and *as* culture; d. The comparative study of musical systems and cultures
2. musicians, musicology, anthropologists
3. False: it has been around for only about twenty-five years
4. comparative musicology, musical ethnology
5. a. the interest in universals balanced by appreciation of infinite variety, b. the emphasis on fieldwork, c. the possibility of notating and analyzing music visually and verbally, d. the insistence that music can be understood only in its cultural context, e. the interest in processes
6. acculturation
7. False: there are what seems to be an infinite number of cultures in the world, and it is seemingly impossible to have data on all of them
8. outsider, insider
9. True
10. composers

## ANSWERS TO SAMPLE TEST QUESTIONS

1. a        2. c        3. a        4. a        5. d

# Listening Form

Student Name_____ I.D. Number_____

Course Name _____ Course Number _____

Date_____ Chapter Number_____ Listening Example Number _____

Record or Tape Number_____ Name of Culture and Location _____

Name of Performer(s)_____

Instructions: place an X, ✓, or • in appropriate boxes; give types; indicate native names.

| performing elements (if vocal) | solo: M/F | duo: M/F | trio: M/F | quartet: M/F | group: M/F | other: M/F | |
|---|---|---|---|---|---|---|---|
| performing elements (if instrumental) | corpophone | idiophone | membrano-phone | aerophone | chordophone | electrophone | other |
| texture | single melody | dense unison | heterophone | imitation | parallelism | disphony | other |
| more texture | with drone | with time indicator | chordal | polyphonic stratification | colotomy | combination | variable |
| melodic contour | static | ascending | descending | conjunct | disjunct | undulating | terraced |
| mode or scale | number of notes | vernacular | using cipher notation (numbers), indicate the mode or scale in ascending order | | | | |
| meter | free | duple | triple | compound | additive | poly | other |
| speed | very slow | slow | moderate | fast | very fast | variable | other |
| amplitude | very soft | soft | moderate | loud | very loud | variable | other |
| timbre (tone color) | clear | breathy | nasal | open | tight | masked | other |
| inflections | no vibrato | slow vibrato | fast vibrato | wide vibrato | falsetto | multiphonics | other |
| formal structure | vernacular name | expanding | reverting | strophic | theme and variations | other | |
| structural or performance techniques | ostinato | responsorial | antiphonal | elastic rhythm | if vocal: syllabic or melismatic | non-synchronous parts | other |

# Evolution and Revolution in Chinese Music

## Kuo-huang Han and Lindy Li Mark

 Introduction

**Purpose**   To introduce basic sociocultural concepts that underlie the historical context of Chinese music, and to present the authors' research plan.

**Guidance**   Historically, music in China was embedded strongly in socio-ideological contexts. Music was mostly programmatic (i.e., for painting a musical picture or evoking other sensory forms) or symbolic (i.e., for expressing philosophical ideas, or ritual and/or social behavior) rather than aesthetic (i.e., for enjoyment in itself). In general, these concepts still apply to modern Chinese music. The authors discuss four kinds of conflicts that have led to the development of Chinese music, creating the diversity of Chinese musical forms and effecting changes in China's musical history. The terms "China" and "Chinese music" are meant to include both Taiwan and the People's Republic of China (and also Hong Kong), and all of the various traditional musics found within them, excluding the certain musics of particular ethnic minorities, such as Islamic and Korean enclaves and the Taiwan native people. Chinese terms in this chapter are romanized with the older Wade Giles system. When appropriate (e.g., under Terms), the newer and official pinyin romanizations are included in parentheses.

**Terms**   Define or identify the following terms or areas, based on readings from the text and/or other sources.

Find People's Republic of China, Republic of China (Taiwan or Formosa), and Hong Kong on a globe and locate Peking (Beijing), Tibet or Tibetan Plateau, Mongolia, Yellow River, great wall of China, and Gobi Desert. Notice the proximity that China has with Korea, Japan, Southeast Asia, India, Russia, and try to imagine possible trade routes between the Middle East and China. Compare China's size with Europe and the United States of America.

**programmatic music**

**absolute music**

**symbolic music**

*Reading Comprehension*    Answer the following questions.

1. In traditional China, music was embedded in _____ and _____ contexts.
2. The notion of "absolute music" in traditional China was quite prevalent. True or False.
3. In traditional China music was mostly _____ or _____.
4. The music of Taiwan and that of China share the same musical heritage. True or False.

#  Acoustic Theory in Chinese History

*Purpose*    To survey the acoustical theories of Chinese music.

*Guidance*    Acoustics is the study of sound. In contrast to ancient Greece, where musical acoustics was the concern of mysticism, musical acoustics in ancient China was associated with politics. This was probably because it was necessary to have certain instruments such as bells and blown tubes (panpipes) be in tune for governmental functions. Three ancient sources about Chinese scale systems are important to remember for their antiquity and their similarity to Greek scales (it us usually thought that European music derived from Greek music). These are the *Rites of the Chou Dynasty* (the earliest, from about 400 B.C.), the *Discourses on the State* (also from about 400 B.C.), and the *Chronicles of the House of Lü* (about 240 B.C.). The basis for the pitches referred to or explained in these literary sources is called the "cycle of fifths," or sometimes the "circle of fifths." Also the term "overblown fifths" is used. A length ratio of 3:2 also explains the concept of relationships between tubes. This concept is difficult to understand without a demonstration using a set of closed tubes, whereby the notes can actually be produced. You can experiment with a 50 inch length of 3/4 inch diameter plastic tubing. Begin by cutting a piece 12 1/2 inches long (pitch C), next cut a piece at 8 3/8 inches (pitch G), then 11 1/4 inches (pitch D), another at 7 1/2 inches (pitch A), and a last one at 10 1/4 inches. Place a cork in the end of each and blow across the top. The lowest pitch you can produce is the fundamental; the next pitch you produce by overblowing is the fifth plus an octave. When you arrange the pipes in a descending order of length you have a raftpipe (panpipe) that plays the

Chinese pentatonic scale. The complexity of acoustics continues when you understand that this system of fifths is actually like a spiral, which means infinity. In other words, you could go on making pipes for the rest of your life, and if they were correctly made according to acoustic theory, you would never repeat the first note (this is what a closed system means). This discovery was made in antiquity by Greek and Chinese scholars at about the same time. Another discovery that occurred at about the same time in Europe and China is called "equal temperament." This is a system whereby all the twelve notes of the chromatic scale are slightly out of tune in order to accommodate playing them together in chordal sequences. Today our ears (really our brains) have accepted this out of tune equal temperament as being in tune.

*Terms*  Define or identify the following terms, based on readings from the text and/or other sources.

**Rites of the Chou Dynasty**

**Discourses on the State**

**Chronicles of the House of Lü**

**yellow bell**

**great tone**

**forest bell**

**resonating bell**

**cycle of fifths**

**pentatonic scale**

**Complete Book of Rules for Music**

**Book of Pitches**

**lü**

*Reading Comprehension*  Answer the following questions.

5. In ancient China, music was from the beginning associated with
   _____.

6. The earliest reference to scale intervals is found in (English name)
   _____.

7. The fundamental or lowest pitch was called (English name)
   _____.

8. Theoretically, pentatonic scales could be constructed upon any of the (Chinese and English terms) _____ or
   _____.

9. According to the Chronicles of the House of Lü, the construction of a set of twelve pitch pipes or tubes was based on the method of the _____.

10. By the _____ century the practice of tuning court instruments to standard pitches well established.

11. An important element of the state ideology was that music could influence the _____ and _____ order.

12. Each new dynasty had restandardized the pitch measurements, although the same names and terminologies were used. True or False.

13. The discovery of a method of equal temperament by prince Chu Tsai-yü in 1584 is unique to Chinese acoustic history. True or False.

##  Historical Survey

*Purpose*   To place Chinese musical instruments, ideas about music, and cultural contexts for music, into a Chinese historical perspective, based on the three major periods called ancient, middle ancient, and late historical.

*Guidance*   *The Ancient Period* (from the Stone Age to about 250 B.C.). There are three ways to obtain some understanding about music from this lengthy period. First, through a study of actual musical instruments excavated by archaeologists we can understand something about the complexity of ancient Chinese music, especially by examining the tuning of instruments with fixed pitch, such as stone chimes. Second, a study of musical instruments and musical activity as shown in pictures or carved in stone yields information of cultural significance. Third, ancient historical writings in China provide important types of musical information. One can appreciate the antiquity of musical thinking in China (for example, the instrument classification system, the relationship of instruments to the seasons, months, directions, and metaphysics, the relationship of music to government, and so forth) by comparing it with Europe at that time. Practically nothing is known about music during the European stone age, for example, and not until the Etruscan and Greek civilizations do musical events appear in painting and sculpture, and not until the Greek and Roman periods do historical accounts appear that explain anything about music.

*The Middle Ancient Period* (from about 250 B.C. to 907 A.D.). Information is obtained about this period by the same methods as for the Ancient Period, that is, through archaeology, music iconography, and historical writings. The latter has revealed that music was divided into three types or divisions: ritual music, secular music, and folk music. The chronological list on text page 14 indicates that many dynasties or kingdoms existed during this period, and music was an important and frequent part of the royal courts. Because of the large number of dynasties during the Middle Ancient Period it is difficult to grasp a feeling of unity of musical development that would define this period as unified. Instead, we see musical activities expanding, with influences from outside cultures via trade, and with the development of governmental musical establishments and court ensembles of enormous sizes.

*The Late Historical Period* (from 907 A.D. to 1911). This period saw a return to certain ancient ideas about music, especially those associated with Confucianism (which originated in the sixth century B.C.) and the ch'in, the zither type of chordophone that was a part of the typical Confucian scholar-gentleman. Nevertheless, the p'i-p'a, a lute type of chordophone that was originally introduced from the Middle East, remained more popular than the ch'in because it was louder and flashier. Chinese drama, which was an early form of opera, became very popular during this period, and two styles existed, the northern and the southern. These were differentiated in three ways: northern style = p'i-p'a (lute), seven tones, one singer; southern style = ti (transverse flute, pronounced *dee*), five tones, many singers. These two styles merged during the 1500s into the K'un opera style. Later, Peking opera, from north-central China, became so popular during the 1800s that it was called the national style.

*Terms*   Define or identify the following terms, based on readings from the text and/or other sources.

**p'i-p'a (pipa)**

**ch'in (qin)**

**shêng (sheng)**

**se**

**Pear Garden**

**Confucianism**

**Yuan drama**

**K'un opera**

**Peking opera (Beijing)**

**Tang dynasty and the Tang emperor**

*Reading Comprehension*   Answer the following questions.

14. Chinese musical instruments had been classified into _____ categories according to the materials from which they were made by the _____ century _____.

15. List the categories of musical instruments:

     a. _____, b. _____,

     c. _____, d. _____,

e. _____, f. _____,

g. _____, h. _____,

16. During the sixth century B.C., musical art was considered a necessary part of the education of a gentleman. True or False.

17. The three major divisions of music that were recognized during the first part of the Middle Ancient Period by the ministry of music were _____, _____, and _____.

18. Give the Chinese names of the following thousand year old musical instruments that were recently excavated by archaeologists in China:
    a. seven-string zither without fret studs called _____,
    b. a twenty-two-pipe mouth organ called _____, and
    c. a twenty-five-string zither called _____.

19. A pear-shaped plucked lute known as the _____ was introduced into China from _____ during the sixth century A.D.

20. During the early Late Historical Period (Sung dynasty) the ch'in was revived and its popularity far surpassed that of the p'i-p'a. True or False.

21. In the northern style of Yuan drama, the _____ was the main accompanying instrument.

22. In the southern style of Yuan drama, the _____ was the main accompanying instrument.

23. The most popular Chinese opera style during the nineteenth century, and which became the national style, was K'un opera. True or False.

24. The emperor of the _____ dynasty became known as the patron deity of musicians and actors.

25. A music academy established in 714 (during the T'ang dynasty) was called the _____.

##  Traditional Music Today

*Purpose*  To describe the most important traditional musical styles and instruments found today in China, using the categories of ritual music, modern classical music, folk song and minstrel music, and theater music.

*Guidance*  *Ritual Music:* The celebration of Confucius' birthday on September 28 in Taiwan is the only occasion when music can be heard that may sound something like ancient Chinese court ritual music. The instruments, costumes, music, rhythm, and dance used during this Taiwanese government-supported ritual are derived from the ritual court musics of several Chinese dynasties, with the tuned stone chimes and bronze bells being the oldest (from possibly 1000 years B.C.). This type of music is no longer heard in the People's Republic of China, since the Republican Revolution of 1911 ended many traditional musical styles, especially those associated with religion.

*Modern Classical Music:* Classical Chinese music today is often a mixture of classical, folk, and popular styles. Musical instruments are also mixed together, including those that traditionally played classical solos with those that performed in opera. One ancient instrument that continues to be played alone is the ch'in, a zither chordophone. The modern instrument, still with seven strings (usually metal today, rather than silk), has thirteen inlayed markings or studs along the strings to indicate finger placement. The ancient instruments (i.e., pre-Han Dynasty) did not have such markings. Since the ch'in has no frets and no bridges to raise the strings, the musician presses the desired string completely down with his left hand fingers (touching the wood underneath it) while plucking it with his or her right hand fingers. Additionally, many types of harmonics (lightly touching the string with the left hand fingers), vibratos, and slides are produced. The ch'in is a very subtle and very soft sounding instrument. The cheng (pronounced with an upward intonation), another zither, has sixteen strings of metal (some had 13 and today some have 22) that are raised from the wooden body by an equal number of movable bridges shaped like an inverted V. The musician plucks the strings with his or her right hand (using little plectrums on his or her fingers) while often pressing the desired string on the left side of the bridge to achieve a vibrato and/or sliding effect. The erh-hu or nan-hu, a popular Chinese fiddle or violin, is unique because the hairs of the bow pass between the two metal strings of the instrument, and cannot be removed unless the bow or the instrument is disassembled. The small resonating chamber of the instrument is usually covered with reptile skin, and its sound is very nasal. Another instrument whose sound is nasal (at least when compared with its Western counterparts) is the ti or ti-tzu, a bamboo transverse or horizontal flute. A special hole between the mouthpiece hole and the fingerholes is covered with a very thin piece of bamboo skin. This skin buzzes like the skin on a kazoo when the instrument is played. These characteristics of tone color alteration (the reptile skin on the fiddle and the bamboo skin on the flute) give the instruments great carrying power, enabling them to be heard during performances of opera, or outside. Both instruments were common in Chinese folk music. Another outdoor instrument is the sona, a double reed instrument like the oboe. This loud instrument originated in the Middle East, and a very similar aerophone is the zurna from Turkey (sona and zurna are almost the same word). The shêng is a mouth organ or harmonica with over twenty pipes that stick straight up out of a gourd windchest (it is classified as a gourd instrument, even though its pipes are made from bamboo). Each of the pipes has a single reed cut into it where it is inserted into the windchest, making the instrument a multiple single-reed aerophone (or a multiple clarinet; the Western harmonica or blues-harp is also a multiple single-reed aerophone). Finally, the yang chin, a hammered dulcimer, is very similar to the Appalachian hammered dulcimer found in the United States. This shows how some musical instruments have migrated, in this case from Persia or Iran east to China and north to Europe and finally to the United States of America.

*Folk Song and Minstrel Music:* One of the popular musical instruments played by minstrels or wondering singers is the san-hsien, a three-stringed lute. This instrument should be remembered because it migrated to Japan via Okinawa, where it is known as the shamisen in Japan and jamisen in Okinawa; both terms, like the name san-hsien, mean three-strings. All three instruments are covered with skin and are therefore somewhat similar to the American banjo.

*Theater Music:* Peking opera is the most widely known of Chinese operatic styles. The authors discuss the style, performance practice, and the function of the instrumental ensemble in Peking opera. It is interesting to contrast the authors' descriptions of Peking opera with European opera because the conventions are so very different. On the one hand Peking opera can be very subtle (for example, the 26 ways to laugh or the 39 ways to stroke the beard), while on the other hand it can be very outgoing (for example, the use of acrobatics and percussion punctuation).

**Terms** Define or identify the following terms, based on readings from the text and/or other sources.

Be able to identify the musical instruments in the pictures.

**cheng (zheng)**

**erh-hu or nan-hu (erhu)**

**ti or ti-tzu (dizi)**

**sona (souna)**

**san-hsien**

**yang chin (yang qin)**

**hsiao or tung hsiao (xiao or dongxiao)**

*Reading Comprehension* Answer the following questions.

26. The only occasion in the People's Republic of China during which ancient court ritual music is heard is the celebration of Confucius' birthday. True or False.

27. The traditional Chinese classical sixteen-stringed instrument known as the _____ is a _____ type chordophone with _____ bridges.

28. The strings of the ch'in, a _____ type chordophone with _____ bridges, are tuned to one of several _____ modes.

29. The Chinese transverse flute known as the _____ has a hole that is covered with _____, which functions like the buzz on a kazoo.

30. The shēng is an instrument with many _____ made from _____; it is classified in China as a _____ instrument because of the material of its body.

#  Contemporary Chinese Music

*Purpose*   To describe the musical situation in mainland China since the Republican Revolution, and the present state of music in Taiwan and Hong Kong.

*Guidance*   There are four periods of history in mainland China in the twentieth century that affected the way music developed there: (1) from the Republican Revolution of 1911 until (2) the founding of the People's Republic of China in 1949, which lasted until (3) the Cultural Revolution from 1966–69, giving way to (4) the modern age to the present. Generally speaking, traditional Chinese music was considered less and less desirable by the government during the first three periods, and European musical concepts and musical instruments gained in popularity. It is an interesting paradox that traditional Chinese music and musical instruments were not acceptable to the communist government, while European ideas were. While the compositions during much of this time are very Western sounding, and range from art songs (the English translation of the German lieder) to symphonies, most music since 1945 has been composed by committees of composers whereby no single individual takes the credit. This is all part of the concept of music for the masses. The Cultural Revolution, however, was a very bleak time for the arts, and the only compositions written were eight revolutionary operas and ballets, in which the singers and dancers are dressed in military fatigues or peasant clothing, and the themes are always about the working masses triumphing over the feudal and bourgeois (capitalist) elite.

The musical situation in Taiwan and Hong Kong has been a contrast to that found in mainland China, largely because composers have been free to do what they want to do. Music in Taiwan, especially, has expressed nationalism (based on folk themes and/or other conventions that depict national pride) because of its long struggle to portray itself as free China. Avant-garde or very modern music has also appeared, often based on traditional Chinese musical, textual, or programmatic ideas. In these ways, twentieth-century Chinese music throughout the People's Republic of China and the Republic of China (Taiwan) has been closely associated with politics and promoting social values, sort of like it had centuries earlier.

In 1993 my wife and I spent about a month in Hong Kong and the People's Republic of China (PRC). At that time we heard several concerts in Hong Kong by the Hong Kong Philharmonic Orchestra, performances of traditional music in the civic center, and snatches of traditional music in various places in Kowloon, on the mainland. Hong Kong is a huge ultra modern city, and encountering traditional music in traditional settings is not easy. Excellent traditional music study opportunities are possible at several universities, especially the Chinese University of Hong Kong, where there is an excellent program in ethnomusicology.

We encountered more traditional music in Beijing than in Hong Kong. I gave several lectures at the Central Conservatory of Music, where I had the opportunity to hear several of its faculty members perform. One moving experience in particular was at the apartment of the yangqin professor, who gave us a private concert that was fascinating. Such virtuosity and musicianship! All the traditional Chinese musical instruments are taught at the Central Conservatory of Music in Beijing, and all the professors are among the best in China. Another memorable experience in Beijing was at the Temple of Heaven. When we were there, a film was being made, and numerous musicians playing souna, erhu, and percussion accompanied several men performing the famous lion dance. We thought they were making an art film about traditional Chinese music and dance, but they were making a cigarette commercial! I never did find out what type of cigarettes the commercial was being made for, and I knew I would never see it on television.

Another great center for Chinese music in the PRC is Shanghai, where a type of music known as "southern silk and bamboo" originated. The Shanghai Conservatory of Music is very famous, not only for traditional music, but for learning Western classical music as well. Shanghai is China's most modern city, after Hong Kong, and it is becoming the financial center of this country of a billion, if not all of East Asia. Like Tokyo, Shanghai has just about everything anybody would want, and finding traditional music can be a difficult task without knowing the right people to guide you.

*Terms*    Define or identify the following terms, based on readings from the text and/or other sources.

**Republican Revolution**

**Cultural Revolution**

**Mao Tse-tung**

**Chiang Ching**

*Reading Comprehension*    Answer the following questions.

31. The purpose of the arts in a socialist country was outlined during a speech in May 1942 by _____.

32. One of the outcomes of the founding of the People's Republic in 1949 was large-scale research of _____.

33. Beginning in 1945 musical creativity in the People's Republic of China was done by _____ of _____.

34. Much of the music composed in Taiwan and Hong Kong uses new techniques to express_____.

35. In general, people in Taiwan and Hong Kong prefer _____ _____ music.

## *Video Viewing*

1. Dizi—flute, with ensemble [erhu, sheng, yangqin, and pipa]: "Gusu-xing" ("Trip to Suzhou") (3-1). *The JVC Video Anthology of World Music and Dance,* East Asia III, Volume 3, China 1 (VTMV-33).

2. Pipa—lute solo: "Shimian maifu" ("Ambush on all sides") (3-2). *The JVC Video Anthology of World Music and Dance,* East Asia III, Volume 3, China 1 (VTMV-33). This composition is often translated as "The Great Ambuscade."

3. Erhu—bowed fiddle with yangqin: "Erquan yingyue" ("The moon reflected in a spring") (3-3). *The JVC Video Anthology of World Music and Dance,* East Asia III, Volume 3, China 1 (VTMV-33).

4. Zheng—zither solo: "Yuzhou changwan" ("The fisherman singing in the evening") (3-4). *The JVC Video Anthology of World Music and Dance,* East Asia III, Volume 3, China 1 (VTMV-33).

5. Instrumental ensemble: "Chunjiang huayueye" ("A beautiful moonlit night by the river in springtime") (3-5). *The JVC Video Anthology of World Music and Dance,* East Asia III, Volume 3, China 1 (VTMV-33).

6. Instrumental ensemble: "Meihuacao" ("Plum blossoms") (3-7). *The JVC Video Anthology of World Music and Dance,* East Asia III, Volume 3, China 1 (VTMV-33).

7. Dongxiao—flute solo: "Huainian" ("Nostalgia") (3-8). *The JVC Video Anthology of World Music and Dance,* East Asia III, Volume 3, China 1 (VTMV-33). This vertical flute, from Fujien in southern China, is related to the Japanese shakuhachi.

8. From *jingju*—Beijing opera: "Bawang biefei" ("The King's parting with his favorite") (3-10). *The JVC Video Anthology of World Music and Dance,* East Asia III, Volume 3, China 1 (VTMV-33).

9. From *Chuanju*—Sichuan opera: "Baishezhan" ("The white snake"), 3-11. *The JVC Video Anthology of World Music and Dance,* East Asia III, Volume 3, China 1 (VTMV-33).

10. *No. 17 Cotton Mill Shanghai Blues: Music in China.* Beats of the Heart series. Jeremy Marre, director and producer.

## SAMPLE TEST QUESTIONS

Multiple choice questions. Only one answer is correct.

1. While the term "symbolic music" is used to express philosophical ideas, ritual, and social behavior, which term is used to express music that evokes other sensory forms? a. absolute, b. programmatic, c. meditative, d. social.

2. Like Pythagoras, the ancient Chinese metaphysical musicians discovered that: a. harmony is to music what beauty is to nature, b. the origin of music is mankind's imitation of nature, c. pitches derived from the cycle of fifths did not form a closed system, d. the tritone was indeed the "devil in music."

3. Which characteristic is *not* a part of traditional Chinese music? a. the notion of absolute music, b. it was embedded in social and ideological contexts, c. it was mostly programmatic, d. it was largely symbolic.

4. The fundamental pitch of Chinese music is called: a. Forest Bell, b. Yellow Bell, c. Bronze Bell, d. Old Standard, e. Mean Tone.

5. Which instrument is vastly different from the other three? a. sheng, b. cheng, c. ch'in, d. p'i-p'a.

6. The ch'in was originally associated with which ideology? a. Buddhism, b. Taoism, c. Hinduism, d. Islam, e. Confucianism.

7. The ch'in is classified in ethnomusicology as: a. plucked lute chordophone, b. struck zither chordophone, c. plucked zither chordophone, d. bowed lute chordophone, e. string instrument.

8. China's own classification of the ch'in is: a. wood, b. bamboo, c. silk, d. metal, e. gourd.

9. One of the techniques of playing the ch'in is: a. striking its wooden body with the plectrum, b. using harmonics, c. striking the drone strings while playing the melody strings, d. pressing the strings in back of the bridges to bend the tones.

10. The bow used to play the erh-hu: a. is made from cat gut, b. shows Western influence, c. is made from human hair, d. passes between the two strings, e. also strikes the body of the instrument to produce a percussive effect.

11. Chinese musical instruments are classified into how many categories according to the traditional Chinese manner? a. 4, b. 5, c. 6, d. 8, e. 10.

12. The sheng is classified as what according to the traditional Chinese manner? a. wood, b. bamboo, c. gourd, d. metal, e. silk.

13. Although it was developed half a century earlier in China than in Europe, the equal tempered scale: a. remained theoretical and dormant, b. was used only in ritual music, c. was used only in Chinese opera, d. was employed by the philosophical Chinese musicians only.

14. In the People's Republic of China, most works, especially recent ones, are created by: a. composers designated by the government, b. national treasures, c. folk musicians, d. committees of composers, e. women, which shows that socialism has no sex discrimination.

15. In historical Chinese literature, professional musicians and actors were considered: a. rich, b. sacred beings, c. strange, d. lowly and unworthy of mention, e. elite.

16. Which type of instrument was not found in late neolithic archaeological sites in China? a. 25-stringed zither, b. stone chimes, c. pottery ocarina, d. bronze bells.

17. The main accompanying instrument in the northern style of Yuan drama is the: a. ch'in, b. ti, c. p'i-p'a, d. sheng, e. cheng.

18. Which of the following is *not* one of the trends first introduced by Mao Tse-tung and realized with the founding of the People's Republic in 1949? a. the return to folk tradition, b. the emphasis on rigorous training in performance, c. the implication of the electronic medium, d. the combination of Western and Chinese elements, e. the infusion of political content in program music.

19. The Chinese hammered dulcimer yang chin: a. is an instrument from the Appalachian mountains that was introduced by Pete Seeger during his tour of China in the 1950s, b. was imported into China from Persia during the eighteenth century, c. is an ancient Chinese instrument that was popular in northern China during the Han dynasty, d. is an important instrument in Peking opera, e. is used only for Chinese mountain music.

20. In which area or group have Chinese musicians *not* kept pace with international trends: a. Chinese communities overseas, b. Hong Kong, c. People's Republic of China, d. Republic of China.

## ANSWERS TO READING COMPREHENSION QUESTIONS

1. social, ideological
2. False: although it exists, it is not nearly as common as program music
3. programmatic, symbolic
4. True
5. politics
6. Rites of the Chou Dynasty
7. yellow bell
8. lü or chromatic pitches
9. cycle of fifths
10. third century B.C.
11. cosmic, social
12. True
13. False: it was also discovered in Europe at about the same time, although some scholars maintain the Europeans learned it from the Chinese
14. eight, third, B.C.
15. a. metal, b. stone, c. silk, d. bamboo, e. gourd, f. pottery or earth, g. leather, h. wood
16. True
17. ritual music, secular music, regional or folk music
18. a. ch'in, b. shêng, c. se
19. p'i-p'a, Central Asia
20. False: the p'i-p'a remained more popular than the ch'in because it could play louder and was more virtuoso

21. p'i-p'a
22. ti
23. False: it was the Peking opera
24. T'ang
25. Pear Garden
26. False: while the statement is true for Taiwan, the People's Republic of China does not celebrate Confucius' birthday
27. cheng, zither, movable
28. zither, no, pentatonic
29. ti or ti-tzu, bamboo skin
30. pipes, bamboo, gourd
31. Mao Tse-tung
32. folk music
33. committees of composers
34. nationalism
35. popular

## ANSWERS TO SAMPLE TEST QUESTIONS

| 1. b | 2. c | 3. a | 4. b |
|------|------|------|------|
| 5. a | 6. e | 7. c | 8. c |
| 9. b | 10. d | 11. d | 12. c |
| 13. a | 14. d | 15. d | 16. a |
| 17. c | 18. c | 19. b | 20. c |

# Listening Form

Student Name_____ I.D. Number_____

Course Name _____ Course Number _____

Date_____ Chapter Number_____ Listening Example Number _____

Record or Tape Number_____ Name of Culture and Location _____

Name of Performer(s)_____

Instructions: place an X, ✓, or • in appropriate boxes; give types; indicate native names.

| performing elements (if vocal) | solo: M/F | duo: M/F | trio: M/F | quartet: M/F | group: M/F | other: M/F | |
|---|---|---|---|---|---|---|---|
| performing elements (if instrumental) | corpophone | idiophone | membrano-phone | aerophone | chordophone | electrophone | other |
| texture | single melody | dense unison | heterophone | imitation | parallelism | disphony | other |
| more texture | with drone | with time indicator | chordal | polyphonic stratification | colotomy | combination | variable |
| melodic contour | static | ascending | descending | conjunct | disjunct | undulating | terraced |
| mode or scale | number of notes | vernacular | using cipher notation (numbers), indicate the mode or scale in ascending order | | | | |
| meter | free | duple | triple | compound | additive | poly | other |
| speed | very slow | slow | moderate | fast | very fast | variable | other |
| amplitude | very soft | soft | moderate | loud | very loud | variable | other |
| timbre (tone color) | clear | breathy | nasal | open | tight | masked | other |
| inflections | no vibrato | slow vibrato | fast vibrato | wide vibrato | falsetto | multiphonics | other |
| formal structure | vernacular name | expanding | reverting | strophic | theme and variations | other | |
| structural or performance techniques | ostinato | responsorial | antiphonal | elastic rhythm | if vocal: syllabic or melismatic | non-synchronous parts | other |

# Trends in the Black Music of South Africa, 1959–1969

## John Blacking

 ## Introduction

***Purpose*** To introduce the sociocultural concepts that underlie the music of black South Africa, and to describe how it changes as the society changes.

***Guidance*** The late John Blacking was a cultural anthropologist, a performing pianist, and an ethnomusicologist who had great insight in the study of music as social behavior. In his introduction he makes several important statements that are important to remember. First he defines music as "a special mode of nonverbal communication," a relatively simple definition that opens the door for discussion. In order to understand the music of a culture, he stresses the need to understand the social system (and more broadly, the sociopolitical context) that produces the music. Then we as outsiders should also be able to learn how to listen to the music as the insiders (music makers and native perceivers) do. This is a lesson that we should adhere to for each chapter in this book and for every music culture that we study.

One important part of the lesson is that outsiders often tend to "dilute" another culture's music and try to make it fit within the outsider's own aesthetic framework. His story about the German Lutheran minister's African church choir is an example. Blacking gives examples of music groups that developed along the lines of the changes that took place in South Africa's social system. In addition to the influence of music from the United States and Europe in the 1960s, the idea of "Black Power" infused South African music with a self-conscious African idiom. Foremost was the collaborative production by whites and blacks of the musical *King Kong* in 1959, which was financially successful, and both composer and performers were black. Thereafter, politics in South Africa became more oppressive to blacks, and music became an agent of political expression partially because of the economic successes of many urban music groups.

*Terms*    Define or identify the following terms or areas, based on readings from the text and/or other sources.

Locate South Africa and Mozambique on a recent African map. Pinpoint the major urban areas and the black townships; be aware of recent changes of political boundaries.

**apartheid**

**Johannesburg**

**Bantu homelands**

**Zulu**

**Xhosa**

**Black power**

**Miriam Makeba**

*Reading Comprehension*    Answer the following questions.

1. The decade in which Black Power came into prominence in South Africa was the_____.

2. The most obvious change in South African music in the 1960s was the infusion of the _____ _____.

3. *King Kong* was a_____ which provided a starring role for

   _____
   _____ and helped to establish her career.

4. South African Freedom Songs came into existence in the

   _____.

5. Blacking defines music as "a special _____-
   _____.

6. LeRoi Jones wrote that music is "the result of certain

   _____ _____, certain specific ways of _____ about the
   _____, and only ultimately about the
   _____ in which music can be made."

#  The Social and Political Background

*Purpose*   To understand the social and political changes of the 1960s in South Africa and the resulting effects on black South Africans and their music.

*Guidance*   Musical activity in South African cities during the 1960s was affected by political changes in several ways. Throughout the country, African people had to be careful not to express political ideas in their song texts. As a result, the music itself became a vehicle for protest, and certain musical elements became unifying factors of the oppressed people. One dance, the Venda pipe dance, is so called because each dancer plays a single-tubed pipe (edge aerophone, like blowing across a soda bottle) made from a piece of steel tubing. The many dancers-musicians interlock their individual notes to create a rhythmical melodic fabric. This communal music making, where the whole is dependent on the parts, is symbolic of the South African native people striving for unity within their diversity.

*Terms*   Define or identify the following terms or areas, based on readings from the text and/or other sources.

**Venda**

**Chopi**

**township**

**pipe dance**

**mine dance**

**Witwatersrand Gold Mines**

*Reading Comprehension*   Answer the following questions.

7. Political changes of the 1960s forced blacks in South Africa to express political sentiments in the _____of their music.

8. The disappearance of the social conditions when certain kinds of music were performed meant that the music was eliminated. True or False.

9. _____ _____ are performed by workers of the Witwatersrand Gold Mines during leisure hours and Sunday mornings.

10. Teams of dancers have a _____, a _____, a _____, and assistants.

11. In most of the mine dances, the _____ are usually played by men, although there are exceptions.

12. Changes in social and political life have often created some of the best performances of traditional South African communal music. True or False.

13. In South Africa, the traditional music is never as politically significant as the event that it accompanies. True or False.

14. List at least five uses for music and dancing in South Africa.

    a. _____,

    b. _____,

    c. _____,

    d. _____,

    e. _____.

15. Managers of dance teams always take part in the dancing themselves. True or False.

16. The dance team director of music is responsible for _____ and _____ each dance.

17. In traditional South Africa, dances are never performed by men and women together. True or False.

18. The dance team director of dance blows a _____ to _____ a change of step and calls out the name of the new _____.

19. In South Africa, everything that sounds like music to us is regarded as music by them. True or False.

20. Some men wear costumes to look like women in South African mine dances, because traditionally these dances were danced by both sexes. True or False.

21. All musical instruments, except for the drums, have their tuning checked by the director of music of the dance team before each performance. True or False.

22. The manager of a dance team is responsible for ensuring that there is beer to drink. True or False.

 # Some Common Elements of the Musical Systems

*Purpose*  To identify, describe, and examine various aspects of South African music and relate them to the various cultures that make them.

*Guidance*  The dynamics of culture, or the "folk" process, affects how all music develops, grows, changes, and even disappears. South Africa provides an interesting case study for change because of the situations discussed in earlier sections of this chapter. Change also took place before the advent of European colonization, although there are no written records to prove it. Today there are new compositions written for Chopi xylophone orchestras each year.

In this section of the chapter, the author uses a number of terms from European music to explain the traditional music of South Africa. The technique of individual, single-pitched instruments interlocking their single notes, discussed in the beginning of the chapter, is also used with voices. While the human voice is not limited to a single note, the technique is employed by other African cultures (Pygmies of the Ituri Forest, for example) and perhaps symbolizes the aspect of communalism or collectivity in living. Blacking defines "scale" as "fixed stores of notes," which is the same as an arbitrary arrangement of notes in descending or ascending order. Pentatonic (five-tone), hexatonic (six-tone), and heptatonic (seven-tone) scales are used by the Venda, and these are not exactly the same as five-, six-, and seven-tone scales in European music, as is obvious when heard. He also uses the terms "harmony" and "tonality," but as in Chapter 10, they do not usually mean European harmony and tonality, except in the case of vocal polyphony where one of the present techniques includes parallel motion and tonic-dominant progressions. All multipart music creates a type of harmony when sounded, and all music has a tonality, meaning it has a note or pitch that functions as a central point of relaxation. Even blocks of notes (chords) create points of tension and/or relaxation, as the author's diagram explains.

South African pop music flourished within that country from 1969 until the release from prison of Nelson Mandela in 1991 and his election as president of South Africa in 1993. South African pop music was an important voice for political and social change, and since the demise of apartheid, it has become increasingly more popular outside that country than within it. A style called township jive was very popular in South Africa in the 1970s, made famous by the Boyoyo Boys. Township jazz was another popular style in the 1970s.

The 1990s have seen important popular musical changes in South Africa. Miriam Mekeba, for example, who was exiled in 1962, returned in 1993. Likewise, Hugh Masekela also returned from exile; they and other jazz-pop artists developed new sounds, such as *mbaqanga,* a type of jazz fusion. After Paul Simon's release of *Graceland,* Joseph Shabala and Ladysmith Black Mambazo became very popular with their style of *mbube,* which is also found in Zimbabwe. Since their first recording in 1973, the group has recorded many albums, including "Shaka Zulu," which won a Grammy award in the World Music category in 1988. Newer pop music styles have been created by the following artists, to name just a few: The Mahotella Queens, a female vocal group employing a contemporary idiom while wearing traditional Zulu clothing as a symbol of identity; Simon "Mahlatini" Nkabinde, whose deep, growling voice is popular; Bubblegum, with singer Chaka Chaka, a group which relies heavily on synthesizers and drum machines for its pop sound; and Busi Mhlongo who has an eclectic style ranging from jazz to Zulu elements.

*Terms*   Define or identify the following terms, based on readings from the text and/or other sources.

**musical bow**

**mbira**

**lamellaphone**

**interlocking technique**

**"folk" tradition**

**tshikona**

*Reading Comprehension*   Answer the following questions.

23. Southern African music remained static for several centuries until European influences affected it. True or False.

24. In South Africa, orally transmitted music is performed less accurately than that which is written down. True or False.

25. In the case of ritual music, every performance may be almost identical. True or False.

26. As a system of socially accepted concepts and conventions, Venda music is a _____ experience.

27. Among the Venda, most music is composed by individuals whose names are not known. True or False.

28. In African music, musical structures are correctly performed when each individual _____ himself or herself and at the same time _____to the "invisible conductor" of the collective.

29. Communal instrumental and communal vocal musics are found in South Africa. True or False.

30. During the pipe dance of the Venda, the men play the _____ and the women and girls play the _____.

31. In African music, successful musical performance depends on the mutual interaction of all the players. True or False.

32. The South African Venda do not recognize the interval of the octave. True or False.

33. In South African traditional cultures, hoeing, threshing, grinding, or pounding maize (corn) have no affect on the metrical patterns of the music that accompanies it. True or False.

34. The musical rules of the Venda are so abstract that children cannot distinguish between the correct and incorrect ways of singing a particular melody. True or False.

35. Because regular _____ is the basic crite-
    rion of music, in song the rhythms of
    _____ are ignored.
36. In South Africa, categories of music are distinguished by their

    _____.

## Video Viewing

1. Lullaby accompanied by musical bow. Republic of South Africa, the
   Zulu (19-18). *The JVC Video Anthology of World Music and Dance,* Middle East and Africa IV (VTMV-49).
2. Wedding ceremony. Republic of South Africa, the Zulu (19-19). *The
   JVC Video Anthology of World Music and Dance,* Middle East and Africa
   IV (VTMV-49).
3. *Graceland: The African Concert.* Paul Simon, Miriam Makeba, Hugh
   Masekela, Ladysmith Black Mambazo. Directed by Michael Lindsay-
   Hogg, produced by Ian Hoblyn. Warner Reprise Video 38136-3.
4. *Rhythm of Resistance: The Black Music of South Africa.* Beats of the Heart
   series. Jeremy Marre, director and producer.
5. *Voices of Sarafina! Songs of Hope and Freedom.* Directed by Nigel Noble.
   Music by Mbongeni Ngema and Hugh Masekela, with Miriam
   Makeba. Lincoln Center Theater/Noble Enterprises (1988).

## SAMPLE TEST QUESTIONS

Multiple choice questions. Only one answer is correct.

1. Apartheid means: a. equality, b. separateness, c. affirmative action for
   minorities, d. all of the above.
2. A musical play produced in South Africa in 1959 as the result of collaboration between whites and blacks is titled: a. *A Streetcar Named
   Hope,* b. *King Kong,* c. *The Zulu Wars,* d. *Apartheid,* e. *Man of the Mines.*
3. The name of the singer who got her career start in the above musical
   play is: a. Shirley Bassey, b. Abia Akita, c. Miriam Makeba, d. Sade,
   e. Winnie Mandela.
4. Blacking defines music as a special mode of what kind of communication? a. verbal, b. nonverbal, c. music, d. instrumental, e. speech.
5. The success of the drama *King Kong* made South African musicians
   and composers realize that a source of strength was in: a. America, not
   Africa, b. Europe, not America, c. Africa, not America, d. Africa, not
   Europe, e. Hollywood.
6. Because of oppression, South African blacks realized they had to
   express political ideas in: a. instrumental sounds, b. words of songs,
   c. theater, d. poetry, e. film.
7. Unity of South African musical expression came from: a. a single
   European tradition, b. American jazz, c. Cuban salsa, d. commonali-
   ties among South African ethnic groups, e. a composite of European
   and American popular traditions.

8. The duties of the director of music on a mine dance team include: a. choosing and leading the songs, b. checking the tuning of the instruments, c. supervising the coordination of music and dance, d. all of the above, e. a and c.

9. The duties of the director of dance on a mine dance team include: a. blowing a whistle to signal a change of step, b. calling out the name of a new step, c. demonstrating new dance steps, d. all of the above, e. a and c.

10. Which is *not* a responsibility of the dance team manager: a. to arrange the rehearsals, b. making sure people attend regularly, c. ensure that there is beer, d. to dance with the team, e. to choose the dance costumes.

11. Which is *not* a responsibility of the dance team director of music: a. choosing the songs, b. leading the songs, c. overseeing the correct performance of the songs, d. making sure the drums are tuned, e. blow whistle to signal dance steps.

12. Among the Venda, vocal polyphony is *not* produced by: a. four-part canonic imitation (a round), b. the overlap of solo and chorus parts in responsorial singing, c. the addition of various parts in counterpoint to the basic melody, d. harmonization with a blend of parallel motion and tonic-dominant progressions, e. the use of voices to produce a total pattern of sound from very short phrases.

13. The *mbira* is a: a. reed flute, b. wooden drum, c. hand piano, d. rattle, e. lute.

14. The Venda national dance, *tshikona,* is played on how many sets of stopped pipes? a. 5 to 7, b. 20 to 24, c. 50 to 60, d. 200, e. 500 or more.

15. One type of South African quasi-percussive polyphonic vocal technique provides accompaniment for the: a. stamping dance, b. girls' initiations, c. gold mining, d. a and b, e. a and c.

16. Chopi xylophone orchestras: a. play newly composed compositions, b. play at mine dances, c. were reported in the sixteenth century, d. a and c, e. all the above.

17. The musical instrument that is most commonly used for the tshikona dance is constructed from what? a. wooden slabs over a frame, b. gourd, c. steel tube, d. cedar wood, e. metal tongues in a frame.

18. A lamellaphone is also classified as what? a. aerophone, b. membranophone, c. chordophone, d. idiophone, e. corpophone.

19. During Venda children's games played at night, someone in disguise comes out while a song is sung and: a. scares the children, b. tells a story, c. plays the drum, d. dances, e. chases the children home.

20. During the *domba*, the dance of the Venda premarital initiation school: a. women and girls play the drums, b. men and boys play the drums, c. women and girls dance without instrumental accompaniment, d. men and boys dance without instrumental accompaniment, e. a Catholic priest presides.

## Answers to Reading Comprehension

1. 1960s
2. African idiom
3. jazz opera, Miriam Makeba
4. 1950s
5. mode of non-verbal communication
6. attitudes, thinking, world, ways
7. sound
8. False: the music acted as a catalyst for new kinds of social activity
9. Mine dances
10. manager, director of music, director of dance
11. drums
12. True
13. False: the music may become more political than the event
14. used to lighten the load of communal labor, for weddings, funerals, initiations, ceremonies, religious rites, to ease the harshness of life, to provide entertainment at a beer party
15. False: they do not usually take part, but stand next to their teams
16. starting, stopping
17. False: several dances are performed by men and women together
18. whistle, signal, step
19. False: just the opposite is true
20. True
21. False: drums also have to be in tune
22. True
23. False: this is inconceivable
24. False: it is supposed to be just as accurate
25. True
26. shared
27. True
28. conducts, submits
29. True
30. pipes, drums
31. True
32. False: the Venda system does recognize it
33. False: they do impose metric patterns on music
34. False: children do distinguish between them
35. meter, speech
36. social function

## Answers to Sample Test Questions

| | | | |
|---|---|---|---|
| 1. b | 2. b | 3. c | 4. b |
| 5. d | 6. a | 7. d | 8. d |
| 9. d | 10. d | 11. e | 12. a |
| 13. c | 14. b | 15. d | 16. e |
| 17. c | 18. d | 19. d | 20. a |

# Listening Form

Student Name_____ I.D. Number_____

Course Name _____ Course Number _____

Date_____ Chapter Number_____ Listening Example Number _____

Record or Tape Number_____ Name of Culture and Location _____

Name of Performer(s)_____

Instructions: place an X, ✓, or • in appropriate boxes; give types; indicate native names.

| performing elements (if vocal) | solo: M/F | duo: M/F | trio: M/F | quartet: M/F | group: M/F | other: M/F | |
|---|---|---|---|---|---|---|---|
| performing elements (if instrumental) | corpophone | idiophone | membrano-phone | aerophone | chordophone | electrophone | other |
| texture | single melody | dense unison | heterophone | imitation | parallelism | disphony | other |
| more texture | with drone | with time indicator | chordal | polyphonic stratification | colotomy | combination | variable |
| melodic contour | static | ascending | descending | conjunct | disjunct | undulating | terraced |
| mode or scale | number of notes | vernacular | using cipher notation (numbers), indicate the mode or scale in ascending order | | | | |
| meter | free | duple | triple | compound | additive | poly | other |
| speed | very slow | slow | moderate | fast | very fast | variable | other |
| amplitude | very soft | soft | moderate | loud | very loud | variable | other |
| timbre (tone color) | clear | breathy | nasal | open | tight | masked | other |
| inflections | no vibrato | slow vibrato | fast vibrato | wide vibrato | falsetto | multiphonics | other |
| formal structure | vernacular name | expanding | reverting | strophic | theme and variations | other | |
| structural or performance techniques | ostinato | responsorial | antiphonal | elastic rhythm | if vocal: syllabic or melismatic | non-synchronous parts | other |

# The Music of Ethiopia

## Cynthia Tse Kimberlin

 Introduction

*Purpose*   To briefly introduce the student to demographic and historical foundations for the study of Ethiopian music.

*Guidance*   The location of Ethiopia in northeastern Africa is important to an understanding of its musical and cultural history. Ethiopia is located in an area known as the "East Horn" of Africa. When you look at a map of the African continent, you will clearly see how the region bordering on the Red Sea and the Gulf of Aden projects eastward like a horn. Although not at the tip of the horn, Ethiopia constitutes a part of that peninsula. As of May 24, 1993, Eritrea is no longer a part of Ethiopia, but is now an independent country.

*Terms*   Define or identify the following terms or areas, based on readings from the text and/or other sources.

Find Ethiopia on a modern map of Africa and on a globe of the world. Notice its proximity to both north Africa and Africa south of the Sahara. Compare Ethiopia's size with other African countries and the United States of America.

**Amharic**

**East Horn**

**Islam**

*Reading Comprehension*   Answer the following questions.

1.  Ethiopia's bravery and past exploits have been celebrated in song. True or False.
2.  One of the musical characteristics one hears when listening to Ethiopian music is infinite _____.
3.  The music of the Amharic people is representative of the entire country of Ethiopia. True or False.

##  Status of the Musician

*Purpose*   To explain the various statuses of musicians in Ethiopia, to briefly introduce how certain musicians learn songs, and to discuss some of the common ways that Ethiopian musicians perform their duties.

*Guidance*   The student is advised to read the third section on musical instruments before reading this section, because several instruments are mentioned even though they have not yet been discussed.

*Terms*   Define or identify the following terms or areas, based on readings from the text and/or other sources.

**azmari**

**Addis Ababa**

**Ethiopian Christian Orthodox Church**

**däbtära**

**krar**

**masinqo**

**bägänna**

*Reading Comprehension*   Answer the following questions.

4.  Although the azmari was originally known as one who would _____ his patron, he later became one who _____ and then one who _____.
5.  All Ethiopians make music during _____ festivities.
6.  The krar is thought of as the instrument of _____ and _____.

7. The usual purpose of the krar is the accompaniment of contemporary religious songs. True or False.

8. Both males and females can become azmari musicians. True or False.

9. To be an Ethiopian azmari is to be in the _____ occupational status, along with _____ who have jobs requiring use of the _____.

10. The most common method of repertory building includes _____ the songs of other azmari.

11. Many Azmari know several texts that are set to one melody. True or False.

12. What are the three ways an azmari can gain popularity and wealth:

    a. _____

    b. _____

    c. _____

13. The Ethiopian musician who plays a Western instrument is considered to be a very low-status person. True or False.

14. The Ethiopian who plays Western instruments becomes _____ and a member of the emerging _____ class.

15. The traditional musical instrument of the Ethiopian nobles and upper class is the krar. True or False.

16. The Ethiopian bägänna is a concert instrument that is played on stage in front of large audiences. True or False.

## ◈ Musical Instruments

*Purpose*   To identify several of the most important musical instruments in Ethiopia.

*Guidance*   The author uses the phonetic alphabet common in linguistics to spell the musical instruments in this section. For some of the most common instruments, you will also find the following spellings (they are presented here according to their numbers in the textbook; the following spellings are from *Roots of Black Music* by Ahenafi Kebede): 3. *tsenatsil,* known as a sistrum in Latin, 8. *begena,* 10. *masinKo* (the K means that it is pronounced with an explosive sound according to Kebede, p. 79), 11. *washint* (a ductless flute similar to the Arabic *nay*), and 12. *embilta.* The drawing of the masinqo is somewhat misleading because the instrument's bridge is collapsed and the bow is stuck under the end string. This is how the instrument is stored and obviously not played. During a performance, the musician passes the bow across the single string like any bowed lute. The raised bridge transmits the vibrations of the string onto the skin and into the resonator. The musician touches the string with his fingers at the points required to change the pitches (he does not press his fingers all the way to the fingerboard).

*Terms*   Define or identify the following terms based on readings from the text and/or other sources, and be able to identify the musical instrument types in the drawings.

**tsenatsil or sistrum**

**begena or bägänna**

**masinKo or masinqo**

**krar**

**washint**

**embilta**

*Reading Comprehension*   Answer the following questions.

17. Instruments of a particular Ethiopian ethnic group are partially _____ determined. Give one example of this: _____.
18. Instruments of a particular Ethiopian ethnic group can also be _____ determined. Give one example of this: _____.
19. Bowls are common shapes for parts of musical instruments in Ethiopia. True or False.
20. Some Ethiopian membranophones are made from old one gallon or five gallon metal containers. True or False.
21. The sound box of the bägänna is covered with _____, and the strings are made from _____ _____.
22. The sound box of the krar may be _____ or _____ shaped.
23. The sound box of the krar is covered with _____, and the strings are made from _____, _____, or _____.

##  Music Examples

*Purpose*   To examine five types of Ethiopian musical genres.

*Guidance*   Although the musical notations are highly technical, the explanations contain valuable descriptive information about cultural contexts for Ethiopian music, musical instrument performance practices, and music theory. The author explains how the embilta flutes are played together in a hocket technique. This is an interlocking method whereby each instrument is played in a manner similar to how bells are played in an American ensemble of bell ringers.

*Reading Comprehension*    Answer the following questions.

24. When performed by an Ethiopian priest, the staff has a movement that imitates the movement of _____ blown gently by the _____.

25. Drumming is not as predominant in Ethiopia as in other parts of Africa. True or False.

26. Women rarely play drums in Ethiopia. True or False.

27. Sometimes accented beating accompanies drumming in Ethiopia. True or False.

28. Washint flutes are made by special artisans and then purchased by flutists. True or False.

29. Embilta flutes are made from _____, _____, or _____, depending on the province where they are made and used.

30. Sometimes embilta flute players _____ in a _____ while playing.

31. The meter employed by the embilta players is _____.

32. Embilta are primarily used for _____ gatherings and _____, and are not usually _____ by other instruments.

33. When a bägänna player tunes his instrument there is no precise _____ range; the player's _____ range determines the _____ range.

34. It is not always necessary for a bägänna player to tune all the strings on his instrument. True or False.

35. Ethiopian music mirrors Ethiopian society and its people. True or False.

# Conclusion

*Purpose*    To make several conclusions of a comparative nature.

*Guidance*    The author concludes by pointing out similarities between Ethiopian music and that of other cultures. It must be emphasized that these similarities are purely coincidental and do not indicate any type of cultural borrowing.

Ethiopian pop music has flourished more among the exiled Ethiopians, especially in the United States, than among the people living in Ethiopia. Since the restoration of democracy in 1991, however, pop music has been revived in the motherland, and new groups have emerged. Probably foremost among them is Ethio Stars, which joins saxophone and brass with electric bass, keyboards, guitar, and drum set, resulting in a funky style—somewhat like a combination of reggae (Jamaica) and soukous (Zaire). Although it is referred to as "Amharic music" by the band members, only the song texts sung in Amharic define many of the songs as Ethiopian. Some of the instrumental compositions, however, are based on Ethiopian scales, such as the ambassel mode mentioned by Kimberlin. An experimental fusion group is the Tukul Band, which uses only traditional Ethiopian musical instruments that have been electronically enhanced (electric lead krar, electric bass krar, electric masinKo, washint, and traditional drums). In addition, the band's musical style is a fusion of traditional ostinatos, improvised solos, heavy bass, and traditional tunings and scales.

One of Ethiopia's leading female singers is Aster Aweke, who records in England and the United States. Her style, accompanied by a driving band of electric keyboards, bass, guitar, trumpet, saxophone, and drums, fluctuates between an almost Caribbean salsa sound to a florid improvisatory solo style derived from traditional Amharic singing. Sometimes she performs with only krar accompaniment, and at other times her band provides a very funky rhythm and blues foundation. Aster Aweke's accompaniment styles are quite varied, while her own vocal work is very florid and traditionally based—therein lies her uniqueness in Ethiopian pop music. This is perhaps only possible because she makes her home outside of Ethiopia (in the United States since 1981). More of a fusion artist is Alemayehu Eshete, one of Ethiopia's leading male vocalists who has recorded in Paris. While the style of his band (trumpet, saxophones, keyboards, bass, drums) can also be funky, with heavy bass and many ostinatos, his keyboardist often plays in a florid style that is a nearly perfect imitation of the krar.

## SAMPLE TEST QUESTIONS

Multiple choice questions. Only one answer is correct.

1. According to the scholar Alan Merriam, the music of the East Horn region of Africa is distinguishable from most of the other music in East Africa by the intensity of which influence: a. Jewish, b. Christian, c. Islamic, d. Shamanistic, e. Buddhist.

2. Ethiopia is susceptible to many musical influences because of: a. location, b. religion, c. ethnic divisions, d. slavery, e. colonialism.

3. Through the years the term *azmari* for the Ethiopian musician has come to mean: a. one who defames, b. one who has loose morals, c. heavenly musician, d. in the king's grace, e. entertainer.

4. An Ethiopian musician will: a. play his music in whichever mode comes mind, b. choose one of the two modes for his music and then seldom change to another mode, c. modulate freely from one mode to another, d. not base his music on a mode.

5. How does the masinqo player learn his instrument? a. from a method book, b. by trial and error, c. from cassette tapes, d. from his father or uncle, e. from a teacher.

6. Which is *not* a method that the masinqo player uses to build his musical repertory? a. to compose his own songs, b. to learn from song books, c. to imitate songs of other musicians as they work, d. to imitate songs played on the radio, e. to imitate songs from recordings.

7. The traditional musical instrument of the Ethiopian nobles and upper class is the: a. tsenatsil or sistrum, b. begena or bägänna, c. masinKo or masinqo, d. krar, e. washint.

8. The traditional musical instrument of Ethiopian pimps and prostitutes is the: a. tsenatsil or sistrum, b. begena or bägänna, c. masinKo or masinqo, d. krar, e. washint.

9. The traditional musical instrument of Ethiopian priests is the: a. tsenatsil or sistrum, b. begena or bägänna, c. masinKo or masinqo, d. krar, e. washint.

10. The traditional musical instrument of Ethiopian shepherds and cowherds is the: a. tsenatsil or sistrum, b. begena or bägänna, c. masinKo or masinqo, d. krar, e. washint.

11. Strings of the Ethiopian krar are never made from: a. metal, b. gut, c. nylon, d. silk.

12. The sound box of the Ethiopian krar: a. can be made from a wooden bowl, b. can be made from a metal bowl, c. is covered with goat skin, d. a and c of the above, e. all of the above.

13. In Ethiopia, Adari women sometimes play the drums during: a. weddings, b. funerals, c. births, d. dinner, e. camel caravans.

14. Which material is never used in manufacturing an Ethiopian embilta? a. plastic, b. wood, c. metal, d. bamboo, e. a and c of the above.

15. The musicians who play which instrument dance in a circle while they play: a. tsenatsil or sistrum, b. embilta, c. masinKo or masinqo, d. krar, e. washint.

## ANSWERS TO READING COMPREHENSION QUESTIONS

1. True
2. melodic variation
3. False: there is not one kind of music that could represent Ethiopia because there are so many ethnic groups that live there
4. praise, criticizes, defames
5. life cycle
6. pimps, prostitutes
7. False: popular songs only
8. False: it is strictly a male profession
9. lowest, illiterates, hands
10. imitating

11. True

12. a. to cut a record and hope it sells, b. to join a performance group and hope it succeeds, c. to leave traditional instruments and take up Western ones

13. False: just the opposite—he is not thought of as low-status

14. sophisticated, middle

15. False: bägänna

16. False: it is seldom played for an audience

17. geographically, no bamboo flutes where there is no bamboo

18. culturally, Muslims or Moslems do not play stringed instruments

19. True

20. True

21. cowhide, sheep's gut

22. trapezoidal, bowl

23. goatskin, gut, metal, nylon

24. grass, wind

25. True

26. False: among some Ethiopian cultures women play drums during wedding celebrations

27. True

28. False: the owner is usually the maker

29. metal, wood, bamboo

30. dance, circle

31. triple

32. social, weddings, accompanied

33. pitch, vocal, instrumental

34. True

35. True

## ANSWERS TO SAMPLE TEST QUESTIONS

| | | | |
|---|---|---|---|
| 1. c | 2. a | 3. a | 4. b |
| 5. e | 6. b | 7. b | 8. d |
| 9. a | 10. e | 11. d | 12. e |
| 13. a | 14. a | 15. b | |

# Listening Form

Student Name_____ I.D. Number_____

Course Name _____ Course Number _____

Date_____ Chapter Number_____ Listening Example Number _____

Record or Tape Number_____ Name of Culture and Location _____

Name of Performer(s)_____

Instructions: place an X, ✓, or • in appropriate boxes; give types; indicate native names.

| performing elements (if vocal) | solo: M/F | duo: M/F | trio: M/F | quartet: M/F | group: M/F | other: M/F | |
|---|---|---|---|---|---|---|---|
| **performing elements** (if instrumental) | corpophone | idiophone | membrano-phone | aerophone | chordophone | electrophone | other |
| **texture** | single melody | dense unison | heterophone | imitation | parallelism | disphony | other |
| **more texture** | with drone | with time indicator | chordal | polyphonic stratification | colotomy | combination | variable |
| **melodic contour** | static | ascending | descending | conjunct | disjunct | undulating | terraced |
| **mode or scale** | number of notes | vernacular | using cipher notation (numbers), indicate the mode or scale in ascending order | | | | |
| **meter** | free | duple | triple | compound | additive | poly | other |
| **speed** | very slow | slow | moderate | fast | very fast | variable | other |
| **amplitude** | very soft | soft | moderate | loud | very loud | variable | other |
| **timbre (tone color)** | clear | breathy | nasal | open | tight | masked | other |
| **inflections** | no vibrato | slow vibrato | fast vibrato | wide vibrato | falsetto | multiphonics | other |
| **formal structure** | vernacular name | expanding | reverting | strophic | theme and variations | other | |
| **structural or performance techniques** | ostinato | responsorial | antiphonal | elastic rhythm | if vocal: syllabic or melismatic | non-synchronous parts | other |

# Classical Iranian Music

*Ella Zonis*

 ## Introduction

*Purpose*   To introduce several sociocultural ideas that have helped to shape the classical music of Iran (Persia).

*Guidance*   This chapter is concerned with the classical musical types of Persian music that are no longer a part of Iranian daily life since the revolution that overthrew the Shah (Pahlavi Empire) in 1979 and established the present orthodox Shiite Islamic government. Since the revolution, Iranian classical music is mostly found outside Iran, in cities where Iranian culture lives in exile, such as Paris, Los Angeles, New York, and elsewhere in the West. Today, this music may seem sad because of the political and cultural changes in Iran; in a traditional sense, however, it is best to consider it pensive and mystical rather than sad. As the author points out, it *is* religious in a sense, although it is not used in worship. Here the line between sacred and secular is not clear cut, and the performance of classical Iranian music *is* often a religiously inspired philosophical expression. It is a music that often moves its traditional listeners to tears because of its profundity and deep Persian cultural ties, which includes religion as inseparable from life itself. Neither the chanting of texts from the Koran nor the Islamic call to prayer are considered to be music by Moslems. Although an Islamic country, Iran is not Arabic. Its history, music, language, and culture are quite different from other countries in the Middle East.

*Terms*   Define or identify the following terms or areas, based on readings from the text and/or other sources.

Find Iran on a world globe and on a map of the Middle East. Notice its
    geographic location at the most easterly part of the Middle East,
    bordering Afghanistan and Central Asia.

Locate Teheran, the capital of Iran.

**Islam**

**Mohammed**

**Persia**

**Farsi**

**dastgah**

**Sufi**

**Koran**

**Omar Khayam**

*Reading Comprehension*   Answer the following questions.

1. Name the five types of non-Western music found in Iran today, and briefly explain each one.

   a. _____
   _____,

   b. _____
   _____,

   c. _____
   _____,

   d. _____
   _____,

   e. _____
   _____.

2. In Iran, among strict Moslems, the rise and fall of a voice chanting the Koran is not considered to be music. True or False.

3. Dastgah, which means _____,
   is religious to traditional Iranians. True or False.

4. The founder of Islam, _____, frowned
   upon "wine, woman, and song," as written in

   _____.

# ✦ History

*Purpose*   To examine the history of Iran and relate it to the classical Persian musical traditions.

*Guidance*   The author again stresses the sadness of Persian music, and uses history to try to explain it. To present another point of view, however, the following passage, written by an Iranian musicologist, should be considered:

> *It is a common tendency to label Persian music . . . as extremely melancholy. Although such judgments are based entirely on personal impressions, it is this writer's belief that if a single adjective describes the emotional quality of Persian music, it is not melancholy. To one who is able to understand the subtleties of this refined art, its spiritual effects seem to transcend such common worldly experiences as sadness or joy. Just as much of the poetry and other fine arts of Persia convey a profound feeling in which all human emotions and thoughts are blended into one, Persian music, as a whole, appears unconcerned with isolated expressions. Perhaps the not altogether lucid adjective mystic is best suited to describe the essence of Persian music. (Homaz Farhat, "Persian Classical Music" in Festival of Oriental Music and the Related Arts, University of California, Los Angeles, 1960, p. 64)*

The same type of careful, emic (from within the culture) scrutiny should also be applied to the Iranian people, as to any culture. To do otherwise is to view a culture, its music and its people, from our own point of view (this is ethnocentrism). Certainly, however, historical events have caused ups and downs in most civilizations, and musical expressions in Iran have been greatly affected by events in Iran's history. Some of these events include foreign domination, as indicated in the author's chronological chart. Many changes, however, have occurred during regimes that have been Iranian. The author's words (not her chart) make it clear, for example, that traditional Persian music was encouraged during the Safavid Kingdom (1501–1736), was discouraged during the rise of the orthodox Shiite (Shi'a) sect of Islam (until 1900), was encouraged during the Pahlavi Empire (1925–1979), and is discouraged today because of orthodox Shiite beliefs. However, during the Iranian Pahlavi Empire, Western musical influences were very strong, with European popular and classical musical forms and performances nearly replacing traditional Iranian music. Today, classical Iranian music is mostly continued outside of Iran. Thus, history and culture (including music) are very dynamic; that is, they are constantly changing.

*Terms*   Define or identify the following terms or people, based on readings from the text and/or other sources.

Know the historical periods.

**Ibn Sina (Avicenna)**

**Safi al-Din**

*Reading Comprehension*   Answer the following questions.

5. The first known major influence on Persian music came from the ancient _____ civilization, dating from about the fourth century B.C. until the second century A.D.

6. During the time of the great Persian theorists Ibn Sina and Safi al-Din, the religious atmosphere was relaxed and allowed for the practice of music to flourish. True or False.

7. The adoption of the Shiite sect of Islam lead to a flourishing state of music-making. True or False.

8. Persian music theory is Arabic in origin. True or False.

9. While the author says that Iranian music is _____, an Iranian musicologist says it is _____. One can also think of Iranian music as _____.

10. Generally, the historical periods in Iranian history were very short. True or False.

#  Classical Iranian Music

*Purpose*   To identify the basic principles of Iranian music—specifically theory, rhythm, and improvisation.

*Guidance*   Persian music is organized into dastgah-ha (the *ha* is the plural form in Farsi), or modes, and each has a name of its own. A performer may play in one dastgah from five minutes to one hour. All of the dast-gahha have unifying elements, such as special notes and specific ending patterns. Classical Iranian music today is basically unmeasured and per-formed in a free style (rubato), relying on the poetry of the text in vocal performances to give some kind of rhythmic structure. Persian music relies heavily on the performers' skill to improvise, within an elaborate scheme that must be followed.

*Terms*   Define or identify the following terms, based on readings from the text and/or other sources.

**dastgah**

**gusheh**

**maqam**

**koron**

**sori**

daramad

radif

iqa'at

mode

zarbi

avaz

*Reading Comprehension*   Answer the following questions.

11. In the classical art music of Iran, the audience, or group of people listening to music in a traditional setting, are totally passive and leave all improvisatory ideas to the performer. True or False.

12. An Iranian musician never modulates from one dastgah to another during the duration of a single piece. True or False.

13. List four English words that may be used to mean dastgah.

    a. _____, b. _____,

    c. _____, d. _____.

14. The term for the total of all the gusheh-ha in all twelve dastgah-ha is called what?

    _____.

15. In classical Iranian vocal music, generally one poetic verse (couplet) is set to a single gusheh. True or False.

16. Though most Iranian classical music is improvisatory, there is a definite scheme for performance ranging from a definite melody or tune, to a section of purely melodic contour, to a section of melodic patterns or motives. True or False.

 Instruments

*Purpose*   To introduce the variety and uses of the musical instruments found in classical Persian music.

*Guidance*   The term "sehtar" means three strings, although today the instrument has four because of Western violin influence. It is plucked with finger nails. The tar is a larger lute with a double-chambered body covered with skin. It is plucked with a plectrum. The sehtar and the Arabic 'ud are comparable (as the author states) only in so far as they are plucked lutes (the former has a long neck, and the latter has a short neck). The santur is a 72-stringed zither that is very similar to the hammered dulcimer popular in the folk music of the United States. Indeed, the hammered dulcimer principle traveled eastward into China (yang ch'in or foreign zither) and northward into Europe. The European piano developed from the Persian santur—the piano is basically a large hammered dulcimer that has mechanical hammers (one for each course of strings, however) attached to a keyboard. The santur and its relative, the Arabic qanun, are both zithers (psaltery is another name for zither), but the former is struck with lightweight hammers, and the latter is plucked. The nay is an end-blown flute without an air duct. The nay musician produces a stream of air in two different ways: for the lower notes he places the edge of the mouthpiece between his two front teeth and blows, and for the upper notes he puckers his lips and blows. The former technique is like whistling between the teeth, and the latter is like whistling with the mouth formed into a pucker. The kamanchay, meaning "little bow," is a bowed lute whose neck pierces the body. Lutes constructed in that fashion are called "spike" or "spiked" when the fingerboard goes straight through the resonating body, from top to bottom, and comes out the bottom as if it were a long spike. The kamanchay, like the sehtar, originally had three strings but today has four. The traditional Iranian membranophone is known by two names, zarb and tombak—the latter term is a good example of onomatopoeia (the name for the instrument is derived from the sound it makes; for example, hitting the drumhead in the center produces "tom" and hitting it on the edge produces "bak").

European musical instruments have found their way into classical Iranian music particularly during this century. The violin, in particular, lends itself well to the music of Iran; it is so popular, in fact, that it is no longer considered a foreign instrument. Also found, particularly in ensembles with traditional instruments, are the clarinet, oboe, flute, trumpet, and the piano (often retuned to one of the Iranian scales).

*Terms*   Define or identify the following terms, based on readings from the text and/or other sources.

Be able to identify the musical instruments. You may have to use sources other than your textbook.

**sehtar**

**tar**

**santur**

**nay**

**kamanchay**

**zarb**

**tombak**

*Reading Comprehension*   Answer the following questions.

17. The Persian tar has triple resonator chambers that are interconnected with a skin membrane. True or False.

18. In ethnomusicology the Persian _____ can be classified as a struck chordophone. It is also called a _____ in English.

19. The kamanchay is called a _____ in English.

20. Which instrument derives its name from the sounds it produces? _____.

 # Classical Persian Music Today

*Purpose*   To examine the state of classical Persian music today.

*Guidance*   The author discusses certain limitations of Persian music. It must always be kept in mind, however, that Persian music is not European music—it never has been, never will be, and does not need to be. Additionally, Persian music should not be discussed in terms of European music. The fact that it does not have measured rhythm (which it does sometimes), harmony (sometimes it has multipart texture, especially the santur), or counterpoint is not a limitation; lacking those elements as they exist in Western music simply shows that Persian music is different from Western music. It stands on its own merits, and will continue to do so. It exists, however, in exile.

None of the major sources on world music pop even mentions Iran. Perhaps because of the musically oppressive Islamic government since the fall of the Pahlavi regime, anything approaching rock or fusion music may be frowned upon. Some pop musicians, however, have remained in Iran, and their styles are conservative yet danceable. Most famous in Iran is Gogoush, a female vocalist who continues to be very popular. Many traditional and pop musicians left Iran during the revolution and scattered throughout Europe and America.

In the United States among Iranian exiles, pop music flourishes on recordings and is performed live during dances, especially in Los Angeles, New York, and other metropolitan areas. Many of the pop musicians live in Los Angeles, where their desires to become recording stars are often unfulfilled. The Iranian pop music cassette industry, however, was big in southern California (replaced now by CDs), and many of the immigrant Iranian singers copy the styles of the more famous musicians. The top male Iranian pop singers in Los Angeles today are Moin, Sattar, and Shahram (pop stars mainly go by a single name), and Shahram even has his own television show. Female Iranian pop singers include Fataneh, Haideh, Ebie, and Deleram. Particularly unique in Iranian pop is the use of electronic keyboards with a variety of stops that can imitate such traditional Persian instruments as the santur, tar, dombak, and others. Depending on the song, keyboard solos that follow verses by the lead singer often produce a traditional instrument timbre, complete with ornamentations such as a tremolo that is reminiscent of the *tahrir* or voice warble. One of the best known Iranian keyboardists is Siavash Ghomeishi (goes by his complete name), who is famous for his interesting piano style and original songs.

### Video Viewing

1. Santur—hammered dulcimer solo: "Nagme-ye karevan" (Iran) (16-11). *The JVC Video Anthology of World Music and Dance,* The Middle East and Africa I (VTMV-16).

### Sample Test Questions

Multiple choice questions. Only one answer is correct.

1. The idea in Iran that Mohammed, the founder of Islam, was against wine, women, and song is found in: a. the Bible, b. the Koran, c. Omar Khayam, d. Zur Khaneh, e. the Torah.

2. Which words best characterize Persian classical music? a. light and carefree, b. slow and majestic, c. gay and boisterous, d. pensive and mystic, e. frenzied.

3. In the seventh through tenth centuries A.D., there was thorough blending of music, instruments, and musical terminology between the Persian culture and the: a. Arabic, b. Eastern Orthodox, c. Turkish, d. Mongolian, e. European.

4. During which Iranian period were musicians publicly respected and public concerts permitted? a. Safavid Kingdom, b. Sassanian Empire, c. Achaemenid Empire, d. Pahlavi Empire, e. Khomeini Regime.

5. At the height of Persian classical culture, music was played only for: a. friends and away from the public, b. the Shah and his court, c. the religious leaders, d. the public in town squares.

6. Iranian music is presently organized into twelve systems called: a. raga, b. dastgah, c. makam, d. koron, e. rasa.

7. In Persian music, the strongest rhythmic factor in music of the radif comes from: a. marching, b. human pulse, c. dance, d. poetry, e. swinging clubs laced with chains.

8. Persian music uses a great deal of: a. measured rhythm, b. harmony, c. counterpoint, d. heterophony, e. improvisation.

9. Which was *not* an effect of Western music in Iran? a. Iranian composers and performers were attracted to Western music rather than to traditional Persian music, b. Iranian composers often grafted features of Western music onto Persian music, c. Iranian composers developed a modern style of composing contemporary music for Persian instruments.

10. For centuries in Iran, musical performance: a. was a family affair, b. was a part of religious worship, c. was performed in towers, d. was written down in notation.

11. Persian music is organized into how many dastgah-ha? a. 2, b. 5, c. 12, d. 25, e. unlimited number.

12. The Persian kamanchay is: a. held close to the musician's body and plucked, b. rested on the ground and bowed, c. rested on the player's knee and bowed, d. rested on a table or stand in front of the player and struck, e. placed under the player's chin and bowed.

13. The Persian nay is played how? a. between the teeth, b. against the puckered lips, c. by buzzing the lips, d. a and b, e. b and c.

14. The sehtar is related to which other Persian instrument? a. tar, b. santur, c. tombak, d. nay, e. kamanchay.

15. Which Persian instrument's name is derived from the sound it produces? a. tar, b. santur, c. tombak, d. nay, e. kamanchay.

## ANSWERS TO READING COMPREHENSION QUESTIONS

1. a. folk music, found outside of Teheran, that belongs to tribal and non-Moslem people
   b. popular music that uses traditional scales and the Farsi language, but Western instruments and rhythms
   c. the music from *Zur Khaneh,* or House of Strength, and *Nagarah Khanah,* or Tower Music
   d. Iranian classical music
   e. "music" that is the chanting of the Koran

2. True

3. melody type, True

4. Mohammed, Omar Khayam

5. Greek

6. False: Islam disapproved of music

7. False: the Shiite sect discouraged music

8. False: it is Greek in origin

9. sad, mystic, pensive

10. False: they generally lasted very long

11. False: they verbally and visually influence the performer

12. True

13. apparatus, mechanism, scheme, framework

14. radif

15. True

16. True

17. False: it has double chambers

18. santur, hammered dulcimer

19. spiked fiddle

20. tombak

# ANSWERS TO SAMPLE TEST QUESTIONS

| | | | |
|---|---|---|---|
| 1. c | 2. d | 3. a | 4. d |
| 5. a | 6. b | 7. d | 8. e |
| 9. c | 10. a | 11. c | 12. c |
| 13. d | 14. a | 15. c | |

# Listening Form

Student Name_____ I.D. Number_____

Course Name _____ Course Number _____

Date_____ Chapter Number_____ Listening Example Number _____

Record or Tape Number_____ Name of Culture and Location _____

Name of Performer(s)_____

Instructions: place an X, ✓, or • in appropriate boxes; give types; indicate native names.

| performing elements (if vocal) | solo: M/F | duo: M/F | trio: M/F | quartet: M/F | group: M/F | other: M/F | |
|---|---|---|---|---|---|---|---|
| performing elements (if instrumental) | corpophone | idiophone | membrano-phone | aerophone | chordophone | electrophone | other |
| texture | single melody | dense unison | heterophone | imitation | parallelism | disphony | other |
| more texture | with drone | with time indicator | chordal | polyphonic stratification | colotomy | combination | variable |
| melodic contour | static | ascending | descending | conjunct | disjunct | undulating | terraced |
| mode or scale | number of notes | vernacular | using cipher notation (numbers), indicate the mode or scale in ascending order | | | | |
| meter | free | duple | triple | compound | additive | poly | other |
| speed | very slow | slow | moderate | fast | very fast | variable | other |
| amplitude | very soft | soft | moderate | loud | very loud | variable | other |
| timbre (tone color) | clear | breathy | nasal | open | tight | masked | other |
| inflections | no vibrato | slow vibrato | fast vibrato | wide vibrato | falsetto | multiphonics | other |
| formal structure | vernacular name | expanding | reverting | strophic | theme and variations | other | |
| structural or performance techniques | ostinato | responsorial | antiphonal | elastic rhythm | if vocal: syllabic or melismatic | non-synchronous parts | other |

# Folk Music of South America—A Musical Mosaic

*Dale A. Olsen*

 Introduction

***Purpose*** To introduce several sociocultural concepts that help to explain the diversity of South America and its music.

***Guidance*** Three recent movements in South America (Tenrikyo, Hallelujah, and Marxism) are mentioned but not discussed. Tenrikyo is a religion that developed in the late 1800s in Japan. Shortly after World War II the religion was brought by Tenrikyo missionaries to Brazil, where today it flourishes among thousands of the over one million Japanese immigrants and their descendants. Tenrikyo is musically very active, and its worship includes playing koto, shamisen, and gagaku. Hallelujah is a syncretic religion found in the interiors of eastern Venezuela and Guyana that comes from the mixing of Native South American shamanism with North American evangelical Protestantism. Marxist ideologies were basically found in Chile, and the important musical result was *Nueva Canción Chilena,* the New Chilean Song movement, which spawned many famous singers and musical groups.

***Terms*** Define or identify the following terms or areas, based on readings from the text and/or other sources.

Find South America on a globe and study where the continent lies with relation to the United States of America. Also study the vastness of its jungle (Amazon), its mountains (Andes), and the locations and sizes of its many countries.

**mestizo**

**mulatto**

**criollo or creole**

zambo

mestization

*Reading Comprehension*   Answer the following questions.

1. Two major divisions that can be made in the oral musical traditions of South America are between the _____ and the to _____ within the past _____ years.

2. List three South American countries where people of Native American descent predominate: _____, _____, and _____.

3. List two South American countries where European descendants predominate: _____ and

   _____.

4. List three South American countries where Black or African-derived characteristics are found in great number:
   a._____,
   b._____, and
   c._____.

5. List five South American countries where the mestizo predominates:
   a._____, b._____,
   c._____, d._____,
   e._____.

## ⬦ European-Derived Folk Music

*Purpose*   To identify some of the important folk musical concepts, instruments, and forms that reveal European characteristics.

*Guidance*   The important concept of musical preservation must be understood, along with the varying degrees of its existence. Some areas of South America function as pocket areas where old musical forms, perhaps similar to those in Spain and/or Portugal, are found. Stringed musical instruments are the most obvious importation by the Spanish and Portuguese. Harps and violins were taught to the Native South Americans by the Jesuits (Spanish missionaries), while the guitar and its many variants were learned from secular musicians. Saxophones and clarinets were introduced by the military in the late 1800s and are played in ensemble with two violins and a harp in central Peru.

Two important musical concepts have to do with rhythm. They are the "colonial rhythm" and the "sesquiáltera." "Sesqui" in Spanish means one and one-half, and "áltera" means alternation. Thus, the "one and one-half alternation" refers to dividing a 3/4 measure (like a fast waltz) in half, which will equal one and one-half beats, or the same as half a measure of 6/8 time. The sequence is usually an alternation of a 3/4 measure with a 6/8 measure, and a good example of this comes from Bernstein's *West Side Story*, with the song "I like to be in America." This can perhaps be sounded out by saying "**dot** dot dot **dot** dot dot **dash dash dash**," or "**1** 2 3 4 5 6 **1** and **2** and **3** and" (emphasize or accent the beats that are boldfaced).

*Terms*   Define or identify the following terms or areas, based on readings from the text and/or other sources.

**villancico**

**romance and romanceros**

**cuatro**

**décima**

**canción**

**tonada**

**modinha**

**tiple**

**violão**

**charango**

*Reading Comprehension*   Answer the following questions.

6.  Spanish-derived song forms that died out in the motherland have been preserved in isolated South American regions to this day. True or False.
7.  Guitar-type folk instruments such as the cuatro, seis, cinco, and cuatro y medio are named after the _____ of _____.
8.  Probably the best-known guitar-type folk instrument, distinctive because of its typical armadillo resonator, is the _____.
9.  Many songs in South America are from the Spanish or Portuguese Renaissance, and they are still found in Spain and Portugal. True or False.
10. The Spanish and Portuguese upper class were responsible for teaching their music to the South American Native Americans. True or False.
11. A type of Christmas song in South America is the _____, which literally meant "rustic song" in Spain where it originated.

12. In some cases some rural black populations in South America are responsible for the preservation of many Spanish and/or Portuguese types of lullabies. True or False.

13. An important determinant of traditional Renaissance musical characteristics in South America is _____.

14. Some lullabies in South America are sung to well-known melodies, such as national anthems. True or False.

15. List in English four regions of South America that are pocket areas for the preservation of colonial Spanish and/or Portuguese musical characteristics:

    a. _____,

    b. _____,

    c. _____,

    d. _____.

16. One reason why Iberian romances continue to be found in many regions of South America is that the romanceros included notations of the music, enabling many people to learn how to sing them. True or False.

17. A common type of song sung between two people is known in English as _____ .

18. Two manners of playing the guitar in South America are known in English as _____ and _____.

19. The polka has been and still is a popular South American dance form. True or False.

20. Shoe tapping is an important element in South American dances of Iberian derivation. True or False.

# ◈ African-Derived Folk Music

*Purpose*   To identify some of the major African-derived musical traditions of South America, and become familiar with their representative characteristics, styles, instruments, and song types.

*Guidance*   Syncretism often occurs when two cultures with somewhat similar cultural characteristics come into contact with one another, developing in the process particular characteristics that are similar to both but still significantly different. The term is most often used to explain the religions of many African-derived cultures in South America and the Caribbean. Some West African cultures, such as the Yoruba (the primary culture to provide slaves for Cuba and Brazil) of Nigeria, have religions that are characterized by a pantheon of gods; these people were dominated by the Spanish and Portuguese Catholics who have a pantheon of saints, leading to a synchronization or fusion of their representative supernatural entities within the new religions known as *lucumí* or *santería* in Cuba and Miami, and *candomblé, macumba,* and *umbanda* in Brazil. Musical syncretism also took place, as African call-and-response joined with Catholic call-and-response, African scales merged with European scales, and so forth. Music of the African Diaspora (scattering) should be studied as a unit that includes all the areas where Black slaves were brought, including South America, Central America, the Caribbean, and North America. Similar syncretic cultures developed in South America and the Caribbean, for example, while a totally different development occurred in North America because of Protestantism. A common drum is a friction drum. The most usual name for this instrument is *cuíca,* and it is characterized by having a smooth stick fastened to its single head inside the drum's body. This stick is rapidly rubbed by a wet rag in the player's hand, which creates a groaning or whining sound so familiar to carnival music in Rio de Janeiro. In the glossary the definitions for the *agida* and the *apinti* are reversed. The apinti resembles the Ghanaian *apintema* drum from which it is derived.

***Terms*** Define or identify the following terms or areas, based on readings from the text and/or other sources.

**syncretism**

**apinti**

**mina**

**currulao**

**batucada**

**cuíca (also puíta)**

**macumba**

**candomblé**

**capoeira**

**berimbau**

**marimba**

**samba (samba de morro, samba da roda)**

**samba school (escola de samba)**

**folk Catholicism**

*Reading Comprehension*   Answer the following questions.

21. South American slave-owners were more determined than their North American counterparts in destroying the African's cultural identity. True or False.

22. An important African characteristic, in which a leader alternates with a chorus, is known as _____ .

23. Syncopation is a reliable indicator of African influence in Afro-South American music. True or False.

24. A dance that is derived from the days when shackled slaves could only kick their oppressors is the _____ .

25. The _____ is a popular rhythmic dance associated with the carnival in Rio de Janeiro, Brazil.

26. The _____ is the favored musical instrument of the blacks living in the Pacific littoral of Colombia, for the currulao dance.

27. The _____ is the favored musical instrument of the Blacks living in Bahia, Brazil, for the capoeira dance.

28. In the music for the Saint John festival in Curiepe, Venezuela, the small drum (curbata) plays the _____ while the large drum (mina) plays_____ .

29. The most important overall characteristic of Afro-South American music is _____ .

30. List four important characteristics of South American dance that reveal African influences:

    a. _____ ,

    b. _____ ,

    c. _____ ,

    d. _____ .

# Amerindian-Derived and -Influenced Musical Folklore

*Purpose*   To examine several types of South American music that show strong Native American influences.

*Guidance*   The information here discusses musical change among Native South Americans, especially in those areas where cultural and musical mixing has taken place for centuries, such as in the Peruvian and northern Chilean Andes. The reason for the differences in terms for the panpipes in the Andes is that *antara* is Quechua (the predominant culture in Peru), *sicu* is Aymara (the predominant culture in Bolivia, parts of southern Peru, and parts of northern Chile), and *zampoña* is Spanish (the predominant language in Chile). It must be pointed out, however, that Native American cultures are not relegated to particular political boundaries, and Aymara people are found in southern Peru and northern Chile, and some Quechua are found in Bolivia. The dancing *chino* flute players in Chilean festivals play their individual notes in hocket.

*Terms*   Define or identify the following terms or areas, based on readings from the text and/or other sources.

**Inca**

**Nazca**

**Moche**

**Quechua**

**Aymara**

**wayno**

**yaraví**

**sicu (*siku*; also zampoña)**

**quena (*kena*)**

**Hallelujah**

**caboclo**

*Reading Comprehension*   Answer the following questions.

31. The pentatonic scale was the only one in use in Inca territory before the Spanish conquest. True or False.
32. The process by which tritonic and pentatonic scales came to more closely resemble Western scales is called _____.
33. A two-step Native American-derived dance that can also be a narrative song form is called the _____.
34. A slow, lamenting Native American song form from the Andes, and often played on the Peruvian harp is the _____.
35. In Brazil, people of mixed Native American and Portuguese heritage are called _____.
36. A folk religion based on North American Protestantism in the Guinea Highlands of South America is called

_____.

37. Certain festivals are held in Chile (and throughout Latin America) in honor of _____ or the _____, and these are characterized by cultural and musical blending.

38. In the Andes, panpipes are known as _____ in much of Peru, _____ in Bolivia (and parts of southern Peru), and _____ in Chile.

39. The chino flutes in certain Chilean festivals play beautiful, lyrical melodies on their instruments. True or False.

##  Musical Synthesis—The Center of the Mosaic

*Purpose*   To examine certain South American musics that represent a synthesis of African, European, and Amerindian elements.

*Guidance*   One could perhaps graphically think of the musics of each South American country (or any country) as a bicycle wheel. At the center of the wheel, the hub, would be the various types of music that are considered by each country as its nationalistic musical and dance expressions. Radiating into the hub are numerous spokes, each representing one of the numerous musical forms from indigenous cultures, African-derived cultures, European cultures, Asian cultures, American, and so forth. Each spoke can be seen in itself as a continuum representing the development of a particular musical form, and in some cases, perhaps, the spokes (musical forms) themselves intertwine and influence one another. One of the most important of these expressions at the hub of the musical wheel is the *Nueva Canción Chilena,* the new protest song movement led by Victor Jara. The movement was begun in the 1960s by Violeta Parra, continued by her children Angel and Isabel, given international fame by the groups Inti Illimani and Quillapayún, and ended with the murder of Victor Jara by the Chilean military in 1973. The music of the New Chilean Song movement continues to be an important expression for many oppressed people of Latin America.

Each country in South America has developed its own unique types of pop music, some of it influenced by European and American rock, some based on Caribbean styles such as reggae and merengue, and still others founded on nationalistic musics. Brazil, which rivals the United States in population, size, and technology, has produced such international pop musicians as Roberto Carlos and Milton Nascimento, while other countries have regional artists who appeal to the hundreds of thousands in their own countries, but are virtually unknown beyond their own borders.

One of the most important pop music movements in Brazil in recent years is known as MPB (música popular brasileira). While there are literally hundreds of artists who produce recordings and tour throughout that country, Chico Buarque is one of the geniuses of Brazilian pop music. He has also written operas, poetry, and books, and has been imprisoned for his expression of political ideas through music. Another extremely popular form of music in Brazil in the 1990s is *música sertanêja,* music originally from the Sertão or Northeast of the country. This is essentially Brazilian country music, and it is currently sweeping the country, urban and rural areas alike. Although Brazilian country music has been around for a long time, it has recently become sophisticated with the technological and marketing advancements of the Brazilian Nashville-like recording industry. *Forro* is another form that originated in Brazil's Northeast. It features an accordion and percussion.

Argentina, the second largest country in South America, still has its tango, which has been modernized and jazzed-up by the late Astor Piazzolla, and experimented with until "tango-rock" was one result. More recent forms are "trash rock" in Buenos Aires and *música cuartetera* in Córdoba. The latter form is a real people's music with a slight Caribbean beat. Argentine jazz/rock tenor saxophonist Gato Barbieri has recorded important fusion albums both in Argentina and the United States. While not a performer on traditional musical instruments himself, he has joined forces with many of South America's greatest folk musicians. "Juana Azurduy," composed by Argentinian composer Ariel Ramirez and recorded in Buenos Aires, features many South American musicians playing such traditional instruments as quena, indigenous harp, charango, siku, erke, and others, as well as electric guitars, bass, and a large battery of drums, all backing up Barbieri's progressive jazz improvisations.

The "Caribbeanization" (influences of reggae, cumbia, merengue, and salsa) of pop music in many parts of South America is a very important phenomenon. Peru has developed its *cumbia andina* or *chicha* music, which is wayno music with a Caribbean beat; Bahia, Brazil has its *samba-reggae* style which is very popular; and salsa can be heard in most urban areas throughout South America. In Colombia the cumbia and a cumbia-styled rural form of music known as *vallenato* is very popular.

Venezuelan *música llanera* (inspired by the Venezuelan plains or llanos) has been modernized by the group Gurrufío, which performs with the traditional *cuatro* and several more urbanized instruments in a highly percussive, harmonically progressive, and virtuosic style. Another current Venezuelan ensemble with a contemporary fusion style is Maroa.

Since the return of democracy in Chile, Andean instruments that were made popular by urban groups such as Inti-Illimani and Quilapayún and outlawed by the oppressive government of the 1970s and 80s, have returned. One of the most recent groups is a fusion rock band known as "Los Jaivas," which uses Andean sikuri panpipes and kena flutes along with electric guitars and synthesizers. Inti-Illimani, after fifteen years of fusing its Andean music with Italian music, is continuing to record contemporary Andean styles in Chile.

Many South American jazz and pop artists living in the United States are either developing important musical fusions or contributing to them. Bernardo Rubaja, from Argentina, composes and performs a type of "pan-American" music that he hopes will unite the Americas. Brazilian Junior Homrich, who composed the film score for *The Emerald Forest,* was the Native American music advisor for the film *Medicine Man,* and who is an honorary member of the Xavante tribe, fuses many Brazilian musical instruments and characteristics into his musical palate.

*Terms*    Define or identify the following terms or areas, based on readings from the text and/or other sources.

**cueca**

**marinera**

**cumbia**

**tango**

**Victor Jara**

**Nueva Canción Chilena**

*Reading Comprehension*    Answer the following questions.

40. A Colombian dance with erotic choreography and with African influence is the _____ .

41. Which dance form was written about in 1914 as being ". . . a reversion to the ape, and a confirmation of the Darwin theory": _____ .

42. The *Misa Incaica* and the *Misa Criolla* are examples of the _____ _____ .

43. The Nueva Canción Chilena is the _____ movement that began in the country of _____ .

44. The Chilean song and dance form known as the _____ shows musical or dance elements from which three cultures or cultural areas: _____, _____, and _____ .

45. Two dance forms that are expressions of the urban elite in Brazil and Argentina respectively are the _____ and the _____ .

## Video Viewing

1. *Mountain Music of Peru.* John Cohen, director and producer.
2. *The Music of the Devil, the Bear, and the Condor.* Mike Akester, director and producer. The Cinema Guild, Inc.
3. *Shotguns and Accordions. Music of the Marijuana Regions of Colombia.* Beats of the Heart series. Jeremy Marre, director and producer.
4. *Spirit of Samba. The Black Music of Brazil.* Beats of the Heart series. Jeremy Marre, director and producer.

5. *Creation of the World: A Samba-Opera.* Vera de Figueiredo, director and producer. The Cinema Guild, Inc.

6. Capoeira dance (Brazil) (28-8). *The JVC Video Anthology of World Music and Dance,* The Americas II, The Music of Latin America (VTMV-28).

7. Candomblé (Brazil) (28-9). *The JVC Video Anthology of World Music and Dance,* The Americas II, The Music of Latin America (VTMV-28).

8. Modern folk song: "Qunapaqui" ("Why?") (Bolivia) (28-10). *The JVC Video Anthology of World Music and Dance,* The Americas II, The Music of Latin America (VTMV-28).

9. Modern folk song: "El Cóndor Pasa" ("The condor passes") (Bolivia) (28-12). *The JVC Video Anthology of World Music and Dance,* The Americas II, The Music of Latin America (VTMV-28).

10. Modern folk song: "Manañachu" ("No longer") (Bolivia) (28-13). *The JVC Video Anthology of World Music and Dance,* The Americas II, The Music of Latin America (VTMV-28).

11. Tango: "El Choclo" ("Corn") (Argentina) (28-15). *The JVC Video Anthology of World Music and Dance,* The Americas II, The Music of Latin America (VTMV-28).

12. *Harawi,* Andean Peru. The JVC/Smithsonian Folkways Video Anthology of Music and Dance of the Americas (1995). Vol. 6, Central and South America, track 13.

13. *Song from Dance of the Pallas,* Andean Peru. The JVC/Smithsonian Folkways Video Anthology of Music and Dance of the Americas (1995). Vol. 6, Central and South America, track 14.

14. *Michicoq (Water Guiding and Cleansing Ritual),* Andean Peru. The JVC/Smithsonian Folkways Video Anthology of Music and Dance of the Americas (1995). Vol. 6, Central and South America, track 15.

15. *Ritual Music and Dance for Marking Cattle, Festival of Santiago,* Andean Peru. The JVC/Smithsonian Folkways Video Anthology of Music and Dance of the Americas (1995). Vol. 6, Central and South America, track 16.

16. *Dance of the Chunchus,* Peru. The JVC/Smithsonian Folkways Video Anthology of Music and Dance of the Americas (1995). Vol. 6, Central and South America, track 17.

17. *Andean Carnival Music,* Peru. The JVC/Smithsonian Folkways Video Anthology of Music and Dance of the Americas (1995). Vol. 6, Central and South America, track 18.

18. *The Festejo, María Ballumbrosio,* Afro-Peru. The JVC/Smithsonian Folkways Video Anthology of Music and Dance of the Americas (1995). Vol. 6, Central and South America, track 19.

19. *Festejo,* Afro-Peru. The JVC/Smithsonian Folkways Video Anthology of Music and Dance of the Americas (1995). Vol. 6, Central and South America, track 20.

20. *Zapateo,* Afro-Peru. The JVC/Smithsonian Folkways Video Anthology of Music and Dance of the Americas (1995). Vol. 6, Central and South America, track 21.

21. *Hatajo de Negritos (Afro-Peruvian Christmas Dance),* Afro-Peru. The JVC/Smithsonian Folkways Video Anthology of Music and Dance of the Americas (1995). Vol. 6, Central and South America, track 22.

22. *Pregón,* Afro-Peru. The JVC/Smithsonian Folkways Video Anthology of Music and Dance of the Americas (1995). Vol. 6, Central and South America, track 23.

23. *Marinera, "Palmero, sube a la palma,"* Afro-Peru. The JVC/Smithsonian Folkways Video Anthology of Music and Dance of the Americas (1995). Vol. 6, Central and South America, track 24.

24. *Joropo, Pajarillo,* Venezuela. The JVC/Smithsonian Folkways Video Anthology of Music and Dance of the Americas (1995). Vol. 6, Central and South America, track 28.

25. *Diablos Danzantes (Devil Dance),* Venezuela. The JVC/Smithsonian Folkways Video Anthology of Music and Dance of the Americas (1995). Vol. 6, Central and South America, track 30.

## SAMPLE TEST QUESTIONS

Multiple choice questions. Only one answer is correct.

1. The villancico and aguinaldo in South America are examples of: a. Christmas songs, b. challenge songs, c. narrative songs, d. lyrical songs.

2. Which is *not* an important characteristic of oral tradition, and one that is useful to the musicologist attempting to find derivation of South American folk musics from Spanish or Portuguese prototypes? a. texts often survive with little change, b. melodies are still recognizable, c. instruments are similar, d. cultural contexts are often similar.

3. From the Spanish romance are derived many kinds of Latin American: a. challenge songs, b. amorous songs, c. narrative songs, d. funerary songs.

4. A South American musical genre that requires spontaneous textual and melodic improvisation, as well as a quick wit, is the: a. romance, b. cowboy song, c. challenge song, d. lullaby.

5. South American narrative songs are commonly used for: a. historical and current events, b. romantic love, c. genealogical histories, d. supernatural powers, e. social control.

6. The charango is unique to: a. Brazil, b. Venezuela and Colombia, c. coastal Argentina and Chile, d. mountains of Peru and Bolivia, e. all of the above.

7. The berimbau is unique to: a. Brazil, b. Venezuela and Colombia, c. coastal Argentina and Chile, d. mountains of Peru and Bolivia, e. all of the above.

8. The guitar is unique to: a. Brazil, b. Venezuela and Colombia, c. coastal Argentina and Chile, d. mountains of Peru and Bolivia, e. all of the above.

9. The cuatro is unique to: a. Brazil, b. Venezuela and Colombia, c. coastal Argentina and Chile, d. mountains of Peru and Bolivia, e. all of the above.

10. In South America, rituals associated with the Roman Catholic feasts of the Lord and the commemoration of the Saints' days were largely introduced by: a. recent missionaries, b. Jesuits, c. Spanish conquerors, d. early minstrels, e. African slaves.

11. In Latin America, the term used to explain the joining of Roman Catholic religious beliefs with those of African slaves is: a. heterophony, b. syncretism, c. enculturation, d. interlocking technique, e. hybridization.

12. Some lullabies in Venezuela have melodies that are based on: a. American rock tunes, b. the national anthem, c. themes by Mozart and Beethoven, d. Brazilian melodies, e. none of the above.

13. The most characteristic African quality of present Afro-South American music is: a. melody, b. reference to African deities, c. percussion, d. cultural context.

14. The marimba dance in Colombia consists of: a. calling the spirits of African deities, b. a tug-of-war between opposing shamans, c. miming the first amorous advances of a couple, d. opponents trying to place blows on each other with their feet, e. use of a handkerchief or scarf by one of the dancers.

15. The capoeira dance in Brazil consists of: a. calling the spirits of African deities, b. a tug-of-war between opposing shamans, c. miming the first amorous advances of a couple, d. opponents trying to place blows on each other with their feet, e. use of a handkerchief or scarf by one of the dancers.

16. The candomblé dance in Brazil consists of: a. calling the spirits of African deities, b. a tug-of-war between opposing shamans, c. miming the first amorous advances of a couple, d. opponents trying to place blows on each other with their feet, e. use of a handkerchief or scarf by one of the dancers.

17. The cueca dance in Chile consists of: a. calling the spirits of African deities, b. a tug-of-war between opposing shamans, c. miming the first amorous advances of a couple, d. opponents trying to place blows on each other with their feet, e. use of a handkerchief or scarf by one of the dancers.

18. Original Native American musical instruments in the Andes do *not* include the: a. kena, b. siku, c. charango, d. drums.

19. A syncretic religious form in South America that is a mixture of Native American shamanism and American Protestantism is: a. macumba, b. Hallelujah, c. candomblé, d. yaraví, e. wayno.

20. Tritonic scales are found more in the South American: a. lowlands where Spanish influence is the greatest, b. the highlands where Indian traditions are stronger, c. coasts where African traditions exist, d. cities where musical mixing has taken place.

21. The yaraví is a: a. quick two-step Native American dance, b. slow mournful Native American song, c. a type of diatonic harp, d. a couple dance featuring colonial rhythm.

22. The new protest song movement of the 1960s took place in which South American country? a. Chile, b. Brazil, c. Argentina, d. Colombia, e. Ecuador.

23. The tango dance craze of the 1910s began in which South American country? a. Chile, b. Brazil, c. Argentina, d. Colombia, e. Ecuador.

24. The cumbia dance craze of this century began in which South American country? a. Chile, b. Brazil, c. Argentina, d. Colombia, e. Ecuador.

25. The Brazilian puíta or cuíca is: a. a friction drum played by rubbing a stick attached to its single skin, b. a musical bow made of wood, with a wire string, c. a small, closed and elongated wicker basket rattle, d. a small guitar with four strings, e. a diatonic xylophone.

## ANSWERS TO READING COMPREHENSION QUESTIONS

1. Native Americans, immigrants, South America, five hundred years
2. Bolivia, Ecuador, Peru
3. Argentina, Chile (also Uruguay)
4. Brazil, Colombia, Venezuela
5. Brazil, Chile, Colombia, Paraguay, Venezuela
6. True
7. number, strings
8. charango
9. False: they have long since died out in their native country
10. False: they were taught by members of the lower classes, such as the conquistadores or conquerors, and the immigrants that followed, plus the Catholic clergy
11. villancico
12. True
13. modality
14. True
15. a. a state located in the dense rain forest of the northern Pacific littoral of Colombia, b. the Caribbean coast of Colombia, c. the dry northeast of Brazil, d. in the mountains of Chile
16. False: the music was never printed, only the words were
17. challenge, duel, or competition song
18. picking, strumming
19. True, although today it has often merged with other dance forms
20. True
21. False: most important to the Catholic South American slave-owners was the soul of the slave; after the slave was converted, he was often allowed to continue many of his African-derived folkways; the North

American slave was often not considered to have a soul, so his culture was virtually destroyed

22. call-and-response or responsorial
23. False: it is found in many types of music, not only African-derived
24. capoeira
25. samba
26. marimba
27. berimbau
28. the ostinato or basic rhythm (steady beat), improvised patterns
29. percussion
30. a. collective ring or circle dancing, b. one person dancing solo in the center of a circle of spectators, c. the dancers half raising their arms, d. dancing in a slightly bent posture
31. False: a tritonic scale and microtonal scales were also used
32. hybridization
33. wayno
34. yaraví
35. caboclo
36. Hallelujah
37. patron saints, Holy Virgin
38. antara, sicu, zampoña
39. False: they collectively play only two notes in hocket (interlocking fashion)
40. cumbia
41. tango
42. folk Mass movement
43. new protest song
44. cueca, African, Spain, Moorish
45. samba, tango

## ANSWERS TO SAMPLE TEST QUESTIONS

| | | | |
|---|---|---|---|
| 1. a | 2. b | 3. c | 4. c |
| 5. a | 6. d | 7. a | 8. e |
| 9. b | 10. b | 11. b | 12. b |
| 13. c | 14. c | 15. d | 16. a |
| 17. e | 18. c | 19. b | 20. b |
| 21. b | 22. a | 23. c | 24. d |
| 25. a | | | |

# SECTION III

# Dance

# Multicultural Dance Education

## Peggy Vissicaro

 ## Introduction

The focus of this textbook is dance as a human cultural phenomenon. Phenomenon refers to an observable fact or event, usually described as any state or process known through the senses.[1] Importantly, dance has existed in all societies throughout geographic space and historical time. With that understanding, we quickly realize how overwhelming a task it is to provide a specific curriculum or set of instructional tools for the purpose of studying dance cultures around the world. It is literally impossible to compile all materials for every type of dance form into a single comprehensive package. Taking an alternative approach, it is realistic to develop key strategies and critical techniques that facilitate learning about this extraordinary behavior as it occurs and has occurred among diverse groups of people. That is the objective of multicultural dance education, which involves collaborative knowledge construction to promote interactions and broaden perspectives.

Dance provides a lens for exploring the world, its people, and their cultures. Evolving from everyday movement, dance is one way that individuals interact with the environment and each other. By nature, people differ, adapting to their dynamic surroundings. Just like our Earth habitat, humans and their behaviors continually change as a result of various conditions. We react to these changes in environment that shape subsequent interactions. Traveling in an ever evolving continuum of events, our past actions inform the present and influence the future.

#  Living in a Multicultural World

We live in a world consisting of people that represent a wide range of viewpoints, traditions, and lifestyles. This diversity increases by the dissemination of ideas generated today from telecommunication systems. Those of you who have access to the Internet know how easy it is to journey across the globe and visit Web sites created by individuals from practically every country on the planet. On a day-to-day basis, it is not always obvious that we are interacting with people who have different cultural frameworks for interpreting information. Like the Internet, our interactions are mostly seamless, with smooth transitions as we pass from one set of values and beliefs to another. Culture is invisible since we usually do not notice or are not consciously aware of its influence upon people's behaviors. Yet of course, if we sit down and think for a moment about why we act the way we do, we realize that indeed there are many differences and factors impacting these variations. The differences have to do with individual information databases that we use to store, interpret, and construct meaning.

This notion of an internal information system that guides our actions is, in fact, how we may describe culture. All humans have a personal cultural system that shapes how they understand the world in which they live. Using that idea, we see ourselves as living in a culturally heterogeneous world, or one with "many cultures."

#  Multicultural Education

Multicultural education today is a result of many historical events. The civil rights movement in the United States is one of these events that began in the mid-twentieth century. This movement stimulated interest in minority concerns, which continued to grow and influence the creation of programs such as affirmative action in the 1960s. Affirmative action policies assisted people who were identified as a minority by providing increased opportunities for employment and promotion, college admissions, and the awarding of government contracts. The term "minority" might include any underrepresented group, especially one defined by race, ethnicity, or sex. Generally, affirmative action has been undertaken by governments, businesses, or educational institutions to remedy the effects of past discrimination against a group, whether by a specific entity, such as a corporation, or by society as a whole. There certainly are advantages and disadvantages for instituting affirmative action programs; however, it is important to recognize that the initiation of these programs fulfilled a need to create and enrich environments, whether in the workplace or in school, with people having a wider range of perspectives about the world.

Discrimination is a complex socio-political issue motivated in large part by ignorance. The most effective way to address ignorance about minority groups is by providing education to increase awareness of and thus place greater value on their unique customs, ways of life, and expressions. This type of education also helps to empower underserved groups by allowing their voices to be heard.

The philosophy of multiculturalism surfaced to diminish the earlier idea of building a social "melting pot." A melting pot ideal encouraged assimilation of minorities into the dominant group and thus became a powerful tool of control. Multiculturalism worked against that concept by embracing diversity and bringing issues of ethnic and cultural identity to the forefront. Multiculturalists, or people whose work emphasized these types of issues, hoped to extinguish minority discrimination especially in school systems with curriculum reform that addressed culturally diverse instructional content. Major attempts at reforming academic institutions occurred throughout the 1980s. This reform was fueled by research about social learning theories, which emphasized the importance of treating students as critical agents who were provided the conditions to speak, write, and assert their own histories and experiences.[2]

Central to multicultural education is the focus on identity—specifically a wide representation of identities that reveal a more accurate picture of the world in which we live. By being exposed to and experiencing different points of view, we attain essential life skills that help us get along with others in an increasingly dynamic social environment. Educator James A. Banks explains that, through a multicultural approach, people become more fulfilled and able to benefit from the total human experience.[3]

However, one problem arises in contrast to the positive aspects of multicultural education. In an attempt to overstress ethno/cultural distinctions, we sometimes promote greater separation between individuals or groups of people. Multiculturalism encourages us to distinguish ourselves from others by placing specific boundaries as a form of identification. This kind of cultural segregation digs trenches which are difficult to cross. For some, the thought of entering boundaries created by ethno/cultural dissimilarities is like encountering a border patrol between national or state lines. In most cases, we are required to pause and recognize our advancement into another territory. The percussive or abrupt stopping of movement that characterizes this observance of difference may be an inhibiting factor that actually prevents us from passing through the border. It is important to realize that often these borders are managed or controlled, usually serving political purposes. Aside from politics, are these boundaries really necessary? Will we lose our identity if we relax our cultural borders? Can we fill the trenches that are perceived to surround us? If so, how?

##  Dance and Multiculturalism

Dance creates a bridge for traversing cultural borders because fundamentally it involves the human body, something that all people have in common. This commonality provides a thread of connection and promotes unity among many people of the Earth. The body is an amazing instrument, extending human perceptions and thoughts. Each person has his or her own particular body for which there is no duplicate (unless cloning is an option). We all move in our special ways through space and time. By observing people move, it is easy to find variations based on multiple factors such as height, weight, age, and clothing. Importantly, movement is a reaction of how a person senses and thinks in relation to their surroundings and what is happening within that environment.

Likewise, every human being dances with idiosyncratic characteristics and qualities, defining that individual. No two people dance the same way. Even in the most synchronous movement activity where dancers try to do the steps in perfect unison, there are always subtle nuances differentiating each person's style.

As previously discussed, all of us possess a personal cultural system that shapes how we make meaning and interact in the world. Culture also impacts the way a person dances. In other words, dance is culturally derived and therefore culture specific. Why, where, when, and especially how you dance is unique because it is your personal cultural system that informs your understanding, and no one else is able to replicate it. Dance can reveal as many different cultural systems as there are people on this planet. Further, any discussion or critical study of dance that includes more than one individual representation, geographic space, and/or historical time is multicultural.

There are two basic ways to employ dance as a tool to explore different cultures. One is as a theoretical approach, which uses conceptual frameworks for looking at dance around the world, as our text provides. The second approach is through the physical application, or doing the actual movement. This type of "trying on" culture is an extremely interesting entry to learning about world perspectives. Perhaps it is the intimacy and vulnerability of using one's body that opens us up to experiencing something new. We may feel uncomfortable at first, but even with limited exposure, movement activities are a most satisfying and pleasurable way to journey across cultural boundaries.

It makes sense that, in a world where we constantly interact with others representing varied cultural perspectives, there is a need for educational opportunities that promote diverse experiences. Multicultural dance education is one fascinating way to explore cultural knowledge as revealed through the body. Movement study, because of its focus on the physical self, offers insight as to how people from different regions understand themselves and each other.

##  Summary

The phenomenon of dance as human behavior is universal in every society. Studying the multiple manifestations of this behavior around the world is a complex process that involves acknowledging the different ways each individual interacts within the environment, informed by a personal knowledge system from which to construct meaning. Dissemination of new ideas impacts the development of these knowledge systems to promote greater diversity. Multicultural dance education includes both the theoretical and practical study of dance to examine viewpoints and learn about people.

## Notes

1. Cognitive Science Laboratory. Princeton University. Word Net. Accessed April 20, 2004 at http://www.cogsci.princeton.edu/cgi-bin/webwn?stage=1&word=phenomenon.
2. Aronowitz, Stanley, & Giroux, Henry A. (1993). *Education still under siege* (2nd ed.). Westport, CT: Bergin & Garvey.
3. Banks, James. (1999). *An introduction to multicultural education.* (2nd ed.). Boston: Allyn and Bacon.

## Discussion Questions/Statements

Write your responses to the following questions in the space provided. Collaborate with one or two other students and explore their ideas to the same questions. Examine similarities and differences in the various responses.

1. When you think of dance, what images come to your mind?

2. How many people have you interacted with in the past 24 hours, week, month, and year that come from areas of the world different than yours? Describe.

3. How would you describe multicultural education and what type of experiences would you include in an educational program geared toward increasing awareness of people around the world?

4. Have you attended any activities or special events in the past that promote multicultural awareness? If so, what were they?

5. What courses or components of courses have you participated in that address multiculturalism? Describe.

6. Have you ever studied dance representing diverse regions of the world? If so, what were they? Describe your feelings toward learning dances that differ from those you knew or were accustomed to doing. If you have not studied any dances from different places around the world, how would you feel about doing so?

## CREATIVE PROJECTS

**Movement Activity**—Try the following experiment: Ask a volunteer in class to move "naturally" from one side of the room to the other. Write down as many details as possible to describe his or her movement. Also have this person describe on paper how he or she felt while moving and in what ways his or her past experiences affected the movement. Now repeat this process with another volunteer. After you have finished, ask both individuals to move at the same time. Again, ask each individual to comment on his or her feelings about moving in conjunction with the other person. Compare "data" by responding to the following questions.

1. What similarities did both individuals exhibit (physical features)? How did these similarities impact the way they moved?
2. What differences were there between the two people? How did these differences influence their movement?
3. How did the classroom space affect the movement of both students?
4. Listen to what each student's response was toward moving alone and with each other, and ask yourself, how did these feelings inform movement?

**Curriculum Design**—Create a proposal, which you will submit to the local Board of Education, requesting the implementation of a Multicultural Dance Education Program for an elementary school (K–5). Your proposed annual budget is $10,000.00. How would you design this proposal and what types of activities would you include? Describe as many details as possible.

**Internet Resources** (a required assignment to be completed by all students)—Surf the Internet and locate one Web site that describes dance culture of people from a country other than the United States. Critically evaluate the site for its authority, accuracy, coverage, and objectivity by responding to the following questions. After assessing your response to these questions, determine to what extent the site increases awareness about this particular dance tradition.

1. Is it clear what organization, individual, company, etc. is responsible for the contents of the page?
2. Does the organization, individual, company, etc. responsible for the site provide credentials or describe qualifications for writing on this topic?
3. Is the material protected by copyright?
4. Are the sources for any factual information clearly listed so they can be verified in another source?
5. Is there a bibliography provided to reference information described?
6. Is the information free of grammatical, spelling, and typographical errors?
7. Do all the links to other pages and/or Web sites work?
8. If there are charts, graphs, photos, video and/or audio clips, are they clearly labeled and easy to read?
9. Are downloads available to support software needed to "read" these media files?
10. Is the information free of advertising? If not, is it clear what the motivation is for advertising on the Web site?
11. Are there dates on the Web site to indicate when the page was written, first placed on the Web, and/or last revised?
12. Is there an indication that the site has been completed and is not under construction?
13. Is the information provided sufficiently described or adequately detailed?
14. Is the site available in multiple languages?
15. Is there a mirror site to facilitate access in various parts of the world?

# Notes

# Humanities and Dance

 Introduction

This chapter situates multicultural dance study in the field of humanities. The questions of how and why dance fits into the scope of that discipline also are examined in more detail. Part of our focus is to construct working definitions of the terms humanities, anthropology, and dance. We also explore historical events and major contributors to the development of dance cultural study.

Dance is a human phenomenon. When we observe dance, we are observing the specific movement of a people. Some individuals think that animals, fish, and/or insects dance. However, it should be emphasized that although these creatures exhibit patterned movements or create certain spatial designs that appear to be dance-like, they are not dancing. The renowned dance scholar, Joann Keali'inohomoku, supports this idea. "So far as is now known, no species other than human formulates ideas about dance or Dance, and no animal other than human willfully attempt to achieve dance skills; neither do they identify themselves as dancers or Dancers."[1] As we provide parameters for understanding what constitutes dance behavior, it is easier to remain focused on germane ideas pertaining to our topic of multicultural dance education.

 Minimal Definitions

### HUMANITIES

The field of humanities broadly refers to discovering knowledge about human nature. Humanities study explores traits, qualities, feelings, thoughts, actions, interests, and values of people as well as their interrelations. From the Latin, *humanus,* humanities are clearly rooted in understanding the human condition.

According to the 1965 National Foundation on the Arts and the Humanities Act, "The term "humanities" includes, but is not limited to, the study of the following: language, both modern and classical; linguistics; literature; history; jurisprudence; philosophy; archaeology; comparative religion; ethics; the history, criticism and theory of the arts; those aspects of social sciences which have humanistic content and employ humanistic methods; and the study and application of the humanities to the human environment with particular attention to reflecting our diverse heritage, traditions, and history and to the relevance of the humanities to the current conditions of national life."[2]

The National Endowment for the Humanities (NEH) uses this information as a guideline for cultural institutions, such as museums, archives, libraries, colleges, universities, public television, and radio stations, and to individual scholars that submit grant proposals. Annually the NEH, an independent grant-making agency authorized by the United States government, requests an appropriation for grants, which for 2004 was $152 million, that (1) strengthen teaching and learning in the humanities in schools and colleges across the nation, (2) facilitate research and original scholarship, (3) provide opportunities for lifelong learning, (4) preserve and provide access to cultural and educational resources, (5) strengthen the institutional base of the humanities. The NEH does not typically fund dance performance or the creation of new work. Rather, they support activities that involve history, literature, philosophy, sociology, and anthropology studies.

## ANTHROPOLOGY

This link to the discipline of anthropology is very important to investigating humanities and dance. Anthropology comes from the Greek words *anthropos* meaning "human" and *logia,* which means "study." Thus, anthropology is a systematic study of humankind in all of its aspects. The work of many researchers and scholars shapes the field. However, it is Franz Boas (1858–1942) who provided the elemental components for building a theoretical foundation for cultural anthropological study. Perhaps Boas's single most significant contribution is the recognition that every group of people has a cultural network or shared knowledge system, which provides social integration as well as a unique history with rules that govern how they operate. His research on the Northwest Pacific Coast Indians at the beginning of the twentieth century reveals that the differences in groups of people are the result of historical, social, and geographic conditions and that all populations have a complete and equally developed set of cultural traits. The concepts of historical particularism and cultural relativism respectively set the stage for comparative human studies that emphasize the "native's point of view."[3] Information about the insider's perspective is necessary to understanding a particular culture.

Boas's work was important for two additional reasons. First, it situated dance research in the social sciences, as a serious academic study. The content of dance "literature" no longer exclusively focused on dance as an art form or entertainment or as a document for historical purposes. Secondly, he introduced the concept that dance was an integral part of human society, woven into the fabric of life. In a lecture presented at a 1942 seminar, directed by Boas's daughter Franziska, he elaborated on ideas in which he observed dance in exactly this type of central role. He wrote that nearly "every aspect of Kwakiutl life is accompanied by some form of dance, from the cradle to the grave."[4] This statement and the seminar in general opened the door to further research about dance as a primary and vital human behavior.

During the 1940s and 1950s, another significant development occurred that influenced the fledging field of dance cultural study. Gertrude Kurath (1903–1992) (fig. 2-2), a dancer, choreographer, teacher, and musician was writing about dance and music traditions in Mexico and in the United States among the Iroquois, Chippewa, and Tewa indigenous people. In 1946 her work about the Los Concheros in the *Journal of American Folklore* marked the beginning of her career as a dance ethnologist.[5] She also was the dance editor of the scholarly journal, *Ethnomusicology,* and published articles in *American Anthropologist, Southwestern Journal of Anthropology,* and *Scientific Monthly.* Kurath coined the term "ethnochoreology," which corresponds to the word "ethnomusicology." These words denote holistic, cross-cultural studies that contextually approach the topics of dance and music.[6] Another key factor informing Kurath's research was the importance she placed on studying relationships between dance and music, working from the perspectives of an ethnochoreologist and ethnomusicologist. This was quite remarkable since few scholars had the ability to conduct both music and dance analyses.[7]

Many people use the term ethnochoreology, most especially those dance researchers who are members of the special section on dance of the International Council on Traditional Music (ICTM). The ICTM is a nongovernmental organization (NGO) in formal consultative relations with the United Nations Educational, Scientific and Cultural Organization (UNESCO). The aims of the ICTM are to further the study, practice, documentation, preservation, and dissemination of traditional music, including folk, popular, classical, and urban music, and dance of all countries.[8] The word "ethnochoreology" is widely used around the world. One reason for such a global acceptance is because interpretation of the combined terms "etno" and "koreo" in other languages generally refers to people and dance, and "ology" or "ologia" is the study of a particular topic. Therefore the term is understood in most Indo-European languages, such as etnokoreologia in Croatian.[9] However, the phrase "dance ethnology" is most common in the United States. Kurath makes ethnochoreology synonymous with dance ethnology, defining it as "the scientific study of ethnic dances in all their cultural significance, religious function or symbolism, or social place."[10] Another useful definition suggests that dance ethnology, as a field in the social sciences, "brings together aspects of anthropology, history, biology, psychology, sociology, and the arts, which combined help to enrich the study of dance as a cultural indicator, a form of human behavior, and a component of human communication codes."[11] These descriptions help to identify the discipline that frames our study of dance cultures around the world.

## DANCE

In addition to situating dance research within humanities, specifically the field of anthropology, it is necessary to define what we mean by dance. Another pioneer in the field of dance ethnology, Joann Keali'inohomoku, provides us with the following definition, which we will refer to through our text because of its universal application to all forms of dance. "Dance is a transient mode of expression, performed in a given form and style by the human body moving in space. Dance occurs through purposefully selected and controlled rhythmic movements; the resulting phenomenon is recognized as dance both by the performer and the observing members of a given group."[12]

The first part of the definition identifies dance as a transient or changing mode of expression. Recognizing dance as dynamic is important because, like culture, there are many influences that shape our ways of living and moving. When people process ideas or adapt behaviors to new situations, they interact differently. Context impacts behaviors that may alter a movement, the meaning of the dance, use of props or extensions of the body, and even the entire dance repertoire of a group. The transitory nature of dance also suggests that it is ephemeral, lasting only for the moment. Feelings, images, interactions, and understandings about the dance come together at a particular point in space and time, never to combine in exactly the same way again. The ongoing transformation of dance is important to acknowledge as we investigate dance cultures representing different geographic regions and throughout history.

The second part of Keali'inohomoku's definition of dance focuses on the idea that dance involves purposefully selected movements that are recognized as dance by the performer and observing members of a given group. We will be examining how dance selectively represents values and beliefs of a specific culture. This concept positions dance as a transmitter of cultural knowledge. The other critical information stated in Keali'inohomoku's definition, and that supports our previous discussion about culture, is that dance emerges as a result of shared meaning. In other words, the dancer and observers use criteria or information from within a particular cultural knowledge system to determine whether a particular phenomenon is or is not dance. That idea transitions us into the next chapter where we will explore comparative frameworks using perspectives inside and outside cultural systems to study the world of dance.

# ◈ Summary

There is tremendous rationale for including multicultural dance education within humanities curricula. First, it focuses on understanding dance as human phenomenon, which reveals the human condition. Humanities studies also provide a link to cultural anthropology, emphasizing shared knowledge systems that guide behavior, such as dance. Finally, anthropological theory informs the development of a universal definition that offers a holistic view for understanding all dance.

## NOTES

1. Keali'inohomoku, Joann W. (1976). *Theory and methods for an anthropological study of dance.* Ph.D. dissertation, Indiana University. *Dissertation Abstracts International 37-04,* #7621511, Pro-Quest, Ann Arbor, MI, p. 2278. The underline emphasizes differences between the lower case "d" referring to relatively unskilled participants and the upper case "D," which involves highly trained specialists.

2. National Endowment for the Humanities web site. Accessed on January 10, 2004 at http://www.neh.fed.us/whoweare/overview.html.

3. Feleppa, Robert. (1990). Emic analysis and the limits of cognitive diversity. In T. Headland, K. Pike, & M. Harris (Eds.), *Emic and etics: The insider/outsider debate* (pp. 100–119). Newbury Park, CA: Sage Publications.

4. Boas, Franz. (1942). Dance and music in the life of the northwest coast Indians of North America. In F. Boas (Ed.) *The function of dance in human society,* 5–19. Brooklyn, NY: Dance Horizons.

5. Snyder, Allegra F. (1992). Past, Present and Future. *UCLA Journal of Dance Ethnology, 16,* 1–28. Mrs. Snyder is a faculty emerita and co-founder of the dance ethnology graduate program at University of California, Los Angeles.

6. Keali'inohomoku, Joann W. (1986). Honoring Gertrude Kurath. *UCLA Journal of Dance Ethnology, 10,* p. 4.

7. McAllester, David P. (1972). Music and dance of the Tewa pueblos by Gertrude Prokosch Kurath and Antonio Garcia (book review). *Ethnomusicology, 16*(3), 546–547. Ann Arbor, Michigan: Society of Ethnomusicology.

8. International Council on Traditional Music. Accessed on January 16, 2004 at http://www.ethnomusic.ucla.edu/ICTM/.

9. Dunin, Elsie. Personal communication, January 15, 2004. Mrs. Dunin is an independent researcher, faculty emerita, and co-founder of the dance ethnology graduate program at University of California, Los Angeles.

10. Kurath, Gertrude. (1960). Panorama of dance ethnology. *Current Anthropology 1*(3), 235.

11. Snyder, Allegra F. (1992). ibid.

12. Keali'inohomoku, Joann W. (1976). A comparative study of dance as a constellation of motor behaviors among African and United States Negroes (with a new introduction). In A. Kaeppler (Ed.), *CORD Research Annual 7* (pp. 1–13), NY: CORD; Keali'inohomoku, Joann W. (1969–1970). An anthropologist looks at ballet as a form of ethnic dance. In M. Van Tuyl (Ed.), *Impulse* (pp. 24–33). San Francisco, CA: Impulse Publications.

## DISCUSSION QUESTIONS/STATEMENTS

Write your responses to the following questions in the space provided. Collaborate with one or two other students and explore their ideas to the same questions. Examine similarities and differences to the various responses.

1. Do you agree with Keali'inohomoku's statement suggesting that dance is only a human phenomenon? Why or why not?

2. In your own words, how would you describe the field of humanities to an 8th grade student? To a 3rd grade student? To a peer? Compare the words and approach you use to explain what humanities is to these different people.

3. Boas's term "historical particularism" is important because it emphasizes how, in the case of dance, cultural knowledge and respective behaviors are specific to the time period in which they occur. What dance or type of dance can you think of that identifies a particular time in history and why? How would you describe characteristics of the dance (movement style, way people relate to each other, physical setting, clothing, etc.)?

4. Describe changes in your understanding of dance from one point in your life to another. How have certain experiences and information to which you have been exposed (besides reading this book) influenced and transformed how you "see" dance?

5. Is dance an integral part of your life? Why or why not? Do you think that dance is/was a central component in the lives of your parents? Your grandparents? Why or why not?

6. Design your own definition of dance. Compare your ideas with one or two other students and discuss what is or is not dance. Then collectively construct a definition of dance that reveals your shared understanding.

## CREATIVE PROJECTS

**Role Playing**—Imagine yourself as an ethnochoreologist who has received a grant to study dance among one group of people somewhere in the world. However you do not speak their language and will need to hire an interpreter to interview the group's leader. What would be the first question that you ask and why? If you could only ask three questions, what would they be? Explain.

**Grant Design**—You are submitting a grant proposal to do a humanities project involving dance cultures and world traditions. Provide a brief description of the project including the audience which this project is geared towards, key objectives, a time line, personnel, materials/resources, and budget.

**Curriculum Awareness**—Access your college/university general catalog and explore what courses constitute humanities education based on the definition discussed at the beginning of this chapter. Investigate what college(s), school(s), department(s), and/or program(s) offers humanities courses. Make a list of these course offerings and compare similarities between them. Identify to what extent dance is included in their content.

# Notes

# The Comparative Framework

 ## Introduction

The investigation of multicultural forms of dance, whether it takes place in a traditional Balinese temple, high school festival in Detroit, Michigan, or Yaqui village in Mexico during the 1600s, involves a comparative process. It is interesting to realize that comparative study has its roots in the beginning of human history. As people with different cultural systems come into contact with each other, they automatically respond to one another by comparing information. It is human nature to assess the details of what is happening around us in this way to find meaning. We compare information with what we "know" through our senses of sight, sound, touch, taste, and smell, which we process in order to make sense. This process of knowing or cognition results from our interactions within the environment.

At theatrical concerts or special events, through travel to various geographic regions, during formal classes, in community settings, or other venues, people experience dance representing diverse cultural systems. Even before we enter into these situations, the comparative process begins. You may ask yourself, "Is this going to be like something I have seen, heard, or felt before?" That type of self-questioning occurs at a conscious, as well as a subconscious, level. After arriving in the actual setting, you selectively examine dance information to notice similarities by finding relationships with previous knowledge. If there are extreme differences with your experience, it is more difficult to explore parallels and make sense. This issue is precisely what the field of comparative studies addresses. Multicultural dance education relies on comparative theory to provide a framework for interpreting dance from varied cultural systems. Without a framework, there is no understanding.

##  Comparative or Cross-Cultural Study

The word "comparative" is relatively easy to understand, which is why it is used to introduce the chapter. However, we will start applying the term "cross-cultural" as a more specific description of multicultural dance study. Cross-cultural study is the comparison of different cultural knowledge systems. Sometimes people confuse this word with multicultural. Individuals may even call themselves cross-cultural dance teachers. Cross-cultural is not a description of someone instructing or doing dances representing diverse cultures.

So much confusion exists over the proper application of the term, "cross-cultural." For instance, you may notice the exchange of words, like inter-cultural, transcultural, and pan-cultural with cross-cultural. Yet, the "attempt to use them synonymously obliterates the value of having terms with differing denotations."[1] "Inter" means between or among, such as the field of intercultural communication, which studies how people from diverse cultural systems communicate. The prefix "trans" means to move across or over, to shift from one to another and implies change, while "pan" indicates a union of several distinct entities sharing something in common. "Cross" denotes a comparative approach that defines and classifies that which is comparable.[2] It also is important to recognize that the comparative method examines correlations and covariations that emerge from studies of similarities and differences.[3]

##  Emic Perspectives

The notion of comparison suggests a structure within which to frame understanding. This frame involves different perspectives, or points of view. Boas's work sets the foundation for acknowledging one of these perspectives, which underlies all cultural theory. In his research, we observe the emphasis on investigating cultural or shared knowledge of a particular group of people with the purpose of discovering how they understand and act upon those understandings. Based on Boas's theory, researchers recognize that criteria selected by members of a group sharing culture dictate how, why, where, when and what type of dance occurs as well as by whom it is performed.

The term "emic," coined by linguist Kenneth Pike in the late 1940s, became an appropriate word to describe the view of someone "inside" a cultural system. He drew from the concept of phonemics, and specifically phoneme, which is the minimum distinctive sound or the smallest sound unit distinguishing meaning in a particular language.[4] The significance of this idea, which he realized when trying to study languages radically different than his own, was that only those who shared the language knew or understood the phonemes. Criteria for understanding came from within the cultural system. That principle supported the rationale for spending in-depth extended periods of time working and living with a community of people to study in context how behaviors and specifically language use revealed meaning.

This practice of in-depth study, known as fieldwork, is a standard part of cultural research. One of the most important objectives of fieldwork is to learn how people within a discrete cultural system construct and share knowledge. "The art of fieldwork is achieved to the extent a fieldworker is able to render from research-oriented personal experience an account that offers to a discerning audience a level of insight and understanding into human social life that exceeds whatever might be achieved through attention solely to gathering and reporting data."[5] Ethnography is the term applied to that type of rendering. An ethnographic report is a synthesis of various interpretations from multiple sources collected through interviews, observations, and other methods. The ethnographer weaves this information together into a "story" that members of the group under study agree is plausible and valid. Importantly, fieldworkers or ethnographers also must consider their own points of view, which influence many factors determining how the rendering occurs.

## PERSONAL EMIC

Each person is unique with different experiences, ideas, and values, affecting how he or she makes sense of the situation. Thus, all understanding is rooted in one's own cultural knowledge or personal emic.[6] The personal emic refers to what is already known to the researcher. That perspective is always a point of departure for comparing what is not known, or outside one's own cultural knowledge system. Comparisons happen constantly, whether you are a researcher doing fieldwork or not. All humans, from the moment they are born to the day they die, comparatively process information using the personal emic as a catalyst to shape how they understand the world around them. This process of finding relationships within existing knowledge structures is highly subjective. No two people share a personal emic. Imagine for a moment the following scenario: Two students attend a local festival featuring dance and music groups representing Africa. They stop and watch a performance by a group of young adult men from Sudan. Student #1 thinks immediately of an experience she had studying dance and drumming with a Ghanaian teacher, although the movements and rhythms are very different from what she learned. Student #2 has no background in dance and drumming from Africa but notices how the men move together in an expression of solidarity. He remembers a step team that performed at his fraternity, which reflected this same type of feeling. Both students have different ways of comparing this experience and finding parallels, guided by their respective views situated within the personal emic.

Importantly, the act of observing a particular event or performance does not by itself constitute cross-cultural study. In the field of comparative studies it is necessary to have more than just basic interactions, involving everyday, automatic comparisons between what one knows and new information. One way to achieve the type of higher level interactions required for cross-cultural investigation is by talking with members of a particular group that share cultural knowledge. However, the suggestion is to go beyond a mere exchange of ideas and move toward a systematic inquiry and recording of responses for later analysis. This describes the ethnographic interview process. Interviewing is a planned activity that incorporates a series of questions, which examine an individual's understanding. More than a "yes" or "no" reply, good interview questions are open-ended enough to prompt a lengthier response, allowing the interviewee to shape and control the direction of his or her answers in a way that is most meaningful.

Questions may explore details about the significance of movements, the dancers and drummers, the time and place the dance occurs, the organization or sequence of movements, and the process by which people learn the dance. The interviewee's response provides an emic or cultural insiders' point of view. It is especially valuable to pay attention to the words and phrases used by "natives" or those members sharing meaning to explain a certain phenomenon. Studying language provides insight to cognition and how people symbolize ideas. Other considerations for interviewing include selecting the informant, as well as determining where and how long the interview will take. These choices significantly impact how information is interpreted. Interviews involve interaction between two people and two emics, that of the person asking questions and the respondent. This type of activity is fundamental to cross-cultural dance studies.

##  Etic Perspectives

Another type of interaction that begins with the personal emic involves comparing information by using a framework derived from outside a specific cultural system. This is referred to as an etic approach. From the word, phonetic, it is a strategy that scientists, scholars, and others use that relies on extrinsic concepts and categories for distinguishing and comparing aspects of multiple cultural systems. "Through the etic lens the analyst views the data in tacit reference to a perspective oriented to all comparable events (whether sounds, ceremonies, activities), of all peoples, of all parts of the earth."[7] Etic perspectives emerge from theories and concepts that have a universal application. In other words, it is possible for a researcher or student to use an etic frame to examine any cultural system and draw parallels between different systems. A specific example of an etic approach for language study is the International Phonetic Alphabet, which provides the academic community worldwide with a notational standard for the phonetic representation of all languages in order to correctly reproduce sounds for word pronunciation. Many dictionaries include phonetic descriptions. For instance, the American Heritage Dictionary lists the word, "dance," followed by the phonetic information, *dăns*.

There is a similar system to record and study human movement called Labanotation, developed by Rudolph von Laban (1879–1958). Labanota-

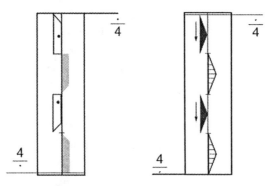

**Cherkessia**, from Israel.
Holding hands in an open circle,
or in a line following the leader.

**FIGURE 3-1.** Labanotation from Ohio State University's LabanLab.

tors around the world use this system, based on graphical representations, to document as well as analyze dance and other movement in space and time. Following is an example of Labanotation (fig. 3-1); Labanotators read the "staff" from the bottom to the top.[8] The symbols refer to Cherkessia movements used in Israeli folk dancing.

It is essential to remember that an etic view is usually a stepping stone for gaining access to emic perspectives or understandings.[9] This reinforces the idea that both positions are necessary for holistic comparisons. Labanotation, for example, is an important tool for studying and comparing movement from different cultural systems. However, critical details about personal motivations for doing the movement, as well as the meaning, history, and other contextual information, also must be obtained. Without that data, any investigation of dance around the world or throughout history will be uni-dimensional and, thus, incomplete. Further, one must remember that the individual's personal emic provides a lens through which he or she interacts and interprets etic perspectives. Simply stated, different people will have different understandings since their background influences how they apply and make sense of a particular etic conceptual or theoretical framework.

##  One Example of Comparative Dance Study

When students encounter an unfamiliar dance form or situation, it is beneficial for them to select from a variety of strategies to analyze information and make sense. Beyond the first and most natural stage of comparison, which consists of the individual trying to find relationships between new and old experiences, there are basically two roads to travel for cross-cultural dance studies. One path involves interactions with cultural "insiders" through interviews to determine how members of a particular group sharing knowledge understand the dance, in other words by investigating emic views. The other path requires having etic approaches that are created and acknowledged by a community of scholars with the purpose of universally comparing dance in diverse settings. This second strategy is more difficult since the novice student does not possess a well developed background or awareness of etic or theoretical frameworks. The following example provides one specific etic perspective for comparative analysis, which adds to the repertoire of tools available for multicultural dance study.

Gertrude Kurath contributes an etic model to the field of cross-cultural dance studies described in her 1960 article that compares how dances develop over time and space. Kurath's model offers several possibilities concerning how people adapt their dances to various contexts. By applying Kurath's framework, we will explore two types of "dynamic processes" relative to the movement form, *capoeira* (cop oh aeh' rra).[10]

*Capoeira* refers to the name of a fight or play that originated in Angola, Southwest Africa *(Jogo de Angola)*. African slaves forced to work in the sugar cane plantations by Portuguese colonialists brought this cultural knowledge to Brazil. The movement form was created as a series of defensive movement techniques among the slaves disguised as rhythmic dance-like behavior. Between 1630 and 1695, African slaves and the Portuguese were at war with each other in the area known as Serra da Barriga (se' hah dah ba he' ga) located between the states of Pernambuco and Alagoas, in Northeast Brazil. This was the first account of the existence of *capoeira* in Brazil.

*Capoeira* could not be openly practiced because law prohibited it into the twentieth century. However, this changed once Master Bimba, often credited for the reformation of *capoeira* in Brazil, developed the movement form into a legitimate sport. In the 1930s, he opened an academy in Salvador, Bahia (bah yee' ah), but only students with good grades and a job could attend. Master Bimba invited President Vargas to Bahia where members of the academy performed *capoeira*. This experience impressed the president so much that he changed his attitude toward *capoeira* and decreed the practice as legal.

Many people around the world resonate with this practice, which have resulted in the establishment of *capoeira* academies and *grupos* in countries around the world. Although there are specific movements and training techniques, every *capoeirista* brings his or her own unique style and defensive strategies to the *roda* (hoh' dah), or circle within which practitioners interact. People of different ages and backgrounds learn *capoeira* in schools, clubs, and community associations.

Kurath suggests that one dynamic process by which dance evolves is diffusion, which implies a dispersion or transmission of "information" from the source. Dances that originate in one part of the world and shared by a particular group of people "travel" across distances, either in their entirety, or perhaps only specific steps, to become a part of another group's repertoire or integrated within another dance.[11] Often, this will happen through individuals migrating to other geographic areas bringing their dance cultural knowledge with them. A certain degree of adaptation always occurs in the new context. In *capoeira*, diffusion takes place as the movement form travels from its place of origin (Southwest Africa) to Brazil in the 1600s—first to the state of Pernambuco and then to various locales throughout the country. Four hundred years later, the diffusion of *capoeira* is extensive, evidenced by the number of classes taught around the world.

A second dynamic process is enrichment that occurs spontaneously, through internal development, or as a result of contact with external forces.[12] Voluntary changes in *capoeira,* such as the addition, deletion, or alteration of movements, the meaning or purpose of the activity, the type of participants, and the space where it is practiced clearly demonstrate the enrichment process. This is especially true as more individuals possessing diverse cultural knowledge become *capoeiristas,* which shapes their actions and specific strategies used to interact with one another, thereby enriching further development of the movement form over time and space.

The dynamic process model, accepted by scholars or experts in the field of comparative studies, is an excellent tool for multicultural dance education. Students apply this etic framework to explore similarities and differences between different cultural systems, informed by their own personal emic lens. This type of "tested" model also may stimulate the design of new etic frameworks and ways of comparing common aspects of dance.

##  Summary

At the heart of multicultural dance study is the cross-cultural or comparative process. This process involves using different perspectives by which to interpret information: the personal emic view, emic viewpoints of cultural "insiders," and etic approaches. The personal emic of individual students or researchers shapes comparisons by interacting with cultural "insiders" through fieldwork and interviews as well as with theories or concepts for universal application and analysis. Importantly, emic and etic interactions provide a multidimensional framework for gaining knowledge about dance cultures around the world.

### Notes

1. Keali'inohomoku, Joann W. (1985, Summer/Autumn). Cross-cultural, inter-cultural, pan-cultural, transcultural. *Cross-Cultural Dance Resources Newsletter 2,* 1.
2. Ford, Clellan S. (Ed.) (1967). *Cross-cultural approaches: Readings in comparative research.* New Haven: Human Relations Area Files Press.
3. Lessa, William A., & Vogt, Evon Z. (1979, 4th ed.). *Reader in comparative religion.* New York: Harper & Row.
4. Lett, James. (1996). Emic/etic distinctions. In D. Levison & M. Embers (Eds.), *Encyclopedia of cultural anthropology* (pp. 382–383). New York: Henry Holt and Company.
5. Wolcott, Harry F. (2001). *The art of fieldwork.* Lanham, MD: Rowman & Littlefield Publishers, Inc.
6. Harris, Marvin. (1990). Emics and etics revisited. In T. Headland, K. Pike, & M. Harris (Eds.), *Emics and etics: The insider/outsider debate* (pp. 48–61). Newbury Park, CA: Sage Publications.

7. Pike, Kenneth. (1954). *Language in relation to a unified theory of the structure of human behavior* (p. 41), Glendale, CA: Summer of Institute of Linguistics.

8. Ohio State University, Department of Dance, Labanlab. Accessed on March 30, 2004 at http://www.dance.ohio-state.edu/labanlab/index.html.

9. Pike, Kenneth. (1990). On the emics and etics of Pike and Harris. In T. Headland, K. Pike, & M. Harris (Eds.), *Emics and etics: The insider/outsider debate* (pp. 28–47). Newbury Park, CA: Sage Publications.

10. The information about *capoeira* is derived from a series of interviews that took place in 1998 with Mestre Aguinaldo Garcia in São Paulo, Brazil and his *grupo*.

11. Kurath, Gertrude. (1960). Panorama of dance ethnology. *Current Anthropology 1*(3), 239.

12. Kurath, Gertrude. (1960). ibid.

## DISCUSSION QUESTIONS/STATEMENTS

Write your responses to the following questions in the space provided. Collaborate with one or two other students and explore their ideas to the same questions. Examine similarities and differences to the various responses.

1. What are the advantages of comparative dance study? How many reasons can you list that support the value of cross-culturally studying dance? Why would you want to develop this skill as a dance performer? Student? Researcher? Teacher?

2. Think about a novel or unique dance experience that was completely unlike anything you had ever done or seen before and describe your feelings. How did the activity compare to previous dance experiences? What relationships did you make between old and new information?

3. Imagine you are conducting an interview with a member of a group sharing dance knowledge, such as a community association that convenes on Friday nights to practice Eastern European social dances. You have identified one of the regular, principal members with whom you will speak. What questions would you ask to explore cultural knowledge relative to the group? What would be your opening question?

4. Thinking about the interview process, describe some techniques you might use to record responses. What "recording" problems can you envision occurring and how will you resolve those? Also, once you have the interview data, how will you analyze this information? What ways or methods can you use to understand or make sense of the material?

5. Consider the variety of etic frameworks that are useful for comparing dance around the world. Draw from your own academic background to describe theories or concepts that might have interesting implications when applied to dance. Scholars from fields such as psychology, sociology, anthropology, education, and art utilize diverse etic frameworks that also are relevant to multicultural dance study. List as many as you know and compare to those of other students in your class.

6. It is not difficult to find dance examples that demonstrate the dynamic process of diffusion. Besides *capoeira*, think about dances that have a specific origin in history or from one place around the world and have traveled to a new context. What examples can you list? Also ask yourself how the dances "moved" from one time and/or space to another. What "vehicles" transmit dance information? How do these change over time and/or space?

## CREATIVE PROJECTS

**Critical Viewing**—Study a photo (from this textbook or elsewhere) of a dance and write down your interpretation of the information. Consider how your background and cultural knowledge shape the way you make sense. In a small group, compare each member's personal emic for understanding. Discuss similarities and differences. Practice this exercise by studying a short video clip of a dance and follow through with the same activities. How does the medium (photo or video) impact the meaning making process?

**Interview** (a required assignment to be completed by all students)—Select a particular group of people that share meaning through dance related activities. Find out when and where they regularly meet. Determine if this time works with your schedule and whether you can attend one of their meetings. Contact the group before you arrive so that they are aware of your intentions to interview one of the members. Perhaps someone interested in participating as an interviewee will step forward, otherwise you will need to ask an individual if he or she will take part in a 30-minute interview that you will conduct to examine "what it's like to be a member of that group." Determine where and when the interview will occur and then record your process from beginning to end. Think carefully about your questions and be sensitive to your interviewee. After the interview, study your data and present your "findings" to the class. Highlight important words used, special emphases, patterns or interesting relationship between ideas, and terms or practices that you find unusual.

**Internet Resources**—Access the Internet and using any search engine, type the key words "cross-cultural." Examine various Web sites to determine which relate most closely to the discussion in our text. Which Web sites present the term improperly? Compare the content or focus of several different Web sites and observe where, when, and by whom these were created. How do various search engines compare? Do the same exercise exploring the term "cross-cultural dance studies."

# Notes

# The Dynamic World

 ## Introduction

Kurath's etic framework of studying the dynamic processes by which dances evolve over time and space provides a perfect introduction to our next discussion. This chapter explores in more detail the scientific theory of dynamism to explain that force or energy is the basic principle of all phenomena throughout the world. Using physics as another etic lens promotes further comparisons between dance and different types of behaviors.

Many people are unaware that physics or other scientific disciplines are useful tools for comparatively studying dance. Yet once we dig deeper and discover ideas about dance not easily visible or common in everyday understanding, we find that there are many underlying surprises. This type of critical viewing also extends one's range of possibilities for making connections between diverse concepts. It is like using a microscope to find out more information than what is obvious to the naked eye.

 ## Physics and Dance

The only constant is change. This adage constitutes our point of departure for examining dynamism, which suggests that everything inherently has energy. The word "energy" comes from the Greek, *energos*, meaning active, at work. Activity implies process, change, or transformation. The study of energy is explored in physics, the scientific discipline concerned with the natural behavior of phenomena in the universe. In physics, energy is a result of subatomic particle activity. As subatomic particles move, they change in reaction to other particles within their immediate environment. Bubble chamber photographs are taken to better understand the movement of these particles by using liquid nitrogen to record particle "tracks."

In the mid-1950s when this technology first appeared, bubble chamber photographs revealed paths of subatomic particle activity that influenced scientists to believe that matter was intrinsically restless. From those early bubble chamber studies, mass was "seen" as energy, which led to a deeper understanding of the dynamic nature of the universe. The ideas of rhythm and dance came to mind as scientists imagined the flow of energy going through patterns that make up the particle world, illustrated in the following quote from *Tao of Physics*.

> *All the material objects in our environment are made of atoms which link up with each other in various ways to form an enormous variety of molecular structures which are not rigid and motionless, but oscillate according to their temperature and in harmony with the thermal vibrations of their environment. Modern physics, then, pictures matter not at all as passive and inert, but as being in a continuous dancing and vibrating motion whose rhythmic patterns are determined by the molecular, atomic, and nuclear structures.*[1]

This notion of "dancing" molecules sets the stage for connecting physics with dance. Physics involves investigation of the building blocks upon which our universe is structured. The behavior of elemental particles demonstrates that energy is the fundamental link between all things, all people, and all places. Like the preceding quote, dance becomes a metaphor for particle activity, as well as the movement of all things. Yet, it is not only the metaphor that supports connection between dance and physics. On the most basic level, dance exemplifies the energy of life. It may be for this reason that dance is a part of all societies around the world throughout history and offers a rationale for comparing these two seemingly disparate topics.

It is interesting to investigate other relationships between dance and physics. For example, envision the following scenario. At a festival, a dance ensemble stands off stage before the performance begins. While they are waiting, members of the group are exemplifying potential energy, or stored energy. As soon as they start moving as dancers on stage, they exhibit kinetic energy. In reality all human action, whether it is walking down the street or eating an ice cream cone, is kinetic. Yet a dancer, by nature of his or her purpose or objective, exhibits kinetic energy once the motion of dancing initiates. Prior to that, there exists potential energy as the dancer prepares to realize or embody the dance.

Once on stage, each dancer moves in relation to others and the environment itself. Sensitivity to the organization of time, space, and energy as well as the conditions of the setting is requisite for being a member of a performance group. The dancers are aware of their surroundings and adjust their movements accordingly. Looking through a physics lens, we may consider Isaac Newton's Third Law of Motion, explaining that for every action, there is an equal and opposite reaction. A good example of this concept is illustrated by tango, a male and female couple's dance originating in Buenos Aires, Argentina. Interactions between the man and woman involve the exertion of forces, which move each other through space. They use energy to travel in various directions and/or articulate their bodies while staying in one place that equals the size or amount of the force they exert. The impetus in Argentine Tango comes from the leader's center of gravity, not from the arms or legs. Some movements use centrifugal force so that the action can happen with the leader being the center axis and the follower is the circumference or vice versa (the follower is the center of the circle), or there is an imaginary center between the two bodies as the action takes place on the circumference of the circle.[2]

Physics applies to the execution of every movement in dance. For instance, the force of gravity influences how we stand, walk, roll, and leap. Earth's gravity produces a downward force that acts at the center of gravity of the body while the floor or ground exerts a vertical upward force on the body through the feet.[3] Balance of the body is possible if the center of gravity lies on a vertical line passing through the area of support (our feet) on the floor. Dance usually involves moving from one foot to the other, which means an individual must find a new center of gravity every time he or she shifts weight. This becomes increasingly more complex as the dancer turns, jumps, or changes vertical alignment of the spine. The dancer and the universe as a whole are bound by specific forces that impact movement and that subsequently influence interactions.

##  Dance and Creation Myths

The study of physics in relation to dance takes us in another direction, besides looking at behavior or motion of the material universe. As we consider origins of the universe, a connection with dance emerges. Physicists continue to develop theories about how the universe was formed. Within the traditions of many people throughout the history of the world, there exists stories to explain the creation of the universe, Earth, people, and other aspects of the natural world. For example, the beliefs of those who practice Hinduism, originating in the area known today as India, directly relate the creation of the universe with dance. According to Hindu beliefs, Shiva, Brahma, and Vishnu form the great triad of Hindu gods. Shiva appears as the King of Dancers or Nataraja, Lord of the Dance, and performs the cosmic dances that typify the ordered movement of the universe. He personifies the destructive forces of the universe, as the dancing destroyer of the ego. His destruction is not simply negative; it is the elimination of old forms to allow new forms to emerge. Thus, he also represents regeneration. He figures in many legends, where he dances to punish enemies, or in some cases to instruct people in right conduct. Shiva is depicted with four arms standing on one leg, with the body of a demon underneath. The upper right hand of the god holds an hour-glass drum to symbolize the primal sound of creation. It beats the pulse of the universe, accompanying Shiva's dance. The upper left bears a tongue of flame, the element of destruction, while the ring of fire and light, which circumscribes the entire image, identifies the field of the dance with the entire universe. The lotus pedestal on which the image rests locates this universe in the heart or consciousness of each person.[4]

Other stories depicting the origins of the universe share a common theme of creation and destruction. Dance is not always directly mentioned; however, the focus is consistently about change, process, and transformation, an inherent characteristic of dance. Dance is ephemeral, or transitory, like all aspects of life and the universe, existing in a particular time and space for the moment. Each subsequent moment of the dance is slightly different than the preceding one. The series of dance moments is like a ceremonial procession, taking the dance and nondance participants into the future. No one moment is the same, and since each preceding moment influences or impacts the next, there is a transformational quality as one "moves" through the dance activity.

Life and dance are synonyms of each other and reflect a linear transformation. In physics, a linear or one-way transformation is explained by the Second Law of Thermodynamics, which states that all things evolve toward disorder or energy dispersion. This is often referred to as entropy. Dance demonstrates this law of physics if one considers the beginning of a dance as having a particular ordering of energy, which progresses until the end when the energy finally disperses. In nature, weather conditions carved the Earth to form the "arches" in Moab, Utah and they also exemplify the same entropic process.

Movement, change, process, and transformation are motifs found in almost every myth related to creation. For example, the Navajo or *Diné* of the Southwestern United States tell a story about Changing Woman (the *Diné* call her by many names such as *Isanakleshe, 'Asdzá · nádle · hé, Asdzáá Nádleehé, Esdzânádle,* and *Estsan-ah-tlehay*). She interacted with Spider Woman, an important figure who helped the *Diné* emerge from the first of four worlds. Today, we are said to live in the fourth or glittering world. In some Navajo sacred narratives, Changing Woman dwells as Whiteshell Woman in her hogan (the name of a traditional Navajo dwelling) in the eastern skies, while her sister in the west, Turquoise Woman, lives in her own hogan. Together, the sisters hold the east-west solar pathway across the heavens. In other sacred stories, Whiteshell Woman and Turquoise Woman, instead of being two different deities, represent different stages, or cycles (youth and maturity), of the same creatress. She lives on earth, but moves freely through time/space. In the skies, she dances out thirty-two spiraling paths through the stars, and in the depths of the ocean, she dances out thirty-two spiraling paths through the waters. There, in a hogan made of whiteshell, turquoise, abalone shell, black jet, and clear quartz, she continues to live. For her, it is a place of dance. Dance is Changing Woman's primary activity in her house, and through dance she manifests blessings, abundance, protection, wisdom, compassion, and everchanging transformations.[5]

Changing Woman also figures prominently in creation stories of the Apache people, another tribe from the Southwestern United States. The *Na'ii'ees* or the Apache Woman's Puberty Ceremony, also known as the Sunrise Ceremony, is a female coming of age communal ritual, reenacting an Apache origin myth based on Changing Woman. Preparations, which are costly and require an enormous amount of time, include the making of ritual paraphernalia and food exchanges. The four-day event involves many ceremonies, dances, and songs as the young girl becomes imbued with the physical and spiritual power of White Painted Woman, and embraces her role as a woman of the Apache nation. For most of the four days and nights, she dances to songs and prayers, as well as runs in the four directions. During this time, she also participates in and conducts sacred rituals, receiving and giving both gifts and blessings, and experiencing her own capacity to heal.[6]

Similar rites of passage ceremonies occur among many American Indian tribes throughout North and South America. Dance is a requisite component of these activities that highlights and heightens the metamorphosis from youth to adulthood. There are dance activities marking other significant moments in life, such as birth, marriage, and death, as well Earth's orbit or travel around the sun.

Rites of passage depend on the events of a particular person, for instance, a young man's bar mitzvah or a child's first communion. They happen because of an occasion that takes place during an individual's life cycle. However, rites of passage differ from rites of intensification, which are intended to reaffirm the society's commitment to a particular set of values and beliefs. For example, activities during rites of intensification like Ramadan, Kwanzaa, St. George's Day, and the summer or winter solstices have no necessary relationship to an individual.[7] Rituals discussed throughout this text include both rites of passage and rites of intensification.

##  Summary

Dynamism, which explains the universe in terms of force or energy, is a fundamental concept of physics. In other words, the basis of all things is energy, and dance is no exception. Energy also implies activity and change. Therefore, dance, or rather the activity of dancing, more clearly illustrates a process rather than a tangible product. Among different people around the world, dance is thought to be the catalyst for cosmic change, like the beginning of the universe or other creations. It is a metaphor for the life force and heightens events that are significant to human and Earth's cycles while furthering social values and beliefs.

### NOTES

1. Capra, Fritjof. (1975). *The tao of physics.* New York: Bantam Books.
2. Borgialli, Daniela. (2004). Personal communication. Ms. Borgialli is an independent Tango performer and teacher working in metropolitan Phoenix, AZ.
3. Laws, Kenneth. (1984). *The physics of dance.* New York: Schirmer Books.
4. Kumar, Nitin. Accessed on March 17, 2004 at http://www.exoticindia.com.

5. Jenks, Kathleen. (2003). Autumn greetings, customs, and lore. Accessed March 15, 2004 at http://www.mythinglinks.org/autumnequinox~archived2001.html.

6. Cody, Ernestine. (1998). The children of changing woman. Accessed March 20, 2004 at http://www.peabody.harvard.edu/maria/Sunrisedance.html.

7. Keali'inohomoku, Joann. (2004). Personal communication.

## DISCUSSION QUESTIONS/STATEMENTS

Write your responses to the following questions in the space provided. Collaborate with one or two other students and explore their ideas to the same questions. Examine similarities and differences to the various responses.

1. Do you think applying physics concepts to learning about dance in a traditional classroom is useful? Why or why not?

2. Go to the Particle Adventure Web site created by the Lawrence Berkeley National Laboratory and selectively read through the information presented (http://particleadventure.org/particleadventure/). Based on that material, what other comparisons can you make between dance and physics?

3. Choose one particular concept in physics and think about how you would demonstrate it to other students using movement or dance. Next, describe it on paper and then verbally explain to a partner what the concept is and how he or she can explore it through movement or dance. Have the other student actually follow the instruction then discuss the outcome of this exercise. Was it clearly explained? How well did the movement or dance activity illustrate the physics concept?

4. The word "dance" is often used as a metaphor for movement as in "the leaf danced with the wind." A metaphor is a figure of speech in which an expression is used to refer to something that it does not literally denote in order to suggest a similarity. How have you heard the word "dance" to refer to movement by other than human activity? What new metaphors can you create using dance?

5. In the stories describing Shiva and Changing Woman, what is the role of nature? How are elements of nature incorporated in the creation myths? Compare similarities and differences between both stories.

6. Think of how dance accents specific rites of passage, either in your own life or that of someone you know. Describe to another person one particular experience that you had or witnessed in which dance was a significant part of the transformation from one stage or situation in life to another.

## CREATIVE PROJECTS

**Art Application**—Work in a small group to design a trademark or logo to represent a dance company using a "physics" theme. Create this visual icon for company letterhead or T-shirts but do not use words/text. Explore color, line, patterns, shape, and size as you develop your ideas. A final rendering will be produced and submitted on white 8 1/2″ × 11″, 20 lb. paper.

**Internet Resources**—Surf the Internet and locate one Web site that has information about a myth or reference in religious literature that involves dance. Write a one-page composition that identifies the source you accessed (full bibliographic citation), explains why you chose that particular source, and describes how the themes of movement or transformation are incorporated within the story or sacred text.

**Literary Activity**—Work in a small group to write a myth in which dance is a tool for creation. Decide how the myth will incorporate values and beliefs of a specific group of people from a particular region of the world or a fictional group of people. Include at least one color illustration. The story should be between 1–2 pages in length (250–500 words).

# Notes

# Human Interaction

 ## Introduction

The topic of interaction provides a bridge between this exploration of the physical and social worlds. One thing that all the natural sciences have in common is an interest in breaking down "matter" or material aspects of the universe into its various component parts to analyze the relationship of those parts. The study of interaction between components not only helps scientists understand the way interlocking pieces fit together, but also provides insight about the nature of physical reality. In the human sciences, the study of interaction among people promotes awareness about the nature of social reality.

This section examines several social theories to create a foundation for investigating what, why, where, when, and how individuals dance, as well as who dances. The theoretical foundation also situates dance as social behavior that is shaped by the context or environment in which it exists. Interaction in a specific context further impacts cognition, the process of knowing. All aspects of our social world influence knowledge construction and, thus, the way we learn dance culture and examine dance around the world.

 ## Social Life

Philosopher Wilhelm Dilthey (1833–1911) contributes to social theory the idea that all human interaction is social action, requiring meaningful orientation to others in any setting. It is natural for people to analyze information about objects within the environment in order to make sense of them. Once we process that information, we take action toward those objects in response to the way we interpret or find meaning.[1] All data including sights, sounds, tastes, smells, textures, and intuition guide our understanding and subsequent behavior. How we act has everything to do with what we know, since prior experience informs the present and future.

Think about the following scenario. It is the beginning of the semester and a group of university students, who registered for an introductory dance course, enter a "classroom space" on campus for the first time. This room has a smooth, wood surface, large floor-to-ceiling mirror on one wall, and no other furniture except for a stereo system on a cart in the corner. The teacher is not present and no instructions are available to offer direction. Even though the students have never been in this space before, they act by observing objects in the room, the room configuration itself, and each other's behavior. One person sits down against the wall opposite the mirror. Everyone else similarly positions themselves along the edges of the room. It does not seem to make sense to sit in the middle of the floor, nor stand and wait. Individuals casually talk with each other, which provides information and influences the sense-making process. Someone enters the room; everyone looks up to see a person walk over to the stereo system, place personal items on the cart, and turn to address the group. The students recognize that this must be the teacher and the class is about to begin.

Each action impacts the next in a continual process that occurs seamlessly from moment to moment. The process of meaning making is mostly subconscious; we do not necessarily calculate each step to decide what action to take. Yet, people usually reflect on what they have done to orient themselves in a particular situation. We have discussed that experience serves to guide understanding. Often the choices of how to act, whether they are based on previous knowledge or not, take into account the individual's sense of what is correct or acceptable and/or feelings of comfort or discomfort in that particular situation.

All interactions between people require a reciprocal exchange or negotiation of information in which individuals fit their own actions to the ongoing actions of one another, shaping each other's behavior. This communication creates a feedback loop in which individuals act in response to how they "read" one's behavior and vice versa. While dancing, people constantly interact through physical or eye contact to negotiate space and time relative to one another. If the goal is to present a certain level of uniformity and one person changes positions, tempo, and/or movements, everyone else must adjust their performance. Conversely, if one person is moving differently, he/she may be forced by the group to move within the pattern, and conform willingly or not. This is seen commonly among line and/or figure dancing in which the odd ball is not tolerated. The person must modify the movement to fit with everyone else, or he/she may be ostracized and/or no longer permitted to dance with the group.

The same type of negotiation process happens between performers and non-dance participants such as musicians, singers, and audience members. For example, in many traditional dances from Ghana, West Africa, the dancers listen to the drum language to execute the correct movements in the proper sequence. The drummers reciprocate by studying the dancers' actions and preparing them with signals to begin new patterns. Realization of an ideal performance usually happens when all those involved with the activity successfully negotiate and share meaning.

## SOCIAL ORGANIZATION

Every human being is born into social organization. Organization implies order or patterns that develop among people over time. Sociological study focuses on these patterns, how they are created, and how they come to influence, direct, or control interactions among people. The process by which individuals learn the rules to become members of a specific organization is known as socialization. This may be defined as the means by which an individual is integrated into society.[2] It differs from enculturation, the process whereby a person adjusts and adapts to his or her total environment.

Social organizations shape the characteristics of interactions that take place as an individual learns appropriate, as well as inappropriate, behaviors within that structure. Sociologist Georg Simmel (1858–1918) states that there are various forms of social organization ranging from dyads, groups, formal organizations, communities, and societies.[3] Dyad patterns come into play when two people interact. In dance, these dyads are usually called duets. Groups refer to interactions between three or more individuals and can last from a few minutes to any duration. Trios, quartets, and quintets are some of the different types of groups in which dancers interact. Larger groups are more complex, which is why it is necessary to devise specific rules that govern behavior. In some group settings, like during an Irish *ceilí* (kay lee), a caller is necessary to announce which movement will be performed next. *Ceilís*, which are a type of party or gathering, usually involves set or figure dances that follow a systematic pattern. However when many people come together for a *ceilí*, the caller ensures organization, an otherwise difficult task for a large group.

Two other types of social organizations are communities and societies. Studying these group formations gives us another tool for comparing dance cultures around the world. Community comes from the Latin word *communis*, meaning common; this also is the origin for the word communication. Community involves more than shared characteristics or affiliations. It implies common activities and sense of purpose that emerge from people whose lives are bound together in symbolic and concrete ways.[4] Family, which includes the nuclear unit (mother, father, and children) as well as extended members (grandparents, uncles, aunts, cousins, etc.), resides at the heart of community and communal relationships. Sociologist Ferdinand Tönnies (1855–1936) explains that community, or *gemeinschaft*, is an essential human will that has an underlying, organic, or instinctive driving force. There is mutual dependence hinging on the group as a whole, and not its individual parts.[5] Membership in *gemeinschaft* is self-propelled, in contrast to *gesellschaft*, or society, where membership is sustained by some definite end, such as remuneration through money or other reward for work or service.[6] Communal, or *gemeinschaft*, groups are usually closed to participation by those who do not share kinship, traditions, geographic space, and/or socio-economic status.[7]

Dance exists in both communal and societal structures. From a community perspective, there are numerous instances in which dance occurs for the benefit of the whole. Family gatherings consisting of dance activities, like at weddings, births, anniversaries, and deaths, as well as religious ceremonies and other events, are community oriented. They promote values of unity and solidarity, strengthening familial bonds and customs. People who share dance traditions, not necessarily related through kinship, also reveal communal organization. Folk dance clubs, where a regular set of participants actively meet, usually are communities. People living in close proximity to one another share common activities and goals and promote community through dance events that take place in neighborhoods, at schools, and in churches. Additionally, there are special populations consisting of individuals that come together for a variety of socio-economic and political reasons. Elderly or retirement-age people, groups, children, and adults with physical disabilities, and asylum seekers/refugees are forming dance communities to adapt and/or cope with their unique situations.[8]

Dance in societal organizations (*gesellschaft*) are much different than communities since they are sometimes larger, involve diverse people from many backgrounds and areas of the world, and have open membership, meaning that anyone in the position to do so may join.[9] These organizations, also referred to as associative groups, often are built on relationships developed through one's profession, educational situation, and/or special interest. Illustrating this type of group is the Royal Scottish Country Dance Society, established in 1923, with the purpose to protect and promote the standards of Scottish country dancing. It is an international organization with over 21,000 members. Society membership is available on an annual basis and is usually obtained through local branches, located in many countries around the world.[10] Another example of associative groups is the Society of Dance History Scholars (SDHS), a not-for-profit organization dedicated to promoting study, research, discussion, performance, and publication in dance history and related fields. Organized in 1978 as a professional network, the society was incorporated in 1983 and has individual and institutional members in the United States and abroad, committed to the (inter)discipline of dance studies.[11] Both the Royal Scottish Country Dance Society and the Society of Dance History Scholars demonstrate *gesellschaft* characteristics because, according to Tönnies, they are artificially contrived or constructed by an "arbitrary will" that is deliberative, purposeful, and goal oriented, instead of being self-fulfilling like the *gemeinschaft* groups.

#  Cognition

The word cognition comes from the Latin *cognitio,* for knowledge. Historically, investigation of cognition begins in the discipline of psychology to understand knowledge acquisition and processing in search of a theory of learning. Early theories of cognition acknowledge the existence of cognitive structures that consist of sets of ideas that are hierarchically arranged.[12] Study of these structures, or schemata, reveals how people organize and retain meaningful materials. Schemata incorporate general knowledge and facilitate interpretation and representation of events and phenomena. Most critically, schemata provide a framework for categorizing "data" and operate as information-processing mechanisms.[13]

As individuals negotiate meaning to interact, they use the appropriate schema to interpret and process information within an environment. The total environment may include people, aspects of nature, and/or human-made objects. In the following example, consider how specific schema organize knowledge about spatial orientation and direct particular actions.

A man and woman visiting Brazil from another country enter a club in the state of Sao Paulo, where couples are dancing *forró* (foh hoh'). This dance and music form, which has many different styles, is popular throughout the country and is performed by people of all ages, socio-economic backgrounds, and ethnicities. Sometimes women will dance as a couple, but most often the duet consists of a male and female. It originated with the *caboclos* (ka bow' klos), individuals with European and indigenous ancestries that worked the sugar cane fields in northeast Brazil. The music, based on Portuguese, Dutch, French, and indigenous Brazilian rhythms, has four beats to a measure. Couples hold hands and torsos, and move together by mirroring each other's steps. They place their weight on one foot opening to the side on the first count, change weight to the other foot in the center for the second count, rock back to the side on count three, and hold the last count to repeat starting with the opposite foot opening to the other side. After observing the dance, the non-Brazilian couple begins moving, but discovers shortly that they are continually bumping into other couples on the dance floor. They stop to reassess their movements, talk about the problems they are having, and then study more carefully the situation as it is happening. They eventually recognize that *forró* is not necessarily a couple's dance. Rather it is a group or collective experience in which everyone moves more or less harmoniously in a counterclockwise direction around the room. Among these people, schemata pertaining to spatial orientation operate to unify and provide order, guiding actions to form a circular pattern. For the non-Brazilian couple, their spatial schemata categorized dance as movement through space that was not group oriented with an arbitrary design and direction.

In the previous example, the non-Brazilian couple interacted with objects in the environment using automatic cognition, a kind of routine or everyday cognition that is implicit, unverbalized, and rapid. When they stopped to analyze their dilemma, their mechanism for information organizing and processing shifted to deliberative cognition, which is more explicit, verbalized, and slow, happening when attention is shifted to a problem or issue.[14] This shift, requiring one to think critically and reflexively, involves the motivation to override existing schemata, and allows variability of time for information processing to occur. Deliberative cognition makes one stop and think about a dissonance or inconsistency between the new and stored information.[15] The same idea is explained by the theory of cognitive dissonance, in which forced or accidental exposure to new information may create cognitive elements that are dissonant with expectations.[16] Often people seek situations to experience cognitive consonance or agreement with what they know. However, during cross-cultural dance study, information does not always fit into our dance schemata pertaining to who dances and when, where, why, and how people dance. Since that may vary radically from one's understanding, it is necessary to develop tools and have opportunities that promote deliberative cognition, a requisite skill for multicultural dance education.

## Social Context

The single greatest influence upon cognitive operations is context. Beginning in the twentieth century, psychologist Lev Vygotsky (1896–1934) suggested that cognitive skills and patterns of thinking are not necessarily prescribed by innate facts, but are determined mostly by the sociocultural context in which the individual interacts. This interaction leads to continuous step-by-step changes in a person's thought and behavior, which may vary greatly from one cultural knowledge system to another.[17] Higher mental functions evolve from social interactions and the negotiation of meaning with others becomes the vehicle through which learning occurs. Thus, knowledge acquisition, information processing, and learning are socially embedded.[18]

The social learning theory of constructivism is based on the idea that people construct knowledge by interacting with their world in order to seek meaning. Interaction with others in the environment encourages an exchange of different interpretations and promotes multiple ways for the sense making to occur, an important aspect of cognitive development.[19] This theory is fundamental to our investigation of dance cultures, as knowledge systems that people socially construct. Constructivism also emphasizes the impact of context and how the environment shapes meaning. In comparative dance study, we may observe that the way individuals or groups understand dance culture is relative to the context, such as where they live or what religious beliefs they practice, and will differ from setting to setting. Interpretation of dance culture changes throughout people's lives, as they continually negotiate meaning and interact with the dynamic world.

# Summary

 Human life is social life that involves interpreting "data" about people and other things within the environment and subsequently interacting in ways that make sense. Experience, as well as context, informs all actions. As humans interact, they organize themselves in different ways to provide meaning and structure. Socialization allows individuals to learn rules that guide behaviors in various types of organizations. Influencing information processing and knowledge acquisition are cognitive operations, specifically schemata, which facilitate interpretation and representation of events and phenomena. The social context in which people interact shapes these operations to influence how they learn. Interaction that encourages an exchange of multiple perspectives enables comparative dance study of cognitively diverse information.

## NOTES

1. Erickson, Frederick. (1986). Qualitative methods in research on teaching. In M. Wittrock (Ed.), *The handbook of research on teaching* (3rd ed., pp. 119–161). New York: MacMillan.

2. Herskovits, Melville. (1948). *Man and his works.* New York: A. A. Knopf.

3. Simmel, Georg. (1908). The isolated individual and the dyad. In K. Wolff (Ed.), *The sociology of Georg Simmel* (pp. 118–144). Glencoe, IL: Free Press.

4. Holtzman, Jon D. (2000). *Nuer journeys, Nuer lives.* Boston: Allyn & Bacon.

5. Tönnies, Ferdinand. (1925). The concept of gemeinschaft. In W. J. Cahnman & R. Herberle (Eds.), *Ferdinand Tönnies on sociology: Pure, applied and empirical selected writings* (pp. 62–72). Chicago: University of Chicago Press.

6. Nisbet, Robert. (1966). *The sociological tradition.* New York: Basic Books, Inc.; Truzzi, Marcello. (1971). *Sociology: The classic statements.* New York: Oxford University Press.

7. Weber, Max. (1947). *The theory of social and economic organization.* (A. M. Henderson & T. Parsons, Trans.). New York: Oxford University Press. (Original work published 1921).

8. Vissicaro, Pegge & Godfrey, Danielle C. (2004, winter). The making of refugee dance communities. *Animated,* 20–23; Vissicaro, Pegge & Godfrey, Danielle C. (2003a). Immigration and refugees: Dance community as healing among East Central Africans in Phoenix, Arizona. *Ethnic Studies Review, 25/2,* 43–56.

9. Weber, Max. (1947). *The theory of social and economic organization.* (A. M. Henderson & T. Parsons, Trans.). New York: Oxford University Press. (Original work published 1921).

10. The Royal Scottish Country Dance Society Web site. Accessed on March 24, 2004 at http://www.scottishdance.org/.

11. Society for Dance History Scholars Web site. (2002). Accessed on February 12, 2004 at http://www.sdhs.org/.

12. Ausubel, David P. (1963). Cognitive structure and the facilitation of meaningful verbal learning. *Journal of Teacher Education, 14,* 217–221.

13. Rumelhart, David E. (1980). Schemata: The building blocks of cognition. In R. J. Spiro, B. C. Bruce, & W. F. Brewer (Eds.), *Theoretical issues in reading comprehension*. Hillsdale, NJ: Erlbaum; Sewell, William H. (1992). A theory of structure: Duality, agency, and transformation. *American Journal of Sociology, 98,* 1–29.

14. D'Andrade, Roy G. (1995). *The development of cognitive anthropology.* New York: Cambridge University Press.

15. Vissicaro, Pegge. (2003b). *Emic etic interaction: Processes of cross-cultural dance study in an on-line learning environment.* Ph.D. dissertation, Arizona State University. *Dissertation Abstracts International, 64-10,* #AAT3109623, ProQuest, Ann Arbor, MI, p. 3588.

16. Festinger, Leon. (1962). *A theory of cognitive dissonance.* Stanford, CA: Stanford University Press.

17. Woolfolk, Anita. (1998). *Educational psychology* (7th ed.). Boston: Allyn & Bacon.

18. Vygotsky, Lev. (1978). *Mind and society: The development of higher psychological processes.* Cambridge, MA: Harvard University Press.

19. Black, John & McClintock, Robbie. (1996). An interpretation construction approach to constructivist design. In B. Wilson (Ed.), *Constructivist learning environments: Case studies in instructional design* (pp. 25–32). Englewood Cliffs, NJ: Educational Technology Publications.

20. Dils, Ann. (2001). Personal communication. Mapping as a classroom activity and instructional tool has been developed extensively by Ann Dils and discussed in her paper, *Mapping: A personal dialogue with culture.*

## Discussion Questions/Statements

Write your responses to the following questions in the space provided. Collaborate with one or two other students and explore their ideas to the same questions. Examine similarities and differences to the various responses.

1. When you enter a theatrical performance space, how does the information you derive from the setting impact the way you interact? Your home? An exercise facility? A dance club? Give examples of the type of "data" you might find in these places and discuss how your interpretation of this information might direct you to act in a certain way.

2. Watch a short video clip (less than 5 minutes) of a person dancing. Write down in as much detail as possible how the individual interacts within the setting. Remember that each action, informed by the previous one, reveals how he or she makes sense in that environment. Discuss your recording of information with another student's observations to compare how you negotiated meaning while watching the video.

3. Do the same exercise watching several video clips, each representing a different group of dancers interacting. Observe carefully the "rules" for appropriate behavior. What happens if someone breaks the "rules?" How do people act similarly or differently in these various configurations?

4. With a partner, take turns teaching each other a short movement phrase. First, create the phrase by using everyday gestures, like washing your face, putting on clothes, and sweeping the floor, or invent your own movements, such as articulating your arms, hands, legs, feet, and torso. After you have developed the sequence, teach your partner non-verbally how to perform the pattern exactly as you did. However, this must be done without words. Explore how both of you must read the other's interpretation to negotiate meaning and understanding. Discuss this process of constructing knowledge after both partners have had a turn to present their phrase.

5. Reflect on situations in which you engaged in or attended a dance activity, but acted differently than the rest of the participants because you were not socialized as a member of that group. Or else, discuss an instance of cognitive dissonance where what you saw, heard, or felt did not agree with your understanding of dance. In either circumstance, explain your feelings about the experience.

6. Watch two video clips of dance performance that take place in different contexts and compare the ways people negotiate meaning. Begin by studying the number of dance and non-dance participants, sex and relative age of all participants, the type of performance environment, and the size of the movement space. How do these factors impact understanding? What other factors can you observe that significantly influence the process of making sense in these settings?

## CREATIVE PROJECTS

**Internet Resources**—Surf the Internet and locate at least three different Web sites that have information about dance and community. Compare similarities and differences between the various sites. How do they reflect characteristics of community discussed in this chapter?

**Critical Design and Artistic Application**—Invent a dance society with an explicit purpose. Determine a name and then construct a mission statement, outlining long-term goals. Clearly articulate membership rules and guidelines. For example, who can join and how much does it cost? Also design a logo for a letterhead on 8 1/2″ × 11″ paper and submit this along with the other information about your dance organization.

**Cognitive/Knowledge Maps**[20] (a required assignment to be completed by all students)—Ask students to make individual cognitive/knowledge maps outlining their concept of dance. Have them begin by writing the word "dance" in the center of a piece of paper. As they think of other words that represent their understanding of dance, they will write those on the paper. Suggest that they group similar ideas together and explore relationships. Compare these maps with other students and with the class as a whole. Examine the way the class works to construct a group knowledge map, representing their collective dance schemata.

# Notes

# The Dynamic Individual

 Introduction

This chapter continues our journey exploring the notion of dynamism, fundamental to human social life and all behavior in the universe. We recognize that people interact for survival and adaptation to every situation in order to make meaning, a necessary and inherent human trait. In the total environment, interaction occurs among people, elements of nature, and/or human-made objects. Those factors are external, influencing how people make sense and act. Yet each individual brings into the setting internal factors that also affect understanding and interactions.

Two internal factors are world view and culture. As we examine these concepts, it is not surprising to find that dynamism, and specifically interaction, impact how internal factors function to guide behaviors. One objective of this section is to question existing ideas about world view and culture. It also is our aim to situate this discussion within a twenty-first century perspective, an important goal for advancing multicultural dance education as a scholarly discipline.

 World View

World view is hard to measure and even more difficult to define because it encompasses the intangible. Yet, it is a critical part of how we describe ourselves. It is the way we know what is real and what is not, and includes individual as well as group understandings. World view is more than seeing the environment around us, or putting on a pair of glasses to explain the way things appear. As a highly generalized structure containing ideas, images, and assumptions about reality, it resides at the deepest, gut-level core of who we are. World view has to do with basic attitudes, values, beliefs about things, including the ultimate questions with which a person is confronted. Issues, such as what is life and death, are examples of concepts that our world view helps us to understand and that are culturally informed.

Philosopher Immanuel Kant (1724–1804) coined the term "world view" or *Weltanschauung* in 1790. *Welt* in German means world and *anschauung* means view. World view describes a consistent (to a varying degree) and integral sense of how people understand reality, although this may vary greatly from person to person and group to group. Importantly, we carry this "baggage" inside of us from one context to the next. Its roots are in human sensory processes, which act as a portal through which our brain receives information to influence interpretation and action.[1]

World view impacts cognitive operations, involving mental structures or schemata that incorporate general knowledge to facilitate processing and interpretation of information. Studying schemata specific to morality and moral codes reveals what a person or group believes is right and wrong. Morality, like other aspects of world view, involves a comprehensive interpretation that does not usually adapt to changing circumstances. This differs from cultural knowledge systems, which may accommodate different meanings and even conflicting constructs depending on the context.[2]

One moral code that guides behavior and ethical conduct among people practicing many of the major organized world religions is the idea of doing unto others as you would have them do unto you. World view informs adherence to this principle and other laws of governance. Failure to abide by moral codes throws one's world view off balance, upsetting cognitive operations. The disruption explains the notion of cognitive dissonance, exemplified by the breaking of taboos or social restrictions on actions that are considered morally wrong by a particular set of people. When this happens, a group's understanding of reality turns inside out, and serious ramifications, including severe punishment, may result.

For instance, among people in most nations where Islam is practiced, dances that involve men and women together in public are usually forbidden. Iranian law, which is largely influenced by Islamic beliefs, does not support the mingling of unrelated men and women. In December 2003 one of Iran's best-known dancers, Farzaneh Kaobli, and 24 of her students were detained as they were performing dances in Tehran, the capital of Iran. Iran's hardline clerics banned the activity, which they considered morally corrupt. The previous year, a court in Tehran barred male dancer, Mohammad Khordadian, for life from giving dance classes and he was forbidden to leave Iran for 10 years. Sweeping social restrictions imposed after the 1979 Islamic revolution have gradually eased since the 1997 election of reformist President Mohammad Khatami. However, the judiciary, controlled by unelected hardliners, does punish anyone who breaks the longtime taboos.[3]

Fundamental to studying world view is religion, a system that represents and orders ideas, feelings, beliefs, and practices, which develop in response to experiencing the sacred, the supernatural, and the spiritual. Religious beliefs significantly influence perceptions of dance throughout history and the world. These understandings of reality form a continuum ranging from one extreme to another, suggesting that dance brings one closer to sacredness or sin as it activates bodily senses. This last idea underlies the motivation by Christian missionaries to restrict certain types of dance activity in the South Pacific and elsewhere, beginning as early as the 1770s with the arrival of Captain Cook. In the Hawaiian Islands, *hula,* a part of ancient religious practices, declined significantly due to Christian attitudes. However, King Kalākaua (1836–1891) reinstated the public performance of hula as a key aspect of Hawaiian cultural knowledge at his coronation where he is honored today by the annual spring Merry Monarch Festival.[4] In Kalākaua's court, the dancers wore Victorian high necked, long gowns *(holoku)* which were stylish at that time in addition to other types of skirts.[5]

As we explore dance cultures around the world, it is good to keep in mind how our personal world view impacts interpretation. For example, among some people influenced by Western European civilization, dance is an individual expression or art. On the other hand, these ideas about dance are not shared by the Hopi, an American Indian tribe located in Arizona. Hopis do not consider themselves dance artists, nor dance for personal satisfaction. Instead, the dances, which strengthen social solidarity of the group, as well as the feeling of clan identity and pride, are done to bring moisture.[6] A Western European perspective may promote the idea that dance represents freedom or reaching up to the sky, in contrast to movement that connects to the Earth or relating down towards the ground. World view always frames our understanding, which is why we must examine our own views in relation to those we are studying. When we peel back personal beliefs, we will find under the surface our world view staring back at us.

##  Cultural Knowledge Systems

The previous discussion of world view sets the stage for studying cultures, or cultural knowledge systems. The concept of culture is confusing and hard to grasp since, like all processes of interpretation and sense making, it is embedded within the social world and changes over time and space. Certain understandings about culture parallel cognitive theory, which suggests that information is input, processed, stored, and output in the form of some learned capability.[7] This idea promotes culture as a cumulative deposit of knowledge, experience, beliefs, values, and assumptions about life that is widely shared among people who have a common heritage.[8] However, a product orientation implies that culture and cognition are a bound collection of shared information resources. That idea reifies culture, by treating it as a structured object about which stereotypes, generalizations, and ethnocentric views may develop.

A focus on process described by anthropologist Melville Herskovits (1895–1963) explains culture as dynamic, manifesting continuous and constant change.[9] The study of cultural processes explores the diversity of personal as well as shared knowledge systems that function by organizing information. People access the information to construct meaning and guide behaviors.[10] From this idea, we may locate culture within cognitive operations in which world view is a consequence.

Each individual has a unique cultural system consisting of negotiated understandings with others, obtained through personal experience in family, work, education, and other social settings. This system is like a tool kit consisting of strategies and techniques that are utilized depending on the context to inform individual interpretations and subsequent interactions.[11] The construction of new knowledge through interactions with various people increases the system's repertoire and broadens the individual's response to different scenarios. Exposure to information presented through media, such as television, radio, newspapers, and the Internet, also contributes to the formation and development of cultural systems. That idea provides rationale for promoting multicultural dance education and the development of comparative skills requisite for living in an increasingly diverse nation, such as the United States.

As a person negotiates meaning in an environment, his or her cultural system provides the individual with appropriate tools to make sense within that particular setting. This concept supports a dynamic constructivist approach to understanding culture as domain specific knowledge structures. It also explains the capacity of individuals to participate in multiple cultural traditions, as well as share and construct new knowledge in varied contexts.[12] For example, the experience of frame switching suggests that individuals shift between interpretive codes rooted in different cultural knowledge systems, responding to cues in the social environment. In the United States, students who speak Spanish as their primary language switch to English and interact using the English language in most public schools. Likewise, learning traditional dance and music of Mexico may be one part of a person's background growing up in the American Southwest and which they continue to experience during family gatherings. That individual also can shift interpretive codes to participate with school friends in line dancing at a club or a mosh pit at a rock and roll concert. This dynamic constructivist approach to culture establishes the ability of each person to have unique interpretations and actions that are situationally cued.

Each context has patterns of behaviors that people who share meaning follow. For example, an individual dancing in a school dance setting adheres to different patterns or ways of behaving than in a family gathering. The patterns are not usually visible or recognizable, but those interacting within the context must learn these in order to adapt to the situation. This process of learning, which every human experiences, is called enculturation.[13] It is through enculturation that we learn dance culture.

## DANCE CULTURE

Keali'inohomoku coined the term "dance culture" in 1972, which refers to an entire configuration rather than just a single performance. This includes the implicit and the explicit aspects of the dance, its reasons for being, as well as the entire conception of the dance within the larger culture.[14] Dance culture is a component of the total cultural knowledge system. Members of dance cultures share knowledge which inform their actions about what constitutes appropriate dance behavior. Because context is ever changing, knowledge construction is an ongoing process, and dance culture, like all cultural knowledge, is dynamic.

Among dance cultures of the world, there are many differences and similarities in terms of how context informs knowledge construction. In some areas, dance culture is a highly structured and integral part of people's lives, such as among the Kaluli speaking people of Papua New Guinea. Anthropologist Edward Schieffelin spent more than four years studying a group identified as the Bosavi *kalu,* who reside in the Bosavi rain forest. He categorized six discrete types of dance and ceremonies, which comprised their dance culture. The Gisaro is the oldest and most widely known, described by Schieffelin in his 1976 monograph. All dances and ceremonies have certain similarities, including social giving and exchanging, which is basic to the Kaluli way of life. Also, songs are made up for each occasion to evoke emotions. These songs project the members of the audience back along their lives, through images of places they have known in the past. The Kaluli do not regard their ceremonies as expressing hostility; instead they are seen as "grand and exciting, deeply affecting, beautiful and sad, but not antagonistic."[15] The anger that motivates an audience member to take a burning torch and plunge it into the body of a dancer is an effect of the songs. This is a measure of the ceremony's efficacy, a drama of opposition in which the actions and feelings of all dance and non-dance participants are brought into mutual relations and understanding with one another.

Dance culture of the Kaluli, a more or less culturally homogenous group, exists as a part of their entire cultural network. Dance culture seems relatively easy to define, but this is changing through contact with the outside world. Dance culture of an American, particularly one who does not have tribal affiliations, is much more difficult to describe. The variations and range of experiences that comprise a person's dance culture can be extremely complex. Through rapid dissemination of information and interaction with different types of people, dance cultures are evolving at light speed.

## THE LANGUAGE OF CULTURE

The study of dance as a component of shared or cultural knowledge systems must include an awareness of how to use the words "culture" and "cultural." Unfortunately, there is tremendous misunderstanding about the usage of these terms. Much of the perplexity relates to the increasingly dynamic world in which we live. One hundred years ago, it was simple to look at a specific set of individuals to observe similar values and beliefs. Today, media, as well as population shifts, promote greater exposure to diverse ideas, which in turn stimulates cultural heterogeneity. Research on shared knowledge systems continues to reach new dimensions and levels of investigation. Being conscious of these changes is important since it ultimately impacts how we relate to one another.

The proper application of language describing culture also helps us to avoid forming generalizations that stratify groups of people based on special abilities or criteria. This may happen when we incorrectly personify culture, suggesting that it is a concrete material object, which acts or behaves in certain ways. As explained earlier in the chapter, reifying culture is a common mistake, illustrated by the phrase "that culture does very theatrical dances." However, culture is not something that takes action. Instead this dynamic process frames interpretation and consequently influences a person's or group's action. It is correct to use the word "culture" if it can be easily replaced by the term "shared knowledge system."

## Summary

It is important to recognize the total environment as an external factor shaping interactions. Additionally, internal factors of world view and cultural knowledge systems, which each individual brings into the setting, also influence interpretation, understanding, and behaviors. These internal factors are located within socio-cognitive operations. Culture involves the ongoing construction of knowledge which people strategically employ to adapt to changing contexts. Together, the study of external and internal factors provides a comprehensive framework for comparing dance cultures worldwide.

### NOTES

1. Kearney, Michael. (1984). *World view.* Novato, CA: Chandler & Sharp Publishers.

2. Hong, Ying-yi, Morris, Michael W., Chiu, Chi-yue, & Benet-Martinez, Veronica. (2000). Multicultural minds: A dynamic constructivist approach to culture and cognition. *American Psychologist, 55*(7), 709–720.

3. Dareini, Ali Akbar. Iran's best-known dancer detained after dancing in public. Accessed on March 22, 2004 at http://cnews.canoe.ca/CNEWS/World/2003/12/25/296739-ap.html.

4. Keali'inohomoku, Joann W. (2004). Personal communication.

5. Ka 'Imi Na'auao O Hawaii Nei, (2004). The history of hula. Accessed on March 24, 2004 at http://www.kaimi.org/history_of_hula.htm.

6. Keali'inohomoku, Joann W. (1972a). Dance culture as a microcosm of holistic culture. In T. Comstock (Ed.), *CORD Research Annual 6,* (pp. 99–106).

7. Driscoll, Marcy. (1994). *Psychology of learning for instruction.* Boston: Allyn & Bacon.

8. Brislin, Richard. (1993). *Understanding culture's influence on behavior.* New York: Harcourt Brace College Publishers; Samovar, Larry A. & Porter, Richard E. (1997). An introduction to intercultural communication. In L. Samovar & R. Porter (Ed.), *Intercultural communication.* Belmont, CA: Wadsworth Publishing Company.

9. Herskovits, Melville. (1948). ibid.

10. Goodenough, William H. (1957). Cultural anthropology and linguistics. In P. Garvin (Ed.), *Report of the seventh annual round table meeting on linguistics and language study.* Washington, D.C.: Georgetown University Monograph Series on Language and Linguistics 9.

11. DiMaggio, Paul. (1997). Culture and cognition. *Annual Review of Sociology, 23,* 263–287.

12. Hong, Ying-yi, Morris, Michael W., Chiu, Chi-yue, & Benet-Martinez, Veronica. (2000). ibid.

13. Herskovits, Melville. (1948). ibid.

14. Keali'inohomoku, Joann W. (1972). ibid.

15. Schieffelin, Edward. (1976). *The sorrow of the lonely and the burning of the dancers.* New York: St. Martin's Press.

## Discussion Questions/Statements

Write your responses to the following questions in the space provided. Collaborate with one or two other students and explore their ideas to the same questions. Examine similarities and differences to the various responses.

1. How do you understand the relationship between dance and the sacred, the spiritual, and/or the supernatural? Use your response as a point of departure in defining your personal world view.

2. From your perspective, what constitutes taboo behavior in terms of dance? Why? How does your world view impact the way you understand dance taboos?

3. Envision yourself doing fieldwork among Kaluli in Papua New Guinea. You experience the ceremony, Gisaro, and observe the activity of burning the dancers. Would this promote cognitive dissonance? Why or why not?

4. Watch one or two video clips representing dance cultures in diverse contexts. Observe how shared knowledge among the group also reveals individual cultural knowledge systems within the total environment. Even though information is similarly understood, what differences emerge in terms of where the dancing occurs, when it occurs, how it is done, and who dances?

5. Think about how switching interpretive frames may apply to your personal life. Is your primary language (what you first learned) different than the one you use in school or at work? Do you have certain traditions and customs that you practice with your family/relatives that are vastly different than what you do when you are away from that environment? How do you shift from understanding and interaction from one situation to the next?

6. Describe your individual dance culture in as much detail as possible. What type of dance experiences have you had or do you have? Where do you dance? When? With whom? Why and how?

## CREATIVE PROJECTS

**Art Application**—Imagine you are giving a Powerpoint presentation and must provide a visual diagram to illustrate the dynamic constructivist approach to culture to support your explanation of this concept. How do you visualize the idea of a personal cultural knowledge tool kit? How might you portray the process of negotiating and sharing meaning in changing contexts? What types of shapes, colors, and lines will you use? What relationships will you emphasize? Render your image on 8½″ × 11″ paper. Then discuss and compare your design with two other people to discover similarities and/or differences between diagrams.

**Internet Resources**—Use a search engine to explore "dance culture" Web sites. Study at least three different resources to determine the extent to which the authors of the sites understand culture as a dynamic knowledge system. How do they connect dance and culture? What similarities and differences occur between the sites? Why? Write your response to these questions in a 250-word essay.

**Critical Thinking**—In small groups discuss the usage of the words culture and cultural in the following sentences. Explain how and why the words are correctly or incorrectly used. As you examine each application, think about whether the idea implied reifies culture.

1. His culture is completely different than hers.
2. Many cultures in North America came from Western Europe.
3. Dance cultures are universal in societies throughout the world and history.
4. Cultural study pertaining to dance in Brazil reveals influences by West African, European, and American Indian traditions.
5. The dances presented at the festival demonstrate great cultural diversity.

6. His dance culture is influenced primarily by the customs of his ancestors.
7. He studied modern dance and ballet but did not know any cultural dances.
8. Dance is not a part of her culture.
9. I'm going to get some culture by attending this event.
10. Her dancing style is culturally informed.

# Notes

# Identity

 Introduction

Renowned master drummer and dancer, Cornelius Kweku Ganyo, or "Uncle C.K." as many knew him, traveled around the world sharing cultural knowledge about the traditions of his people, the Ewe of Ghana, Togo, Benin, and Nigeria, as well as other ethnic groups with whom he lived and researched in West Africa. His motto was "We are all ONE in music and dance." This notion of unity was an attempt to deemphasize separation and segregation between people. C.K.'s lifelong mission in teaching dance and music highlighted positive human virtues by which to live in harmony as citizens of the world. He recognized similarities as a way to open doors that spread peace through increased awareness.

The concept of unity affirms our identity as *homo sapiens,* inhabiting planet Earth. Beyond this idea, there may be many other identities, both individual and collective. An individual identity is like a fingerprint, since no two are alike. When several people have certain types of similarities, they may form a collective identity. One of the most common types of collective identities is culture, in which a set of people shares knowledge and acts upon how they make sense of that information. As we will continue discussing throughout this text, dance reveals cultural identity by demonstrating the shared knowledge that people use to define themselves in relation to others. Preservation, dissemination, and/or creation of cultural identity occur through dance cultural processes. People maintain dance culture with current shared knowledge, bring past shared knowledge to the present, and encourage the production of future or new shared knowledge.

# Race

Collective identities may promote accord within a group while at other times they become divisive and produce situations of inequity. In past centuries, race has been considered a type of collective identity based on membership to a particular group. Caucasian, Mongoloid, and Negroid were terms used to describe three large categories by which to classify humans and relate to each other. Popular conceptualizations of race are rooted in nineteenth and early twentieth century scientific thought in which scientists used observations of racial differences to support racist doctrines. Racism, stemming from the erroneous concept of biological racial superiority, has had and continues to have a tremendous effect on how people interact with one another. Race in the United States is a social and political construct and has no basis in science.

The biological concept of race is now believed by many to be untenable. Research by the International Human Genome Sequencing Consortium shows that any two people are 99.9 percent identical at the genetic level. However, the 0.1 percent difference is important only because it helps explain why one person is more susceptible to a specific disease.[1] By studying the patterns of these genetic differences, or genetic variations, in many people, researchers expect to identify which differences are related to disease.[2] This concept is irrelevant, however, for the purpose of multicultural dance education.

Deep-seated beliefs about race are difficult to change even with current scientific understandings about the human genome. This insight about the relatedness of all humankind may strengthen the concept of one race, the human race, which aims to fill the trenches isolating people and discouraging interaction. Among the *Diné*, or Navajo, there exists the notion of one race, "the five-fingered people" as told in creation stories.[3] The Miwok, an indigenous group located in California, also have a creation myth explaining how *Os-sā'-le*, the Coyote-man, and *Pe-tā'-le*, the Lizard-man, who are the first people, made humans with five fingers so they could eat and hold things.[4]

World dynamics further complicate and make more ambiguous the notion of race, since more and more children are born of parents with various types of skin color and other physical features. The mixture of these characteristics generates even greater diversity, making so-called racial classification next to impossible. This is quite obvious in countries such as Brazil. More than half of the population has a varied ancestral background that includes some combination of African, European, Asian, and/or indigenous American descent. Unlike the United States, Brazil has not had the same type of emphasis in educational or government applications that require data based on race, although discrimination is clearly evident in terms of advantages provided for "lighter skinned" people, particularly in higher levels of administration.

Race may be understood as an artificially contrived tool of power and has become a cultural construct, promoting racial differentiation. The notion of race influences how people share information and understand themselves in relation to others. This understanding leads to various actions and behaviors, including those that promote group identity as well as discrimination. Dance classified by so-called racial distinctions is not instructive. By attempting to identify traits that differentiate dances on this basis, we propagate the construct of race, leading to appropriation of power. Any terms that endorse racial classification are insignificant for comparative study, implying extreme ambiguity and generality, which lead to misinformation and stereotyping.

## Nationality

Nationality is another collective identity that connects people in terms of birthplace. Individuals may have more than one nationality or change nationality through a process of naturalization, which requires prolonged stay in a particular nation. Nations have physical, empirical delineation such that the people within those boundaries are controlled by the jurisdiction of a specific government. Since these geographic borders are negotiated, they may change over time. Negotiations occur through economic trade and/or war. Japan, Cambodia, Vietnam, and Afghanistan are all countries in the continent of Asia. People born in these countries are respectively Japanese, Cambodian, Vietnamese, and Afghan. If travel occurs from one country to another, they are required to have a passport or other official document demonstrating their national identity.

National dances are becoming more and more difficult to categorize. A century ago, there was greater emphasis on the study of dance of a particular nation. Much of this interest was fueled by feelings of nationalism or patriotism through which people demonstrated their devotion to their birth nation. However, today's national qualities or characteristics may not adequately describe dances. This is due in large part to dissemination of information through media and immigration influencing shared knowledge systems. American dance is diverse and nearly impossible to define. This same statement is true in relation to many other nations around the world. Therefore, nationality, like race, as a category to describe dance, may become inconsequential.

One example where nationality is an identity marker for dance culture is among refugee groups. This is particularly true among the Dinka and Nuer people from Sudan, Africa's largest country. In Sudan, intermittent periods of civil war have existed for decades between different groups. Two groups in the southern portion of this country are the Dinka and Nuer, influenced by Christianity but faithful to traditional ways. Both groups subsist as cattle, sheep, and goat herders and are generally nomadic, following their herds' migrations. On the other hand, they have distinct languages, and similarly, distinct dance and music.

Many of these people have fled as refugees from their homeland, leaving established ways of life behind. In some instances, social service intervention has helped to relocate the refugees to host countries. In the U.S.,

Dinka and Nuer, who have come to be known as the Lost Boys of the Sudan, interact with other refugees and share certain cultural knowledge, like the English language, food choices, dress, and popular music. In Phoenix, Arizona, they have formed the group Sudanese Voices United as a community organization through which they reaffirm national identity. Although Dinka and Nuer maintain traditional dance cultures distinct from each other, they collectively participate in special events and perform dance and music traditions under the auspice of Sudanese Voices United.[5]

## ❖ Ethnicity

A third type of collective identity that connects people is ethnicity. *Ethnos,* a Greek term, from which the word "ethnic" derives, refers to a group of people that has in common biological and cultural ties, with a special emphasis on tradition.[6] Biological similarities may be physical size and shape, hair and eye color, and skin tone. Cultural characteristics, or shared knowledge among people sharing ethnic ties, may include language, world view, religious beliefs, political values, social organization, dress and food/eating customs, music, and dance. Examples of ethnic groups are Celt (United Kingdom), Hmong (China, Laos, Myanmar, Thailand, and Vietnam), Arara (Brazil), Basque (Spain/France), Inuit (Canada/Alaska), and Ibo (Nigeria). Sometimes a particular ethnic group constitutes the nation of its origin, such as ethnic Slovakians in the nation of Slovakia. In contrast, several different ethnic groups exist simultaneously in one area, like the Ga, Akan, Ewe, and Twi people within the national boundaries of Ghana.

The explicitness of ethnic identity varies significantly depending on the time and place of study. For example, one hundred years ago, ethnic groups in Europe were more easily observed than today. Interethnic marriages, immigration, nationalism, and globalism have diffused or placed less emphasis on ethnic group identities. In some cases, ethnic identity is no longer distinguishable. Keali'inohomoku raises further questions about whether ethnic dance is identified by the style, the ethnicity of the performer, or the context in which it is presented.[7]

The United States, as a multiethnic society, is complicated in terms of studying ethnic identity. Sometimes ethnic groups are not clearly defined because people have adapted to new settings and lost or consciously relinquished their traditional ways. In fact, not long ago, there was a fear that the U.S., as a melting pot of many different types of people, might lead to homogenization, where all ethnic identities would blend together. Renewed interest in diversity issues, especially in the 1980s, led to increased ethnic awareness and pride. This became a focal point in education and civic activities. Today most major cities in the U.S. have annual festivals and are developing community centers to promote various ethnic groups.

In some cases around the world, ethnic identity is as clear in the twenty-first century as it was hundreds of years ago. Regardless of external influences, specific languages and ways of life persist. For the Yaqui or Yoeme, indigenous people of the American Southwest, *pascola* dances are a treasured part of their heritage. Their traditional homeland is in the state of Sonora, Mexico, although socioeconomic persecution forced some of them to relocate and establish communities in and around Tucson and Phoenix, Arizona.

The word *pascola* means "old man of the fiesta or ceremony" and is a Spanish version of the Yaqui word *pahko'ola*. Taught through oral and movement traditions and passed down through the generations, the *pascola* learns the dances by apprenticing with another *pascola*. Much of their inspiration to dance comes through visions, usually in a dream. The *pascola*, a unique part of Yaqui dance culture, performs at all major occasions, including feasts, weddings, and sacred occasions. Sometimes, he is the host of the event and, in addition to dancing, will pantomime, clown, and tell stories to the crowds. A harpist, a violinist, and a drummer-flutist usually accompany the *pascola*, who wears a large blanket tied around his waist, a belt of metal bells, and cocoon rattles around his ankles. The *pascola* also carries a wooden rattle and wears a mask, carved of wood and usually painted black or brown. The mask is made to resemble the face of either a human, a goat, or other animals, with a beard and eyebrows made of either hair or fibers. The tradition of mask making also is passed through generations and taught through apprenticeship.[8]

Ethnicity is a subcategory within the larger classification of culture. Although members of a specific ethnic group have biological similarities, this information is only one component pertaining to their shared or cultural knowledge system, which influences how they make sense of themselves in relation to others and informs their actions. The study of ethnic dances, as dances from ethnically distinct groups of people, is still possible and important. Dances of the Yaqui reveal ethnic identity. However, a shift in perspective is taking place that no longer focuses exclusively on ethnic dance as a category of study. Instead, emphasis on dance as a cultural knowledge system begins to "even the field" since universally ethnicity is becoming less and less an identifying factor worldwide.

One such example is popular dances, such as hiphop, which are complex and difficult to understand ethnically. This also is true for studying ballet or modern dance as ethnic dances, especially today, when each dance form borrows heavily from other dance traditions around the world. By examining the origin of ballet, it is possible to discover common ethnic roots, as Keali'inohomoku observed in her well-known article on that topic. She explains how the language, performance space, customs reenacted on stage, choreographic themes, roles, aesthetic values, and scenic elements reveal a Western European civilization heritage. However, if some dances are considered ethnic and others are not, there emerges a type of hierarchy in which ethnic dance may be more or less valued. This attitude powerfully impacts how people look at and understand dance around the world.

# ◈ Summary

Dance reveals unique characteristics by which people identify themselves. These characteristics also make it possible to recognize a particular person or group through their dance culture. Dance, a form of self-identity, is as diverse as the number of people in the world. Individuals with common traits form collective identities. Yet, categories based on race and national identity (in some cases) are not beneficial to the philosophy underlying multicultural dance education, since this type of identification often leads to generalizations about dance behaviors that are stereotyped and promote misinformation. Worldwide, there are many examples of dance cultures illustrating ethnic identity. Nonetheless, ethnicity does not provide a universal framework for comparative study of dance. Diffusion of dance cultural knowledge due to intermarriage and population shifts is making ethnic identification increasingly more difficult.

## NOTES

1. National Human Genome Research Institute. (2002). International consortium launches genetic variation mapping project. Accessed August 21, 2002 at http://www.genome.gov/10005336.

2. Bamshad, Michael, & Olson, Steve E. (2003, December). Does race exist? *Scientific American, 289/6,* 78–85.

3. Zah, Peterson. (2003). Personal communication. Mr. Zah is the Former Chair of the Navajo Nation.

4. Judson, Katharine B. (Ed.) (1994). Myths & legends of California and the old Southwest. Lincoln, NE: University of Nebraska Press.

5. Vissicaro, Pegge, & Godfrey, Danielle C. (2004). African refugee dance communities: Parity in the aftermath of civil war. *African Studies Quarterly,* (in press).

6. Keali'inohomoku, Joann W. (1969–1970). An anthropologist looks at ballet as a form of ethnic dance. In M. Van Tuyl (Ed.), *Impulse* (pp. 24–33). San Francisco, CA: Impulse Publications.

7. Keali'inohomoku, Joann W. (1990, Summer). Angst over ethnic dance. *Cross-Cultural Dance Resources Newsletter, 10,* 1–6.

8. Maldonaldo, Merced. (2004). Personal communication. Mr. Maldonaldo is a Yaqui Pascola and artist living in Guadalupe, AZ; The Yaqui today. Heard Museum. Accessed March 23, 2004 at http://www.heard.org/rain/cultura5/raincu11.html.

## DISCUSSION QUESTIONS/STATEMENTS

Write your responses to the following questions in the space provided. Collaborate with one or two other students and explore their ideas to the same questions. Examine similarities and differences to the various responses.

1. In what ways does dance reflect your cultural identity? To what extent do you share dance cultural knowledge with your family? Peers? With another group of people?

2. Think about how many times you have seen job or school applications that ask for information regarding race. White, Black, Hispanic, Indian may be some of the terms listed, however, none of the words accurately describe race. The term white is not an appropriate label for describing a group of people, nor is the term black. The words Hispanic and American Indian also do not accurately refer to a race of people. Without a scientific basis by which to understand significant variables, why does the concept of race continue to exist as a criterion to assess someone for an application? As humans heighten their awareness about the political construct of racial distinction, how will that change the way people relate to one another? What action should be taken now, as we move forward in the twenty-first century?

3. What value does ethnic identity have in your own life? How has interethnic marriage, immigration, nationalism, and/or globalism impacted your ethnic identity? Which ways does dance reveal your ethnic identity?

4. How do you think people interpret, understand, and take action toward dance performance groups that identify themselves on the basis of racial, national, and/or ethnic characteristics? What examples can you provide, both positive and negative, that may relate to your own experience or observations?

5. What is your nationality? How does this identity impact the way you make sense of dance as a part of your cultural knowledge system?

6. Name one specific ethnic group to which you may belong and discuss whether or not that identity influences your dance culture.

## CREATIVE PROJECTS

**Family Genealogy** (a required assignment to be completed by all students)—With the help of family members, list as many ethnic groups to which your family is associated in the form of a genealogical chart or tree (principally your mother's and father's parents, grandparents, and great-grandparents). You may have to dig deep to locate specific areas from where your ancestors originated to determine their ethnicities. If it is absolutely impossible to identify specific ethnic groups, you may refer more generally to nations or regions (for example, Ireland or Andalusia). After researching this information, write a short essay (250 words) describing the extent to which your share cultural characteristics (language, food, dance, dress, religion, etc.) with other members of each ethnic group you listed. After each individual has designed their chart, compare the information with two or three other students. Finally, develop a class tree that visually illustrates similarities as well as the range of different ethnicities among the group.

**Literary Application**—Develop a short story for children between the ages of 2–4 using a reference to dance, which is new or expands on an existing story that pertains to the notion of one race or one people. The objective is to promote peace through unity. Include a title and at least one color illustration.

**Critical Viewing**—Observe two video clips of groups of people interacting through dance. Study which characteristics the individuals in each group share. What type of identity or identities do you think or know that these characteristics demonstrate? How are the groups similar or different? Discuss your ideas with one or two people.

# Notes

# ◈ Maps

# The Nations of the World

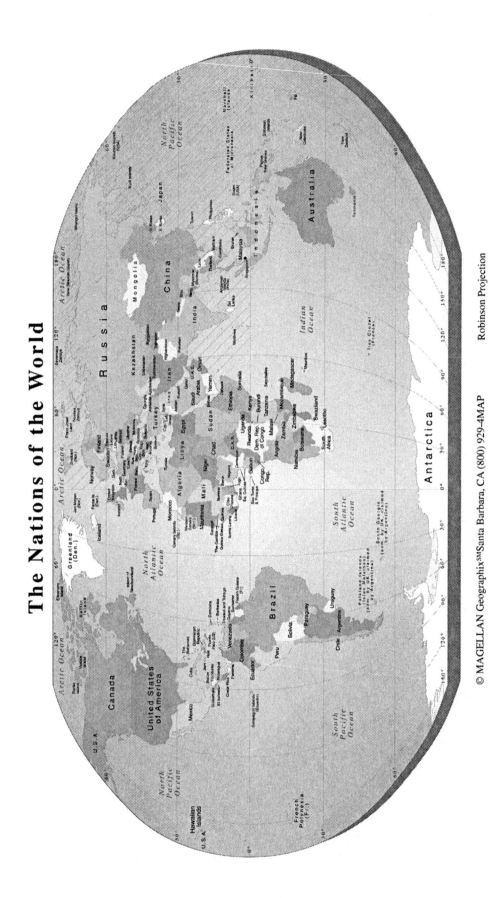

© MAGELLAN Geographix℠Santa Barbara, CA (800) 929-4MAP    Robinson Projection

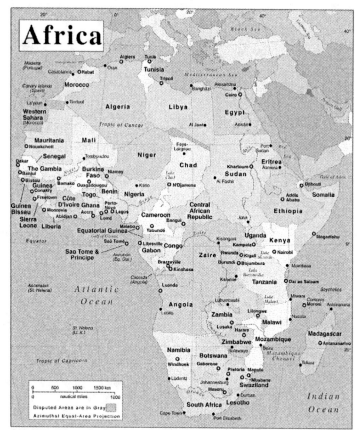

© MAGELLAN Geographix℠Santa Barbara, CA (800) 929-4MAP

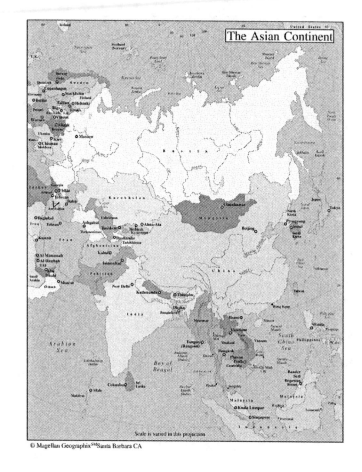

© Magellan Geographix℠Santa Barbara CA

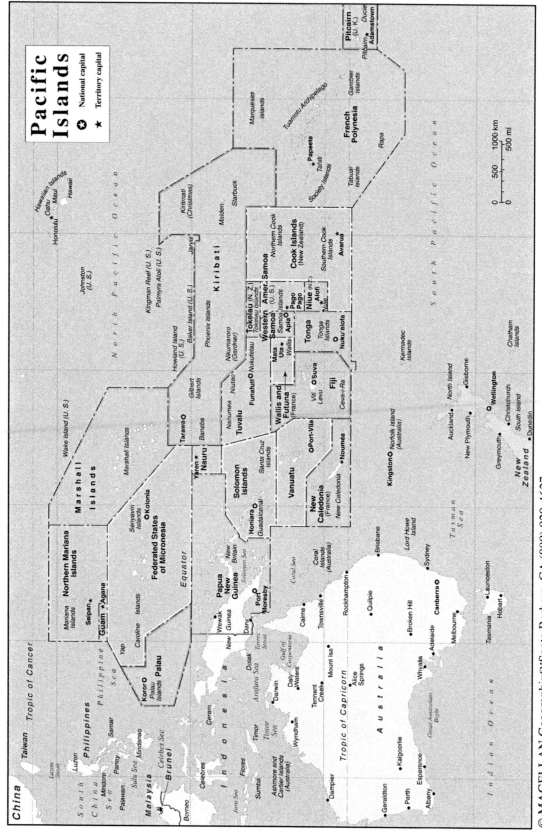

# Pacific Islands

⊛ National capital
★ Territory capital

© MAGELLAN Geographix℠Santa Barbara, CA (800) 929-4627

© MAGELLAN Geographix℠Santa Barbara, CA (800) 929-4627

# SECTION IV

# Art Criticism

# Arts in Society

 A Guide to Attending the Theater

### What's Playing

Your syllabus for Arts in Society: Theater will probably designate several theater performances for you to see. However, if you need to look for an alternative, several good sources list current plays and musicals in metro Atlanta.

The **Atlanta Journal & Constitution** runs a list of theater offerings in the Friday "Weekend" section. The newspaper is widely available, and can also be found in the KSU library. It is also on line at: *www.accessatlanta.com*. On this site you can browse the recent entertainment listings.

Kennesaw State University is a member of the **Atlanta Coalition of Performing Arts.** They have an excellent online calendar at *www:atlantatheatres.org,* which lists theater and dance events, and a few music events. They also sponsor Atlanta's only half-price ticket booth (see the section on Freebies and Discounts in "The Atlanta Arts Scene"). Their telephone hotline, 770-521-8338, provides information about local auditions.

**Creative Loafing,** a free weekly newspaper, also runs a list of theater offerings. The "Loaf is published on Thursdays and can be found in the newspaper boxes outside the KSU bookstore or at various bookstores and coffee shops around the city.

From *Arts in Society* by Kennesaw State University, Department of Theatre and Performance Studies; Editors: John S. Gentile and Karen Robinson; Contributing Writers: Ming Chen, Amy Howton, Kurt Daw, Hillary Hight, Julia Matthews, Karen Robinson, and Dan Shea. Copyright © 2002 by Kennesaw State University Theatre Department. Reprinted by permission of Kendall/Hunt Publishing Company and the author.

## PREPARING FOR THE SHOW

Once you've found out about a play that's taking place on a convenient night, you may still want to get a little more information. For instance, you may want to know whether this is a good selection for you and your 10-year-old to see together. Or you may want to know about the nearest MARTA stop, or parking availability.

Call the theater's box office with your questions, or send an e-mail. (Most box office numbers for the area theaters are listed in "The Atlanta Arts Scene.") *Many box offices are not open in the morning.*

You might also like to read a review before you attend. The *Atlanta Journal & Constitution, Creative Loafing,* and various smaller papers regularly send critics to the local productions. The AJC website (*www.access atlanta.com*) may help you get started. The KSU library also has back issues of the AJC.

## GETTING YOUR TICKET

It is *very important* for your success in this class that you book your tickets *well in advance.* If an event is sold out, you will want to know well ahead of time so that you can find another option. Keep an eye on the calendar and get your tickets early.

### Theaters

To purchase a ticket, you should contact the box office, either by phone, e-mail, or in person. (See the listings above for box office information.) You will need to know the performance you wish to attend and the number of tickets you require. Ask about student discounts! Usually you will need to pay in advance or provide a credit card number.

### Types of Tickets

"*Reserved seating*" means that you have a ticket for a specific seat at a particular location. You can request to sit in a particular area of the theater when you reserve your ticket (on the front row, or on the aisle, for example). Most theaters that use reserved seating have different ticket prices for different areas of the theater, and in general the seats with the best view of the stage cost the most.

"*General seating*" or "*open seating*" means that you have a ticket to see the performance, but not from any particular seat. These performances are first-come first-served: the audience members who arrive first have their choice of seats; those who arrive last have little or no choice. If you want to sit with friends, plan to arrive early. Ask the box office "when the house opens" to find out when audience members are allowed to enter the seating area.

### Refunds and Exchanges

Many theaters *will not* refund ticket purchases. You may be able to exchange tickets in advance for another performance, but in many cases ticket sales are final.

### Special Needs

If you or your companions need wheelchair accommodation, audio enhancement, or special attention of some sort, call the box office in advance. The theater staff will be happy to accommodate you appropriately. Many theaters offer occasional performances with simultaneous translation into sign language—don't hesitate to ask if this is available for the show that interests you.

## GETTING DRESSED

Most American audiences are fairly casual. Nonetheless, theater is a social event, and most people like to dress more formally for a performance than they would to relax at home.

In general, the more expensive the ticket, the more "dressy" the occasion will be. Friday and Saturday nights tend to be a little more dressed-up than weeknights or matinees. If you would like to dress up for the theater, go right ahead!

For a medium-priced or college theater, however, casual clothes will be fine. Many audience members wear casual pants and shirts, but cut-off shorts and torn t-shirts would be *too* casual. Baseball caps are usually not appropriate.

Beware of strong perfumes and colognes! You will be sitting close to other people, and those with allergies will appreciate your discretion.

## ARRIVING AT THE THEATER

### Be on Time

Plan to arrive at least 15 minutes early, so that you can find your seat, collect your program, and get comfortable. If you are late, ushers may not admit you until a suitable break in the performance—and sometimes, that break does not come until intermission! In larger professional theaters, you may be able to view the scenes you are missing on a video monitor in the lobby.

### Collecting Your Ticket

If you have not reserved your tickets in person, you will need to arrive early at the theater to collect them from the box office. If there is a cashier's window labeled "Will Call," this is where you should go. You should pick them up at least 15 minutes before the performance. *Some theaters will re-sell tickets that have not been claimed 15 minutes beforehand.*

### Checking Your Coat

Some theaters may have cloakrooms, although they are becoming less common. Most unsupervised cloakrooms are free. There may be a small fee to leave your coat with an attendant. You are always free to carry your coat into the auditorium with you, but try not to let it bother the people around you.

### Entering the Auditorium

As you enter the auditorium, you will usually be met by ushers who will tear your ticket and offer you a program. They will help you find your seat, and they can tell you where to find a restroom. *For assignments in THTR 1107, you will need to submit your ticket stub and program as proof of attendance, so keep them somewhere safe!*

If you or your companions have special needs (such as wheelchair access), ask the ushers or the house manager for assistance.

### Pagers and Cell Phones

If you need to be available to pages or phone calls during a performance, *leave the phone or pager with an usher or house manager.* They will make a note of your seat, and contact you discreetly if you receive a page. Otherwise, silence all pagers and cell phones!

## THEATER ETIQUETTE

Good behavior for the theater is based on the same principle as good manners anywhere else—that is, respect for the comfort of others around you. Since a theater audience is essentially watching and listening, try not to block their view or distract their hearing. Do unto others as you would have others do unto you in the theater.

- Arrive on time, and take your seat before the house lights dim. Crawling over the people in your row disrupts their pleasure in the performance.
- Silence all pagers, cell phones, and watch-alarms during the performance. Alarms and beeps disrupt the show for everyone. These interruptions are disrespectful and rude to the performers and the other spectators, and embarrassing to the offender. *NEVER receive a call or carry on a conversation during a performance.*
- Applaud, laugh, and cry as the performance moves you, but don't talk or even whisper with your companion during the performance. Even if you think you are being very quiet, your conversation is being heard by those around you.
- Unwrap your cough-drops before the play begins. The rustling of plastic wrappers annoys the people seated around you. If you have a terrible coughing fit, leave the auditorium as quietly as you can. Don't reclaim your seat until the next suitable break in the performance.
- Don't tape, photograph, or record the performance unless you have received permission in advance from the house manager. (If you need a photo for a newspaper story or a review, theaters are usually willing to make an arrangement with you.)
- Remain in your seat until the house lights come on at the end of the act or the end of the curtain call. Although you may be tempted to race for the parking lot, restrain yourself! It is rude to the performers and to the people around you.

# ◈ Attending Dance Events

One of the most exciting things about performance dance is that it encompasses all the arts. Included are, of course, the movement or moving sculpture, but also visual arts in the scenery, props, and costuming, as well as music, and drama in the acting and staging.

## ATTENDING A LIVE DANCE PERFORMANCE

An evening of dance should be a special event for each member of the audience. Live dance is not repeatable; the performance you are about to see is unique. A dance performance should be a conversation between the dancers and the audience, so think of yourself as a participant rather than just a spectator. The three-dimensional movement images presented to you will be filtered through your own knowledge and experiences. Your responses to the performers can affect the outcome of the performance by inspiring the dancers to reach new heights of excellence.

When you enter the theater you may find that quiet music is being played in the house (the part of the theater where the seats are found). In any case, it is appropriate to talk in a low voice with the person(s) with whom you came to the performance until the **concert** begins. After the performance begins, conversations in the audience should end.

## THE PROGRAM

You will want to look at your program book. Inside it you may find information about the dancers, **choreographers,** and technical design staff, as well as explanatory material that will help you better understand what is going to happen on the stage. If the performance has an historical basis, for example, historical notes will probably be provided. Sometimes a choreographer uses a poem or a story as inspiration for the work. The poem chosen or a synopsis of the story may be included. You will certainly find the names of the choreographer and dancers for each work, and usually the composer of the music is listed as well. There may be material about the dance company itself and often short biographies of the dancers and staff. Often, a calendar of upcoming events is also included somewhere in the program copy.

## DANCE PERFORMANCE ETIQUETTE

There are a few things you will notice about dance performance etiquette that differ from protocols for dramatic theater or music concerts. One is that it is appropriate to applaud at any time during the performance if you are favorably impressed by what you are seeing on the stage. Dance is visual, so your applause does not prevent other members of the audience from enjoying the movement. As in dramatic theater or musical performances, it is also appropriate to laugh at humorous moments or to stand at the end of a performance if it was of particularly excellent quality. In some cases, the audience is invited to participate in the dance; sometimes the audience spontaneously rises to its feet during a particularly moving or inspiring portion of the performance. The members of the audience may clap, sway to the music, or tap their feet. Alvin Ailey's *Revelations* often elicits these types of responses from the audience.

You will also notice that dancers often turn their backs on the audience as they are dancing. This is acceptable in dance theater because the dancers are not speaking lines, which could be difficult to hear if not spoken directly to the audience. In fact, the dancers are offering you the opportunity to see their bodies as three-dimensional shapes. Sometimes the movement is most interesting from the back, or from a variety of angles.

## TYPES OF DANCE PERFORMANCES

There are basically two types of dance performances. Traditional dance, including **classical ballet,** is often presented in the format of an evening-long production with a story line. *The Nutcracker,* a favorite Christmas ballet, is this type of performance.

While the dance may be divided into several or many sections with a variety of musical and choreographic themes, there is a continuing story throughout the entire performance, and there are central characters that appear throughout it, as well. Traditional **romantic** and **classical** ballets were created prior to this century and came from an era when people had more leisure time and were willing to spend time to allow the story to develop.

## THE INFLUENCES OF SOCIETY UPON DANCE PERFORMANCES

With the turn of the century, audiences were more impatient as their lives became more hectic. They were reluctant to give up a whole evening to one story. An astute **impresario,** Serge Diaghilev, recognized this new trend and encouraged the choreographers he hired for his *Ballets Russes* to create one-act ballets for the enjoyment of Paris dance audiences.

In this way, he was able to present up to three different ballets in one evening, offering the audience "more for their money." As this trend developed, choreographers felt more able to create ballets that were simply about movement, rather than needing to rely on a story to carry the evening. Michel Fokine's famous ballet, *Les Sylphides,* is an example of this type of ballet, which is still performed frequently today.

In today's theater, it is very common to find a "mixed repertoire" performance that may include three or more dance works. They may all be of one type of dance or they may not; they may have stories or they may not.

The works found in an evening of dance may or may not be in the classical ballet style. Also around 1900, choreographers began experimenting with new ways of moving: They broke the rules so strongly enforced by classical ballet choreographers. Movement became more natural and less formal, but it also became more abstract. Some critics feel that **modern dance,** as this style of dance has been called, requires the greatest amount of dance education for the audience of any of the styles of performance dance.

## THE INFLUENCE OF THE MOTION PICTURE ON DANCE PERFORMANCE

With the advent of motion pictures and the Great Depression, a very wide audience was introduced to dance. Just as with fans of today's sitcoms, many of these audience members wanted only to be amused or entertained. They did not want to have to think a great deal about the choreographer's intentions. Dance purely for entertainment became popular. **Tap dance** and the modern dance offshoots now called **jazz dance** became the dance styles of choice in motion pictures, music videos, and on Broadway. These styles often hold the most appeal for general audiences today, and many dance companies choose to include one or more in a mixed repertoire performance.

## OTHER TYPES OF DANCE PERFORMANCE

Sometimes you might attend a performance of ethnic or folk dances that have been staged for a viewing audience. This is often a wonderful way to discover the folk art and culture of another country.

## YOUR ROLE AS DANCE CRITIC

When you watch a dance concert, you will first want to identify the styles of dance being presented. Is the performance an evening-long event with a story or a unifying theme, or is it a mixed repertoire concert? You will want to observe all the elements of the performance, not just the movement itself. Are there stage sets or backdrops? What sorts of costumes are being used? Do the costumes enhance the movement or define the historical period or other parameters of the dance?

Do the colors chosen for the sets and/or costumes influence your emotional or intellectual response to the work? Are the dancers wearing shoes? Do the shoes, or lack of shoes, determine the type of movement the choreographer has created? Are the dancers working with any kind of props, or using the set or costumes as props? What lighting colors have been chosen, or do you see only "normal," or white light? Are there projections being used in the theater or on the stage?

Are the dancers dancing on a proscenium stage, on a thrust stage, in a round theater or in a non-theater space? Are they dancing alone, in groups, or with partners? All of these factors affect the way the members of the audience perceive the dance and, to some degree, how involved they feel in the movement occurring around them.

When you critique a dance work, the most important thing you must determine is whether you like the work. Why did you like it, or why did you not like it? Evaluating the dance may help you isolate the elements of the dance that appealed to you or that you disliked. There are, of course, other factors that may influence your opinion, but some common elements are listed below.

- Is there a historical basis for the piece?
- What knowledge do you think the choreographer needed to create this work?

- How did the choreographer utilize the available stage space? Was this use of space effective for you?
- What contrasts do you see in the choreography? [Consider levels, energy, number of dancers, body shapes, floor patterns, speed, and any other issues you perceive.]
- What were the strongest images in the dance?
- What was the climax of the dance? How did the choreographer achieve it?
- How did the non-dance elements contribute to the meaningfulness of this work? [Discuss music, costumes, stage set, audience reactions, etc.]

### AFTER THE PERFORMANCE

After the concert, you will leave the theater with the rest of the audience. You will not usually see the dancers after the performance. They will change clothes and leave the theater by the stage door in order to "preserve the magic" they created on the stage. You will want to write your critique soon after the performance so that you can remember as many details as possible. Hopefully, you will have enjoyed the performance so much that you will be looking forward to your next opportunity to attend a dance concert.

### WRITING A DANCE CRITIQUE

A formal critique is written in essay form. An informal critique may be placed on a prepared form or discussed in class. In either case, you should remember two very important points. First, assume your audience or reader has not seen the performance and knows little about the art of dance. Explain things in detail so this person can easily understand what you are trying to say. Second, express your opinions freely, but make sure it is clear that they are your subjective opinions, not facts.

#  Attending the Classical Music Concert

### WHY GO TO A LIVE CONCERT?

In a time when recorded music is readily available, the first question that comes to mind, is why go to a concert at all? It is true that some of the greatest performances of any given piece of music are available on CD, and that some pieces of music that would otherwise be almost never available are now easily accessible in recorded form. These are the great virtues of recordings, and we applaud them. Still, going to a live concert, like attending live theater, has specific advantages not available in any other format.

When you attend a concert, you are getting the "real" thing. Recordings are often doctored to remove any and all imperfections, losing much of the spontaneity of live performance. You can be sure that the tenor will hit the high "C" on a recording, but the excitement and risk of the live performance is missing.

Purists will say that live sound is better and more complex than recorded sound. This is true but it may be beyond the ability of most of us to make such a distinction. There are some things, however, that anyone can discern. In live performance there is a visual counterpart to the sound being heard. It is fascinating to watch musicians at work. In a live performance, the reality of the physical work of the musician is there to see. Few novices realize that opera singers are creating enough sound to fill an opera house *without amplification*. They are doing something remarkable, but it may not be clear on a recording, where volume is just a matter of turning a dial to a higher position.

## What Is the Difference between "Classical" and "Popular" Music?

Most of us are very familiar with the kind of music played on our local radio stations and, in many cases, have attended concerts by rock, country/ western, or hip-hop performers. These kinds of music, along with many other categories, are called "popular." With a few notable exceptions called "cross-over" performers, classical music is usually presented by, and attended by, a different group of people than is popular music. (Within the music world this difference is much more pronounced than it is in theater, where the classical and the contemporary exist side by side at the same theater, often using the same performers.) Pop music is not really different from classical music in a fundamental sense. Music is music. If you regularly enjoy pop music, you have access to the basic skills that will help you enjoy classical music. There is, however, quite a bit of difference in the standard ways in which these two types of music are *presented* to the public.

In presentations of popular music, be it on video or in concert, the emphasis is on the performers, how they dress, and on visual spectacle. Some performers, like Cher and Madonna for example, have made their primary reputation by dressing outlandishly. Others, like Garth Brooks, have become famous for stunt-filled concerts that are visual extravaganzas. By contrast, we rarely know who composed the music we are hearing. It would be a rare pop music tour now that did not spend huge amounts on sets, costumes, lights, and other very theatrical elements. Programs discussing, or even listing the music are rare. Music, *per se,* is a less important part of the event than the performers. It is the medium through which the personality of the performer is projected. That is not to say that there is not a lot of music presented, but it is of limited sophistication and complexity. Pop star Rod Stewart, for example, once claimed that he could only play three chords on the guitar, but that was all that was necessary for his concerts. That is, no doubt, an overstatement (or understatement, depending on whether he was bragging or complaining) but contains just enough truth to illustrate the point.

Classical music concerts emphasize the music above all. The "rules" of presentation are loosening up in our time, but traditionally musicians have dressed in a very standard manner, in black and white formalwear, to de-emphasize their individuality. The clothes for any concert are completely interchangeable with any other, and so in some sense, are the musicians. It was the sound that mattered. Stages are kept simple and uncluttered. Programs are almost always available (more on this later) listing the composers and keeping our attention firmly focused on the primacy of the music over all other elements.

Of course, both of these descriptions are extremes where musical presentation really lies on a continuum, but they serve as a helpful starting place as we think about the events we are to attend.

## WHY ATTEND A CLASSICAL CONCERT?

The assignment for this class is to attend a formal concert (usually classical but sometimes jazz presented in this format) rather than a popular concert. This is not a value judgment, and no one is suggesting that you must choose between these forms. One of the authors of this chapter is a music professor and classical musician who regularly listens to and enjoys many types of pop music as well.

The assignment is based on the supposition, however, that you may have much more experience with, and exposure to, pop music than classical music. The assignment is urging you to try something new and get a new perspective. Serving the purposes of education, we want you to broaden your horizons. Of course, you may already be a classical music fan, or even performer. Whether you have a lot of experience with formal presentations of classical music, or none whatsoever, the experience can help you better understand the role of arts in society.

## VARIOUS KINDS OF PERFORMANCES

Having contrasted classical music presentations with pop ones, you may have the impression that there is only one kind of classical music out there, but actually there is quite a range and variety of concert and recital types available for you to attend. Here is a quick guide to various kinds of classically based performances:

*Symphonic Concerts:* A concert presented by a large group of between 50 to 100 instrumental performers under the leadership of a conductor (a symphony orchestra) is the most familiar image of a "classical" event. This type of concert will usually feature three or four long pieces of music and last about two hours plus intermissions. There may be guest performers appearing as featured soloists for some or all of the pieces. There may be singers appearing with the orchestra as soloists or as a choral group. One of the most common musical forms presented at instrumental concerts is the symphony, which usually comes in four parts, called movements. Between each of these parts there is a small break, but it is traditional not to clap until all four parts are complete. (More about this later.) The concerto is also common. This is a work for a soloist accompanied by the full orchestra. Concertos usually come in three movements, where again it is traditional to applaud only after the last. Near the end of the third movement of a concerto there is usually a moment where it seems like things have ended when suddenly the soloist will play a last flurry of unaccompanied music called a cadenza. Don't let the second of silence before it begins fool you into applauding. It is particularly important to forgo applause here and wait until the piece ends, which is often very shortly after the cadenza.

*Chamber Music Concerts:*  Similar to symphonic concerts, but featuring fewer musicians in a smaller space, chamber music events are intense concerts usually attended by dedicated music fans. Chamber events usually feature between three and fifteen musicians. They usually play about the same amount of music as is played at the symphonic concert, but it is often divided into more pieces of shorter length. There may be a conductor at chamber music concerts, but often one of the players gives a few signals that begin and end the otherwise unconducted pieces. Observance of rules of decorum is particularly strong at chamber events because of the extreme intimacy of the format.

*Early Music Concerts:*  Around the time of Shakespeare, music became a more public art form but it was more than a hundred years later that most instruments took on their modern form. Music written during this time period (from approximately 1580 to 1700) is called early music and has seen a resurgence of popularity within the last 50 years. Sometimes it is played on instruments in their old forms, but more often it is played on modern instruments. There is rarely a conductor at an early music concert, because historically this music was written before the advent of conductors, so there are few clues about when pieces of music are beginning and ending as opposed to just switching from one movement to another. The audience for these historically fascinating concerts is extremely specialized. Go and enjoy yourself, but let others take the lead in matters of decorum until you learn the "rules."

*Choral Concerts:*  Concerts that feature a singing ensemble accompanied usually by a piano and/or a small number of instruments are called choral concerts. Choral concerts are still formal events, but they are generally looser in their overall adherence to decorum than are instrumental concerts. Choral works take a large variety of forms, but two of the most common are masses (settings, usually in Latin, of the Roman Catholic Mass) and requiems (settings of special masses composed for funerals). These are now performed outside of their religious contexts (even when, as they often are, presented by church choirs in churches as special events) and are meant as musical events instead of religious worship. Nonetheless, the religious tradition behind these events often makes their presentation, and audience behavior, more solemn than at other types of choral concerts. Choral concerts are usually a bit shorter than instrumental events.

*Recitals:*    Musical events where a single performer presents a body of work with the assistance of one or more accompanists are called recitals. Occasionally small groups such as duos or trios will also present recitals. Song recitals are commonly presented by a single singer accompanied by a piano. Because of the nature of songs, there is often a fairly large number of two- to three-minute songs. These are presented in the language in which they were originally written, and it is common practice for a singer to demonstrate a familiarity with several languages. Most recitals feature at least a couple of songs in French, German, and Italian. Songs in English generally appear on this type of recital near the end of the program. Instrumental recitals often feature fewer pieces, but they are longer. In either case, the amount of music on a recital is closer to an hour's worth, rather than the two hours of a symphonic concert. A recital is a demonstration of skill on the part of the solo performer, so it is also common practice to begin with some early music and offer at least one piece of music from all the major historical periods between then and now. The ability to handle a wide variety of musical styles is especially valued.

*Opera:*    Of all the classical forms, opera is closest to theater, in that it is a play in which much or all of the dialogue is set to music and sung. Opera is essentially a theatrical form, and the rules of decorum are those of the theater instead of classical music. Most operas were written in foreign languages and are performed in the original language. It has become nearly universal practice now to project the words of the English translation above or below the stage during the performance.

## PREPARING TO ATTEND: TICKETS, APPROPRIATE DRESS, AND PLANNING

Once you have selected an event to attend, there are a few preparations to make. Because they are usually one-night events rather than long runs, tickets for musical events often sell out well in advance, so it is important to check with the box office and see if there are seats for the performance and the night you want to attend. Don't just go to an event hoping to be seated. More often than not, you will be disappointed. *This is true even for free events. You may need a ticket, even though you don't have to pay for it.* Be sure to ask if student discounts are available, or if you can see the performance for free in exchange for ushering if you are trying to control costs.

While on the telephone to the box office, ask about directions and parking. The box office should be able to give you good, easy-to-follow directions from whichever direction you are coming. They will also be able to suggest where to park safely and conveniently. Since there is often a charge for parking, ask if they know the approximate hourly cost of nearby lots. In most cases it is strictly forbidden to have a pager or a telephone in the event, so also ask if they have an emergency message system number to leave with sitters, businesses, or others that must reach you.

Finally, you may want to get some assistance with planning your timing. Many theaters close the doors at the beginning of the concert and will not allow latecomers to enter until intermission. Be sure you know the correct starting time of the event, the seating policy, and the suggested arrival time. The box office will also be able to tell you the total length of time for the event. Students who are used to more casually oriented events chronically underestimate the travel time to events and are frequently disappointed to find that the concerns of avid concert goers are much more highly considered than the needs of latecomers. Your instructors will not understand your missing half or more of a concert because of arriving late and being denied entrance.

Influenced by the formalwear of the musicians, most concert goers opt to dress up a bit. You will see everything from tuxedos to jeans on men and formal gowns to warm-up suits on women, but the standard dress for a concert generally settles on business wear. A shirt and tie for men, a nice dress or suit for a woman will always be appropriate. Standard classroom dress, T-shirts and jeans, is generally a bit on the casual side for a formal concert. Hats, especially baseball-type caps, are almost always inappropriate, as is torn clothing (however fashionable it may be).

## THE MUSIC IS THE THING: CONDUCT AND APPLAUSE AT THE CONCERT

Rules of behavior at formal concerts can seem stuffy and confusing to the first-time concert attendee, but they are actually all related to a single idea: the music is the most important thing. Arriving late is bad form, because it disturbs others as you get to your seat. In fact, moving to or from your seat any time music is playing interferes with the concert. Eating and drinking anything, especially wrapped candies and gum, disturbs others around you by making sound when they are trying to listen. The basic rules for decorum are as simple as trying to maintain silence so that the music can be heard. For those going to a formal concert for the first time, especially if they have experience with pop concerts, this can seem very surprising. At pop concerts, people eat, drink, smoke, scream, stomp, applaud, and respond wildly, often at the moment the new piece of music is starting. That is the moment in a classical concert when total silence is required.

Beyond what common sense would dictate about keeping the silence (moving about to use the restroom or get a drink only at intermissions, for example) there is only one other consideration: applause at musical events is governed by rules that seem arbitrary until you get the hang of them.

In a musical event, it is traditional to applaud when the conductor enters, or re-renters the stage or orchestra pit. In opera performances, you may not be able to see this unless you are sitting in the balcony. It can be very disconcerting for the whole audience to burst into applause for no apparent reason! Usually the conductor has entered without your noticing.

Soloists also get applause each time they enter, or re-enter the stage.

Music is applauded, but only at the end of the entire piece. This is where it is important to remember that symphonies and concertos are composed in multiple movements. Just because the musicians have stopped playing momentarily does not mean the piece is over. Just one section of it is over. Wait until all the sections are finished before you applaud the work. This is easy to tell in concerts where there is a conductor. At the end of the piece, he or she will turn around to face the audience, step off the podium, and bow. At conductor-less events this is trickier to determine. Wait until the whole audience begins to applaud before you jump in. If in doubt, just don't start the applause and you'll be fine.

## WHAT WILL HAPPEN AT THE CONCERT

Because there is a variety of kinds of concerts, there are several different kinds of concert plans, but overall most concerts follow a consistent pattern. At the beginning of a large event, the musicians will begin to wander onto the stage one by one. They will warm up by playing a few notes or phrases on their instruments. At this point they are generally ignored. At length, the last instrumentalist will enter the stage. This person is the *concertmaster*, the head violinist, and he or she is considered the symbolic representation of the whole orchestra. The appearance of the concertmaster is greeted by applause, and then silence follows while the orchestra "tunes." They all play the same note to determine that their instruments are all playing in the same precise key. This is more complicated than it sounds, and can take a bit of work. The audience is silent for the tuning, because the musicians need to be able to hear their instruments.

In a concert with a small number of players, say five or six, they will all simply enter at the same time, greeted by applause, and may then tune.

Singers do not "tune" so they will simply enter and prepare to perform.

When the tuning is complete and the concert requires a conductor, he or she will enter and receive applause. If there is a soloist, that person will enter with the conductor.

At this point, the music will finally begin. The audience will fall completely silent, and from this point the rules concerning silence (including the exclusion of latecomers) will commence. In conducted concerts, the conductor steps up on a small platform in front of the players (called the podium) and begins the concert. In recitals or concerts without a conductor, the music will begin with less formal signaling. The music will continue until the end of the first full piece, or in song recitals, until the end of the first *group* of songs. The musicians will turn to face the audience, and the applause will begin. The conductor may shake the concertmaster's hand, symbolically thanking the whole orchestra. At the end of the applause some or all of the musicians will leave the stage. There will be a brief pause of perhaps two to three minutes, but unless indicated in the program, this will not be the intermission. Nonetheless, if you must slip out for any reason, this is the time to do so.

For the second part of the concert, the whole process will start over again. The musicians and conductor will re-enter. They will receive applause again, and bow again, before starting the music. Once they begin again, all the rules about silence go into effect again.

This process will proceed until the end of the evening, with intermission included as indicated in the program. At the very end of the evening there may be a few additional pieces of music played, called *encores,* which will be discussed below.

## THE PROGRAM AND WHAT'S IN IT

At most concerts there is a printed list of all the music to be presented, called the *program.* Keep your program. Not only do you need to attach it to your report form, it is also the best guide you can have to the evening.

A good concert program contains a lot of useful information. At very least it will contain the title and composer of all the pieces to be played, the names of the soloists, and whether there is an intermission. Many programs also contain the birth and death dates of the composers, or the actual dates of composition of the pieces of music.

Musical selections with more than one movement are traditionally listed so that you can tell the number and order of the movements.

A typical example might look something like this:

*Concerto in B minor for*
*Cello and Orchestra*     Anton Dvorák
  *Op. 104 (1895)*

  *Allegro*
  *Adagio ma non troppo*
  *Rondo: Allegro Moderato*

    *Robert Shaw, Conductor*
    *Mstislav Rostropovich, Cello*

This entry tells us the name of the piece of music. You can see from the title that it is a concerto, which you will recall is a form for a soloist accompanied by an orchestra. Further down you will see the names of both the conductor and the soloist involved. *Concerti* traditionally have three movements, as does this one. You can tell because just under the name of the piece you will see the three movements listed. As is often the case, each movement is identified by the Italian words describing the speed at which it is to be played. You don't have to understand these words to make use of them. Simply count the number of entries to get the number of movements. Remember that the final movement will feature a *cadenza.* This will give you a good sense of when the piece is finishing, and when to applaud.

The are other bits of useful information here also. The composer's name follows the piece (Dvorák). There is also an opus number, which is a chronological listing of all of the composer's works. In this case, this is the 104th piece by this composer. It was composed in 1895. Some programs will tell you the birth and death dates of the composer (1841–1904) instead of (or as well as) the date of composition.

When performed by an orchestra, this would probably be one of two or three pieces played in the evening, but the entries for the others would probably be similar.

If you are an inexperienced concert goer, this may all look a bit intimidating, but getting a feel for how many pieces are being played, how many sections each has, and some idea of when they were written can really help you settle in to listen carefully. A piece like this one lasting nearly 40 minutes can be hard to attend to when you are used to songs of two to three minutes in length. There will actually be a lot of unity to the piece, however. Specific musical phrases, called themes, will reoccur over the space of the evening giving you some familiar "landmarks" for which to listen. You will also notice the piece has the same shape as a dramatic composition, with an opening section, rising intensity, a climax, and a short denouement.

## WHAT'S NOT IN THE PROGRAM: ENCORES

At the end of the evening (usually a solo concert), when all the pieces listed on the program have been played the concert may not yet be over. In fact, the very best part may just be beginning.

Famous musicians are apt to return for additional pieces called *encores*. Encores are supposed to be spontaneous responses to an audience that is begging for more music, so it would be bad form to list them on the program, thereby assuming the audience will want more. In practice, however, encores are usually thoroughly planned and rehearsed, and the musicians have actually decided in advance that the audience *will* want more.

Encores are usually the signature piece of the specific musician/s featured on the night's concert. These are the pieces for which they are most famous. Another reason they are not listed is because, rightly or wrongly, it is assumed that the pieces being played are very familiar. Even if you do not know much about music you may realize suddenly that you have heard an encore piece many times before.

Don't be in a hurry to leave a concert when the program is complete, but stay with the clapping audience and see if the musician reappears to play more pieces. The encores are often the most fun and familiar moments of the evening. If you really want to get your money's worth, join in the clapping and keep it up until the musician returns.

## A FEW SUGGESTIONS FOR WORKING ON YOUR REPORT FORM

When all is said and done, your instructor wants primarily to know that you attended the complete concert and did your best to listen to it carefully. You will do yourself—and your instructor—a favor if you do a few simple things.

First, use your program to help you craft answers that are specific and make use of musical terminology. Don't write "the third piece was my favorite" when you could take just a second to look it up on the program and be able to write, "The Dvořák concerto was my favorite, especially the *allegro* movement."

You may also find information in the program that helps you to understand a piece better. Knowing Dvořák was a Czech, for example, may help you to hear and identify the Slavic sound of many of his pieces. To say something had a distinct eastern European sound is better than saying it sounded "weird" or "awesome."

Second, be careful about the words you use. Only sung works are songs. Instrumental pieces can also be called selections or works to avoid repeating the word "piece" too often. You can also refer to the name or the genre of the work for more variety.

Write about what you heard and the impression it made on you. Sometimes student report forms are so vague that an instructor is unsure if the student even attended the concert. Go ahead and describe the actual events and sounds of the concert to make your responses more compelling and interesting. Use musical terminology if you know it.

Don't worry if you are not an expert. You don't have to be to know what was interesting about the concert. If you do your best to fulfill the assignment, which is to have a fresh experience with classical music, and you write about it clearly, your report will be a good one.

##  Visiting the Art Exhibition

### EXPECTING THE UNEXPECTED

When you visit an art museum or gallery, have you ever had the experience of being puzzled or shocked by artwork that goes far beyond your expectations? If so, you are not alone.

The question "What is art?" has been debated by artists, art critics and historians for generations if not centuries. There are many controversial opinions regarding its purpose, social function, style and definition. For instance, in our individualistic age, our notions of art may stress self-expression. But this notion might never occur to the artists who lived in the Middle Ages, when the only acceptable purpose of art was to express the glory of God. Contemporary artist Cai Guo Qiang uses gunpowder and gunpowder fuses to create fascinating spectacles in grand scale. His works shocked many. Yet, to him, the very act of art is to show the artist's determination to break away from the past and create anew (see picture III-8 on page 53). As we visit the art galleries and museums we should view the art works with open minds and be aware of the fact that others may not share our own notions of art. "I do not know what is art, but I do know what I like" may very well be a valid answer to "what is art" for you.

### PUTTING ARTWORKS INTO CATEGORIES

Artworks vary in form, type, medium, purpose, function, and the way the images are rendered in their relationships to nature. Trying to put the piece that you choose to discuss into certain categories is a way to identify the uniqueness of the artwork.

*Form:* Some of the artworks are two-dimensional (height + width) such as painting, drawing, and book illustrations and some are three-dimensional (height + width + depth) such as sculpture and furniture, whereas others invite you to experience them through time, the fourth dimension! Architecture and mobile art are such examples. Artist

Zhen-Huan Lu created an illusion of 3D depth in his 2D oil painting *Snow Fence*. Chen Zhen's installation *Round Table*, although displayed in this book as a 2D picture, was originally created in a 3D art form. Cai Guo Qiang's *Parting of the Sea* requires the viewers to experience the changes made by gunpowder explosions throughout the viewing process. Just as when you watch a movie or a play, the time element is important to the artwork that changes and evolves during the viewing process.

***Type:*** To identify the type, ask yourself: "Is this piece watercolor, drawing, painting, sculpture, or installation art?"

***Medium:*** Identifying the material and tools the artist employed to create the work of art is a starting point for reaching an understanding of the technique and process involved in the creation of the piece. Is this piece watercolor, oil on canvas, polished bronze, or mixed media? Look at the label by the work on display. It usually informs you about the name of the artist, the medium of the work, the title, and sometimes even the size of the piece.

***Purpose/Function:*** If the art piece is intended solely for visual appreciation, it is considered a piece of *fine* art. If it is created primarily for a practical purpose (to be used) and/or a commercial purpose, then it is called *applied* art. In general, drawing, painting, and sculpture are examples of fine art, whereas industrial design, clothing design, commercial ads, and interior design are examples of applied art.

***Relation to Nature:*** *Objective (figurative) art* consists of artworks that describe the objects in a somewhat realistic fashion. *Non-objective (non-figurative) art* consists of artworks that do not suggest any object from the world of our experience. Cai Guo Qiang's *Sakurajima Volcano Time/Space Reversion Project* is such an example. *Abstract* art is a relatively more sophisticated term. On a superficial level, it refers to an art piece that suggests a known object with great economy. For instance, a single inward spiral line may be used to suggest a ballet dancer. On a deeper level, abstract art refers to works by those who aim at probing beneath the surface of life, making visible the invisible. Ayokunle Odeleye's *Harmony, Balance and Order* speaks to the interconnectedness among things. The trio of images—face, bird, and fish representing land, air, and water resources—serves as a metaphor for the flight and fluidity of the human spirit and its inter-relatedness to the physical world.

In his installation work *Round Table,* Chen Zhen uses familiar objects—a round table and twenty-nine chairs collected from five different continents across the world—but he extracts the essence of the known objects and rearranges them in a disjointed fashion to reveal the dilemma the United Nation faces on a daily basis. The round table, a ready-made, is a symbolic image derived from the Chinese "festive meal" and suggests unity, harmony, and dialogue; it also references the international "round table" conference, implying discussion, negotiation, political meetings, and power constraints. At first glance, the round table with the chairs placed around it appears to be an ideal setting for a gathering. People can sit around the table, each on a par with another, to the satisfaction of all. Yet ironically enough, as one looks into the piece more carefully, the strangeness of the relationships between the table and chairs surfaces: The chairs in the piece are embedded in the tabletop with one chair facing away from the table! How could anyone ever sit at the table? Are dialogue and agreement ever possible? As the artist puts it: "The metaphor of the 'round table' was aimed not only at the operating capabilities and the scope of power, but also at the various inequality issues in the development of the human kind." The ready-mades are familiar objects, but the artist uses them in ways that utter unspeakable ideas, and thus he guides the viewers on a journey into a realm beyond the obvious.[1]

## OBSERVING BUILDING BLOCKS OF ART

Another way to appreciate an artwork is to look at its building blocks and the way the artist applies those blocks to fabricate the visual edifice. Unlike verbal language, visual language is thought to be universal. Horizontal lines suggest repose, stability, and peace. No matter which country we live in, we lie down horizontally when we sleep. When the calmness of the sea allows us to see the horizon line from a great distance, we feel relaxed and restful. The color red excites us. We use it to suggest passion, to alert us to a dangerous situation, for it is the color of our blood and the fire. Artists use lines, shapes, space, texture and color as the building blocks to shape viewers' experiences and to create visual images that seek viewers' emotional and intellectual involvement and responses.

*Line:* We are most familiar with lines drawn by pens and pencils or formed by strings and wires. Artists use them to describe the objects or to express their feelings for the objects. For instance, in Ming Chen's costume design for Iris, the designer drew long, curved lines to suggest the folds of the costume and the soft and flowing quality of the fabric. In her set sketch for *Who's Afraid of Virginia Woolf,* a play by American playwright Edward Albee, Ming Chen employed short broken lines, diagonals, and cross diagonals to express the cruelties a husband and wife (the leading characters in the play) devise for torturing one another; this use of lines also emphasizes the degree of their violence and maliciousness as well as the depth of hatred conveyed throughout their conversations.

Lines can also be perceived when two values of the same color meet, two different colors meet, or even when they are just implied. In Zhen-Huan Lu's *Snow Fence* the horizon line, at which ocean and sky mingle, the rolls of sea foam and the fences in the distance bring calmness and peace to the picture. In the meantime, the outlines of the fences in the foreground and their shadows form curved lines that waltz toward the coast in the distance, adding a sense of liveliness, grace, and romance to the composition.

---

1. Chen Zhen, "Chen Zhen: Transexperiences," Center for Contemporary Art CCA Kitakyushu + Korinsha Press & Co., Ltd.

*Shape:*    Shapes are spaces enclosed by lines. They assume the qualities of lines that surround them. Triangles have diagonal lines and sharp corners. They are usually more aggressive and less inviting. On the contrary, soft rounds and ovals are sensuous, warm, and huggable. They remind us of a mother's body, stuffed animals, pillows, and gentle waves in the ocean. When looking into an artwork you may ask yourself, "Are the shapes in the picture geometric shapes?" "Do they resemble the objects?" Or, "Do they have no reference, whatsoever, to anything in the world of our experience?" "What are the personalities of those shapes?" "How do they make me feel?"

*Space:*    You may also ask yourself while observing an artwork: "Does the artist work with real 3D space or does he create the illusion of 3D space on a 2D surface?" Some artists make use of perspective painting techniques to describe 3D objects or vast spatial distances on 2D surfaces. In the oil painting *Snow Fence*, can you find some techniques the artist applied to suggest 3D objects and vast distance?

*Texture:*    The word texture refers to the tactile quality and surface characteristics of any material or object. Since each material or object is made of specific substances and constructed in a unique way, it possesses a special quality experienced by touching or handling. For instance, glass is smooth, hard, crisp, and cold, while in comparison, fur is rough, soft, flexible, and warm.

Tactile sensation is a human being's response to the textural material. It is the feeling we get by touch. However, by the time we are adults, we no longer need to touch to understand the texture. Merely by seeing the object, we are able to register a sensation for a given texture. Some artists deliberately use, describe, even enlarge or exaggerate the texture of the material to evoke viewers' tactile responses to the piece. For example: Cai Guo Qiang used gunpowder and gunpowder fuses to get the textural effect of the burning paper in his sketch for *Sakurajima Volcano Time/Space Reversion Project*. Ayokunle Odeleye's *Birthplace of Exceptional Men* is made of teak. The sensuous, flowing organic form, an image of cosmic existence,

### Perspective Painting Technique

- Things that are in the distance appear smaller are blurry and have less color intensity and or less value or color contrast.
- Things that are up close seem to be larger, clearer, and have more color intensity, and/or more value or color contrast.
- Things in the picture that are overlapping the tops of one another or nestling behind each other suggest spatial depth.
- Convergence of parallel lines into a point (or more) on the horizon line in a picture conveys a sense of distance.

is further enhanced by the beauty of the natural wood grain, the warmth of the material, and the smoothness of the surface texture brought out by the artist through sanding, staining, and polishing the piece in the working process.

*Color:*   Color has three properties, *hue* (the family name for a color—red, green, and blue, etc.), *value* (the darkness and lightness of a color), and *intensity* (the dullness or purity of a color). Each color can be described according to these properties. A rusty rose describes a purplish-red hue with a medium-dark value and a dull tone. Based on our physical reactions and our psychological, social, and cultural associations with color, we endow color with symbolic meanings. For instance, artists may use white to suggest purity, blue to suggest serenity and peace. Yellow reminds us of disloyalty in western culture; it is, however, the color designated for the ancient Chinese Emperors. It means, therefore, power and royalty to the Chinese.

Despite the fact that an individual color may have its own symbolic meanings, color is often seen in relation to the other colors that surround it. Examining the color combination will facilitate our perceptions of the overall emotional tone of an artwork. Bright, complementary colors form a scheme that arouses excitement and bold feelings, while soft pastel colors and monochromatic tones bring gentleness and quietness to a piece.

## UNDERSTANDING COMPOSITIONAL PRINCIPLES OF ART

Art theorists and artists have long tried to discern the rules behind great masterpieces and how they affect the viewer. It is generally accepted that the compositional principles of art and design include unity, variety, rhythm, balance, emphasis, and economy. These principles are organizational guidelines that focus on the relationships and interactions between the various visual elements in a piece rather than on individual elements by themselves. Here are some examples:

*Balance:*   Visual balance is a sense of stability established by means of an even distribution of weight and force in a composition. A composition without balance tends to appear haphazard and unsettling. There are generally three types of balance: *horizontal* balance, *vertical* balance, and *radial* balance. *Horizontal* balance is the balance between the left and right sides of the central dividing line. *Vertical* balance is the balance between the upper and lower parts of the composition. *Radial* balance is the combination of the two. Dome design is such an example. Some artists use left-to right mirror images (horizontal, symmetrical balance) in their works to convey a sense of authority, seriousness, or grandeur. Others try to avoid the static effect of a mirror image and instead compose images that look different on each side of the central dividing line yet still achieve a sense of even distribution of horizontal weight (asymmetrically balanced design). Zhen-Huan Lu's painting *Snow Fence* is such an example. To achieve a more dynamic and lively effect, the artist used more sea-waves on the left side to counter-balance the larger fence section on the right side of the composition.

*Emphasis:* Emphasis refers to a focal point or an area in a design to which other areas are subordinate, just as in the composition of a term paper your thesis statement is the focus of your paper, and all the evidence and descriptions are built around it. The center position is usually the natural focal point of a visual piece. However, a skillfully designed artwork can move the center of the attention from where the viewers' eyes would naturally fall to a desired area in the composition. In his *Snow Fence*, the artist uses ocean waves, fences and a path with converging lines to push the viewers' eye toward the seashore; in the original painting, he gave the beach chair and towel a glaze of red, the hottest color in the composition, so as to draw the attention of the viewer to the place where human activities are implied.

## Summarizing and Evaluating Your Viewing Experience

*Mood:* By answering a question such as whether the artist establishes a consistent emotional tone throughout the piece, you start to shift your attention away from a conscious, meticulous analysis of the artwork, and instead trust your instinctive and immediate response to the piece. The artist's choices of texture, color, and lighting quality will, no doubt, strongly affect the emotional tone of the piece, whether it is cheerful, mysterious, murky, or horrifying.

*Movement:* It may sound odd to discuss movement in a static artwork, but studies have shown us that the center of our attention does move as we take in an art piece. Revolving movement suggests mechanical energy and makes us feel disoriented and dizzy. Cascading movement suggests lightness and sprightliness. Converging movement draws us inward and implies consolidation. And descending movement puts crushing weight on us and makes us feel doomed and full of grief.

*Idea:* Is there a message that you think the artist is trying to send through his or her work? Some artists do have a strong message in mind when they create the piece, some are more open to the interpretations of the viewers, while others reject the notion that art should serve as a tool for social change. However, as a viewer, your response is always valid. Since, art is a way of communicating, the artwork can not be considered complete without the viewer's mental participation.

# ◈ Class Assignments

## REPORT FORMS

It is our belief that one's enjoyment of the arts can be enhanced by means of heightened perception of the creative process and the results that it yields. The following **Theater, Art Gallery,** and **Music REPORT FORMS** represent your opportunity to reflect upon the artistic choices being made in the various live events that you attend. They are a significant part of your work in Theater 1107. Please prepare them thoughtfully and carefully.

### I. Instructions:

- Re-read each report form before attending the performance or exhibit to remind yourself what you are being asked to critique in the arts event.
- Jot down specific observations and strong impressions during intermission(s) or soon after the performance if you are at a performance event. When attending a gallery exhibit you may write notes while viewing the work. These will help jog your memory when you write the actual report.
- All reports must be typed.
- Be sure that you answer each section of every question.
- When the question invites you to write a response, be as specific and detailed as you can. Use your own thoughts and words: This is **INDIVIDUAL** work.
- Look back at your notes from the pertinent lectures and practice using the appropriate dance, theater, or visual art vocabulary in your answers.
- Submit your report(s) in a pocket folder. Attach your ticket stub (for theater, dance, and music events) to the left-hand pocket, and put your program(s) in this left pocket. Put your report(s) in the right pocket. **Five points will be deducted for each missing item.**
- Papers are due **NO LATER** than the end of the class period on the due date. All late papers will be penalized by 10 points. Late reports will only be accepted on one alternate date. (See your syllabus.)
- Online gallery exhibits and music, and filmed dance, theater, and music performances are not acceptable events for these reports.
- In the event that you are unable to attend the specific dance or theater production that is assigned, you are permitted to substitute another **professional** performance. However, please note that you are only allowed **one** event substitution. You must fill out an **Event Substitution** form and obtain your professor's approval prior to attending the event. Submit the Event Substitution form along with your report form. The form can be found at the end of this section.

## II. Grading Criteria:

Your instructors will grade your reports according to the following criteria:

| Required Elements for Reports | F | D | C | B | A |
|---|---|---|---|---|---|
| **Thoroughness** | Leaves two or more 10-point questions blank or fails to answer 4 questions completely. | Leaves one entire 10-point question blank and/or 3–5 questions partially answered. | Neglects to answer parts of 3–5 questions, and/or answers all questions minimally. | Neglects to answer parts of 1–3 questions, or answers all questions but some minimally. | Answers all parts of each question completely and persuasively. May omit part of one question. |
| **Examples Based on Observations** | Only a couple of details, which are vaguely expressed and/or inappropriate. | A few examples are included, but they are either inappropriate or very generalized. | Examples are provided when asked for but they are minimal. | Examples are provided for almost all of the answers; some are vivid. | Vivid, clear, and appropriate examples are given for all answers. May omit a minor detail. |
| **Knowledge and Comprehension** | Does not use arts terms; there is no evidence that the text or notes were used for definitions. Many factual errors. | Terms are used without a demonstration of understanding, and they are often applied incorrectly. Many factual errors. | Terms are used when required, with a few errors. Several factual errors. | Terms are used with accuracy and frequency with a couple of errors. One or two factual errors. | Terms are frequently, with comprehension based on notes and textbook, and correct application. Facts are accurate. |
| **Mechanics and Presentation** | Spelling and/or grammatical errors in nearly every question. Many answers are difficult to read and/or comprehend. | Spelling and grammatical errors in most of the questions. Some answers are difficult to comprehend. Sloppy presentation. | Five to seven spelling and/or grammatical errors that do not affect comprehension. | Three or four minor grammatical or spelling errors. Neat presentation. | One or two minor grammatical or spelling errors. Neat presentation. |

- **Thoroughness:** The substantive questions in **Part II** of the reports have several components. Read carefully, and make certain that you address **every** aspect of the question.
- **Specific examples:** Include **specific** and **detailed** examples you have observed in the performances; the more concrete examples you include, the better your grade will be. Assume your instructor has not attended the event and needs very vivid and clear descriptions.
- **Comprehension:** Demonstrate accurate knowledge of all fact-based questions and terms. Make appropriate connections between terms and observed examples.
- **Mechanics or Writing Style:** While you will not be penalized for a spelling error here and there, your grade will suffer if there are numerous spelling and grammatical errors. Write in complete sentences in Part II, maintain correct spelling, and write neatly.
- **Remember** that 10 points are deducted for lateness and 5 points for each missing item.

# Arts in Society\*\*Theater Report A\*\*Acting and Directing\*\* Worth 40 Points

READ CAREFULLY ALL of the INSTRUCTIONS and GRADING CRITERIA at the beginning of this section in your book. Due Date: See Your Syllabus.

**Name:** _____

## I. FACTS (1 point each):

1. Title of production:

2. Name of theater building:

3. Name of theater *company:*

4. Name of playwright:

5. Name of director:

6. Size of theater (circle one):

   Large (@4,000–600 seats)        Medium (@599–99)        Small (@99 or less)

7. Staging format:

8. Format of curtain call (order and arrangement of bows):

9. Genre of play:

## II. The following questions require more thought and time, and are worth 10 points each. Be detailed and specific. Imagine your reader has not seen the production. One-word responses are not acceptable:

10. What acting moment made a significant impression on you? Why? Identify the actor AND character (by names), the **moment in the story,** and explain in detail what the actor did with his/her **body, voice,** and **emotions** that caught your attention.

11. Describe TWO moments where the director (through his/her use of blocking) created effective stage pictures (see glossary for definition). Explain why and how these stage pictures
    a. were visually compelling;
    b. supported the dramatic situation. (Answer in terms of story-line, emotions, character relationships.)

12. Review **concept** in your notes and in the glossary of this textbook. Describe what you think was the main idea of this production and explain WHY. Your answer should include descriptions of an acting moment, scenic elements, and costumes that helped to convey this interpretation. **NOTE:** If you did not discuss the director's concept beforehand, you must answer the question by incorporating ideas from the director's notes in the program and/or what you thought the production was attempting to communicate. If you were told the director's 'concept' prior to attending the production, state that concept and evaluate how effectively that concept was conveyed by means of acting, scenery, costumes, and at least **one** other production element (lighting, music, blocking). Give examples.

# Arts in Society**Theater Report B**Design & Production**
## Worth 40 Points

READ CAREFULLY ALL of the INSTRUCTIONS and GRADING CRITERIA at the beginning of this section in your book. Due Date: See Your Syllabus.

**Name:** _____

### I. FACTS (1 point each):

1. Title of production:

2. Name of theater building:

3. Name of theater *company:*

4. Name of playwright:

5. Name of director:

6. Size of theater (circle one):

   Large (@4,000–600 seats)        Medium (@599–99)        Small (@99 or less)

7. Staging format:

8. Format of curtain call (describe it, including the order and arrangement of bows):

9. Genre of play:

10. Names of scenic, lighting, sound, and costume designers:

### II. The following questions require more thought and time, and are worth 10 points each. Be detailed and specific. Imagine your reader has not seen the production. One-word responses are not acceptable:

11. Describe the SCENERY in detail, commenting on elements that were visually interesting and/or significant. (If there were multiple sets, choose **one**.) How did it help to make the production more effective? How did it contribute to the story/the theme of the play and/or the situation of the characters? Were any elements of the setting symbolic? Identify them and what they symbolized.

12. Choose ONE COSTUME that you thought was particularly effective and explain how it conveyed:
    a.  character traits (personality/age/gender); don't forget to identify the character.
    b.  period and locale

    Describe the costume in detail (i.e., articles of clothing, colors, types of fabric, the way it fit).

13. Choose **one** of the following two questions:

    As you watch the play, remember to listen for MUSIC and SOUND EFFECTS.* Select one instance where *each* was used to help a) enhance emotional impact; and b) help suggest location/atmosphere. Describe in each case what the music and/or sound conveyed, and judge its effectiveness. *SOUND EFFECTS are sounds other than musical underscoring that help create location, atmosphere, time of day (i.e., bells, clocks, outdoor sounds, etc.).

    Watch carefully how the LIGHTS are used: Look for colors, motion, expressive use of shadow, fast or slow changes in lighting, whether there are visible light sources, isolated pools of light. Using these features (and any others that might strike you), describe one moment where a lighting effect served to accentuate the storyline and/or an emotional moment.

# Arts in Society**Theater Report C**Musical Theater**
## Worth 40 Points

READ CAREFULLY ALL of the INSTRUCTIONS and GRADING CRITERIA at the beginning of this section in your book. Due Date: See Your Syllabus.

**Name:** _____

### I. FACTS (1 point each):

1. Title of production:

2. Musical Form (circle one):      musical comedy      musical drama
   musical revue opera     operetta     rock opera

3. Name of theater company:

4. Name of composer:

5. Name of lyricist

6. Name of book-writer

7. Name of director:

8. Size of theater (circle one):

   Large (@4,000–600 seats)      Medium (@599–99)      Small (@99 or less)

9. Staging format:

10. Format of curtain call (order and arrangement of bows):

### II. The following questions require more thought and time, and are worth 10 points each. Be detailed and specific. Imagine your reader has not seen the production. One-word responses are not acceptable:

11. Discuss a song that was particularly effective in expanding emotions beyond what is possible in a spoken drama or comedy. Identify the song, the character(s), the emotions, and describe how the music and lyrics expressed those emotions. Discuss where the song occurs in the story, and offer an explanation for why it is placed there.

12. Choose one dance number, and describe in detail how it
    a. was visually compelling
    b. contributed to mood
    c. helped to establish situation and/or tell the story

13. Is this musical designed primarily for entertainment? Did it contain a thought-provoking message? Both? How so? Explain your answer and give specific examples of songs, dance numbers, scenery, and costumes to support your point of view.

# Arts in Society**Theater Report D**Storytelling
## Worth 40 Points

READ CAREFULLY ALL of the INSTRUCTIONS and GRADING CRITERIA at the beginning of this section in your book. Due Date: See Your Syllabus.

**Name:** _____

### I. FACTS (1 point each):

1. Title of storytelling event:

2. Location and date of storytelling event:

3. Sponsoring organization(s):

4. Title of individual storytelling session attended:

5. Name of **all** individual people on the program of the session attended:

6. Size of audience (circle one):

   Large (@4,000–600 seats)     Medium (@599–99)     Small (@99 or less)

7. Name of emcee:

### II. The following questions require more thought and time and are worth 10 points each. Be detailed and specific. Imagine your reader has not attended the storytelling program. One-word responses are not acceptable.

8. Pick ONE teller to discuss: What makes this person an effective storyteller? How does the teller use **suspense,** build a **rapport with this audience,** or use his/her **body** and **voice** that is distinctive and memorable? **(10 points)**

9. Which story (or part of a story) carried the most meaning and relevance for you? Why? Describe the story/moment and the elements that created the connection. Incorporate the concept of 'empathy' into your response. **(10 points)**

10. Choose **TWO different stories** told in the session you attended (either by one teller or two different tellers) and compare and contrast HOW the stories were told AND WHAT the stories offered in content that made them compelling as narratives. **(10 points)**

# Arts in Society**Theater Report E**Production Critique
## Worth 50 Points

READ CAREFULLY ALL of the INSTRUCTIONS and GRADING CRITERIA at the beginning of this section in your book. Due Date: See Your Syllabus.

**Name:** _____

### I. FACTS (1 point each):

1. Title of production:

2. Name of theater building:

3. Name of theater company:

4. Name of playwright:

5. Name of director:

6. Names of scenic, costume, lighting and sound designers:

7. Size of theater (circle one):

   Large (@4,000–600 seats)          Medium (@599–99)          Small (@99 or less)

8. Staging format:

9. Genre of play:

### II. The following questions require more thought and time and are worth 10 points each. Be detailed and specific. Imagine your reader has not seen the production. One-word responses are not acceptable. Attach extra piece of paper as needed.

10. Pick ONE performer to discuss:

   a. Why do you think this performer was cast in his/her role? Include a description of the **character** in your answer and discuss what is appropriate and interesting about this casting.

   b. Describe by means of examples what the actor did with his/her **voice** and **body** to become the character.

   c. What was particularly compelling about this actor's performance?

11. Describe TWO moments where the director (through his/her use of **blocking**) created effective *stage pictures*. Explain why and how these stage pictures a. were visually compelling; b. supported the dramatic situation. (Answer in terms of storyline, emotions, character relationships.)

12. Describe the SCENERY in detail, commenting on elements which were visually interesting and/or significant. How did it help to make the production more effective? How did it *contribute* to the story/theme of the play and/or the situation of the characters? Were any elements of the setting symbolic? Identify them and what they symbolized.

13. **PICK *ONE* of the three questions below (5 points):** Choose ONE COSTUME that you thought was particularly effective and explain how it conveyed:
    a. character traits (personality/age/gender); don't forget to identify the character.
    b. historical time period, and location

    Describe the costume in detail (articles of clothing, colors, types of fabric, the way it fits).

    OR: *MUSIC AND SOUND EFFECTS.** Select one instance where *each* was used to help a) *enhance emotional impact;* and b) help suggest location/atmosphere. Describe in each case what the music and/or sound conveyed, and judge its effectiveness. *SOUND EFFECTS are sounds other than musical underscoring which help create location, atmosphere, time of day (i.e., bells, clocks, outdoor sounds, etc.).

    OR: Watch carefully how the *LIGHTS* are used: Look for colors, motion, expressive use of shadow, fast or slow changes in lighting, whether or not there are visible light sources, isolated pools of light. Using these features (and any others that might strike you), describe TWO moments where a lighting effect served to accentuate the storyline and/or an emotional moment.

14. How was this production relevant to our lives today? **(5 points)** Support your conclusion with TWO examples drawn from the acting, directing and/or design elements.

# Arts in Society** Classical or Jazz Music Concert Report**
## Worth 40 Points

READ CAREFULLY ALL of the INSTRUCTIONS and GRADING CRITERIA at the beginning of this section in your book. Due Date: See Your Syllabus.

**Name:** _____

### I. FACTS (1 point each, 10 points for this section):

1. What musician or group of musicians gave this concert?

2. Where did you go to hear it? (Name of concert hall or building):

3. Name the titles and composers of the pieces:

4. Identify the types of music performed in the concert (i.e., solo? chamber or orchestral music? choral music, band music?):

5. Identify the types of musical instruments used in each piece (i.e., strings, percussion, brass, woodwinds, voices, etc.):

6. Was there a conductor? If yes, who was she/he? If there was not, how did the performers stay together musically?

**II. The following questions require more thought and time and are worth 10 points each.** Be detailed and specific. Imagine your reader has not attended the concert. One-word responses are not acceptable:

7. Which piece of music made the greatest impression on you and why? In answering this question, discuss the following details: the types and numbers of instruments (remember, a voice is also an instrument); the length; the number of sections. Listen for **contrasts, similarities, repetition.** Incorporate descriptions of the following musical elements in your answer:

    **Rhythm** (the time aspect of the piece; arrangements of long/short notes):

    **Melody** (catchy? simple? complicated? repetitive? pretty?):

    **Dynamics** (the volume, as in relative softness and loudness, and how it varies):

    **Tone color** (the *quality* of the sound as determined by the instruments used; find your own adjectives to describe these qualities; e.g., bright, smooth, rich, harsh, hollow):

    **Tempo** (the pace, or speed of the music and how it varies):

8. Now that you have carefully described the way the composer and musicians have combined musical elements, describe the emotional qualities of this piece of music. Give several examples as to HOW these were evoked by the music and/or players. If the music conjured up visual images for you, describe those here.

9. Which performer made the greatest impression on you? Why? (If the concert featured only one performer, discuss his/her performance here.) Evaluate the effectiveness of that person's performance musically, emotionally, and in terms of stage presence. Describe three specific moments in the concert to support your answer.

# Arts in Society**Art Gallery Report**
## Worth 40 Points

READ CAREFULLY ALL of the INSTRUCTIONS and GRADING CRITERIA at the beginning of this section in your book. Due Date: See Your Syllabus.

**Name:** _____

I. **FACTS (1 point each):**

1. Gallery or museum visited:

2. Name of the exhibition visited:

3. Commercial exhibition or non-profit exhibition (circle one)

4. General nature of the exhibit (for example, an exhibit of watercolors, oils, photos, sculptures, installations, etc.):

5. Group show or solo exhibition (circle one)

6. Name of a specific piece you are choosing to discuss:

7. Name of the artist:

8. Form of the piece (2D, 3D, or 4D—time—as in mobile art; video is an example):

9. Medium of the work (watercolor, oil on canvas, mixed media, etc.):

10. Fine art or applied art (circle one). Consult the glossary.

II. **The following questions require more thought and time. Be detailed and specific.** Imagine your reader has not seen the exhibit. One-word responses are not acceptable:

11. Discuss in detail the CONTENT or subject matter of the piece. Imagine your reader has not viewed the work, and describe precisely what you see. (Save commentary on meaning for #13.) What is being depicted? In answering this question, consider the piece's relationship to nature: Does the artist present objects/persons as we see them in life; if so to what degree? Or does he/she depart from objects as we perceive them; if so to what degree? STATE whether the piece is representational (objective), abstract, or nonrepresentational. (10 points)

12. Now describe some of the following **visual aspects** of the piece **as well as your emotional responses** to the visual effects that have resulted from the choices of the artist:
    a. **Color** What colors are used; how are they juxtaposed?
    b. **Line** (diagonal? short? long? flowing? curves? horizontal? vertical?):
    c. **Shape(s)** (geometric shapes? invented shapes? skinny shapes? bulky shapes? shapes that have straight edges and sharp corners? shapes that have round, soft edges?):
    d. **Texture** (surface characteristics; material used to evoke the sense of touch):
    e. **Space** (suggestive of distance? open or enclosed space? 3-dimensional space?):
       (15 points)

13. Purpose/Ideas: What do you think the artist is trying to say with this work of art? Justify your response with examples of details. Be specific! (7 points)

# Event Substitution Form

**If you are unable to see an event, you should make every effort to attend another perform-
ance of the same production, and turn in your report on the established deadline.**

However, if you are unable to attend one of these events, you must submit this form and have it
signed by your faculty administrator. Only then may you substitute another **professional** event for
the event you miss. Please note that the events must remain in the same artistic field. (That is, only
another professional theater production may substitute for the required theater event.) You must
include this signed form in your report packet when you turn it in on the established deadline. *Permission to substitute events in no way implies permission to turn in a report later than the established
deadline.*

All late reports are penalized.

Please note that you may use the substitution option only **once** during the semester.

**Name:** _____

**Date:** _____

Which event will you miss?

Why must you miss this event?

What event will you see instead?

What professional group is producing this event?

Faculty approval of substitution: _____

Be sure to secure faculty approval for substitutions **before** you purchase tickets or expend resources
on an event. Approval is not automatic, and you do not want to be holding non-
refundable tickets for an event that your administrative faculty will not approve.

# *Arts in Society* Group Project

Each group is required to create a **five-minute** theater piece utilizing the concepts of theater we have studied throughout this semester.

Each member of the group must participate in some quantifiable, documented way. Each member does not have to perform, but his/her contribution must be specifically indicated in the program and represented in the Group Portfolio.

*Theme:*   Each group will choose one binding theme from the list below:

1) Dreams     2) Childhood     3) War     5) Fire     6) Love     7) Angels     8) Death

*Words:*   The Words of the piece must include words from:

1. **Shakespeare:** It can be from a play or a sonnet and may be as few as three words, or as many as three hundred.
2. **Original Words:** These words must be created by the members or member of the group: dialogue, a poem, a song, a paragraph, a thought, etc.
3. **Newspaper or Magazine:** It must have been published within the last month and pertain to the theme.
4. **Quotation:** A quotation that pertains to the theme. This quote must appear in the Program and may or may not appear in the script.

*Music:*   Your play must incorporate music—

1. It may be recorded or live. It can be as complex as a concerto or as simple as "Happy Birthday."
2. If the music has words in it, it may be counted as part of the words requirement.
3. There must be a music cue for the curtain call.

*Movement:*   This must be part of the overall fabric of the piece—as simple as hand clapping games, as complex as a rumba. It might simply be a piece that is carefully blocked by the director.

*Program:*   You must create a program; it should be visually interesting, and it must be typed. It must include:

1. A list of participants, their biographies and their responsibilities;
2. A quotation based on the binding theme;
3. An appropriate picture or graphic;
4. Director's notes.

*Design:*   COSTUMES/SCENERY/PROPS/SOUND/LIGHTS
You are responsible for everything the audience sees and hears. You do not have to build or create any costumes or scenery, but you should consider how the space in which the performers perform and how the costumes of the performers will affect the outcome of the piece. Consider how lighting or sound can affect the audience.

## GUIDELINES FOR GROUP PORTFOLIO

At the time of your performance (TBA), your group must turn in one thin **three-ring binder** that includes the following neatly arranged and **tabbed**:

1. Cover page for the portfolio;
2. Index of the portfolio;
3. Director's Notes. These should include comments about the significance of the 'binding theme,' your creative process, the challenges you've faced, the relevance of your play;
4. Blocking notes (either on the script, or clearly outlined on separate pieces of paper);
5. Scene design: A **ground-plan** (a drawing of the set and what it looks like from above);
6. Costume design descriptions and rationales for choices;
7. Sound design and notes, including the music used and your rationale for choices;
8. Lighting Design and notes (use the diagram we provide; it's on the web-site also.);
9. Properties Master's list of props;
10. The Script;
11. Immediately following it, a list that includes:
    a. The Theme;
    b. The Quotation which relates to your theme (Remember: this must also be included in your program.);
    c. The Shakespeare Words;
    d. The Newspaper/Magazine words.
12. Actors: each actor must type out his/her Character's Objectives (what his/her Character wants) and at least one Obstacle (something that stands in the way of getting what she/he wants);
13. Rehearsal Log: Record all your meetings and who attended. Record what happened in each meeting;
14. Your Program.

**Your Group Number and class day/time must appear on the front. Failure to turn in a Group Portfolio at the time of performance will result in a grade of "0" for the entire group.**

## SOME SUGGESTIONS

*Cast List:*  Positions one might hold in this project (if you think of another, contact your instructors):

   Director, Actors, Designers (Set/Costume/Lights/Sound/Props), Playwright(s), Program Designer.

If you have a large group, you can assign a separate person to design Set, Costumes, etc. If you have a small group, some of these tasks may be lumped together.

   **Remember, EVERYBODY has to participate in some QUANTIFIABLE way. Also remember that Theater is the art of collaboration. Therefore, YOU WILL BE GRADED AS A GROUP.**

1. GETTING STARTED:
2. Start by appointing a director. This person's responsibility is to make choices—let him/her.
3. Identify strengths/talents within the group. Who wants to perform, research, write, create programs, etc.? Any special talents?

4. You are granted in-class rehearsal time for this project. If you can meet outside, fine, but you have enough time (if used wisely) to complete the project in class. Come prepared (scripts written, lines learned, designs ready, etc.

5. Every production, company, and school has a weak link. The customer, student, and audience will not let you get away with that excuse and neither will we. Make the project work based on the strengths you have.

## GRADING

You are graded on the quality of your creative process and your Portfolios. That means commitment, a positive attitude, timely contributions and a collaborative spirit. Portfolios are graded according to how thoroughly you fulfill the guidelines listed above. If a group member's name is missing from your Program/Portfolio and that group member has been consistently absent, he/she will receive a 0 for the project. It is the group's responsibility to inform your professors both verbally and in writing if a group member is not collaborating and cooperating fully. That particular member's grade will be adjusted; the rest of the group's grade will not be affected.

*Each group of three absences that are not communicated in advance and that affect that group member's ability to contribute to the project will result in the loss of a letter grade for that student.*

# Class Activities

**The Arts in Society**
- Exercise #1: Valuing Art

**What Is Theater?**
- Exercise #2: What Is Theater?
- Exercise #3: The Theatrical Experience

**What Is a Play?**
- Exercise #4: Reading a Play
- Exercise #5: Creating a Plot Structure

**The Actor**
- Exercise #6: Acting in your Own Play

**The Director**
- Exercise #7: The Casting Process
- Exercise #8: Creating a Concept

**The Designers**
- Exercise #9: Costume Design
- Exercise #10: Character and Setting

- Exercise #11: Conveying the Mood with Lighting
- Exercise #12: Viewing Set Design
- Exercise #13: Viewing Costume Design
- Exercise #14: Viewing Lighting Design

**The Theatrical Process**
- Exercise #15: From Page to Stage: Creating a Theatrical Production

**The Producer**
- Exercise #16: Planning a Theatre Company

**The Audience**
- Exercise #17: Contemporary Theater

**Storytelling**
- Exercise #18: Storytelling: Telling Your Story

# Class Activity
# Valuing Art

**Your Name:** _____

In this class we will concentrate on your responses to the following selections of theater, visual art and music. Please focus on the work of art, and then jot down answers to the following questions.

### I. THEATER

Name of excerpt: _____, by
_____

After viewing the selection, write down descriptions of:

1. Your **gut** response to the scene:

2. What **happened** to you during the performance?

3. What did the scene **mean** to you?

## II. VISUAL ART

Jot down brief responses to each of the following questions as you look at each painting/sculpture:

1. Describe your sensations when viewing this work (emotional and/or physical);

2. What might this work of art mean? What elements communicate that meaning?

## III. MUSIC

1. What mood does the piece of music convey to you?

2. What visual images did it conjure up for you?

## IV. Are there connections between these three art forms? Jot down three things they have in common.

## V. Why do human beings need to experience and/or create art?

Jot down several reasons.

# Class Activity
# What Is Theater?

**Your Name:** _____

1. Write a definition of THEATER so that someone who has no earthly idea what it is will have a clear understanding.

2. Look back at your definition: What elements did you put in it that are ABSOLUTELY NECES-SARY to create theater? Jot them down in list form, and add any that you left out of #1. Like-wise, eliminate any which aren't absolutely essential.

3. Who makes theater? Make a list.

4. What distinguishes theater from other human activities?

5. Create a 60 second piece of theater which incorporates the elements you listed in #2.

# Class Activity
# The Theatrical Experience

**Your Name:** _____

## *Theater Terms*

The Curtain Call

Critiquing the Production

Actors Impersonating

Reservations and tickets

Willing Suspension of Disbelief

Publicity and Marketing

Resolution or *denouement*

Empathy

Ushers and Seating

House Lights Dim

Using the above list, write the "Order of a Theatrical Experience" in a step-by-step fashion in the blank spaces below:

1. _____

2. _____

3. _____

4. _____

5. _____

6. _____

7. _____

8. _____

9. _____

10. _____

# Class Activity
# Reading a Play

**Your Name:** _____

As you read the play you have been assigned, jot down impressions and questions. When you have finished, answer the following questions. (You will be turning this in.)

1. Describe the setting: Where does the play take place? (Give both the geographical location AND the specific locale.) Does the setting for the play change locations, or does it all take place in one locale? When does the play take place? Besides the *stage directions*, find clues in the dialogue which give details about the setting. Jot down TWO quotes (and page numbers) which give you information.

2. Which character did you EMPATHIZE with most, and why?

3. Describe a moment of TENSION in the play.

4. Write down a quote which communicates a THEME you have found in the play, and briefly explain what that theme is.

5. Write down two questions you have about the play.

# Class Activity
# Playwriting: Creating a Plot Structure

**Your Name:** _____

I. Jot down the definition of PLOT:

II. The following incidents are the "bare bones" of a plot; they are not put in the most effective order. Your task is to re-arrange the events below to create the most compelling plot structure.

1. Man on bench. Bubba enters, glares. Bubba slowly walks towards the Man. Someone's gonna get hurt. . . .

2. Fast food place. Bubba ordering. Man enters, stands behind Bubba. Bubba sees Man's ring, turns, looks at Man and says, "Where'd you get that ring?!" and leaves. (**Man has to give actress ring before scene 3**).

3. Sidewalk. Man and Woman pass, bump into each other. They smile as they walk away.

4. Bubba and Woman. Bubba: "I'll be right back." He leaves. Man enters, he and Woman steal a moment. She tells him he has to leave, they don't have much time (very Romeo and Juliet). Man gives her a ring and leaves, Bubba re-enters, sees the ring. Uh-oh . . .

5. Bubba and Woman on bench. "I catch you lookin' at another guy I'll kill you!"

III. Write down the new order below:

IV. Try writing your own plot structure, keeping in mind that you want to have a clear beginning, build suspense, and create some sort of resolution.

# Class Activity
## Acting in Your Own Play

Below you will see what we call an "OPEN" scene. It is waiting, full of possibilities for you to make some CHOICES and bring it to life!

DECIDE: Which one of you is A and which one B.

1. Read through the scene once. Your objective is to tell a clear story with the scene by means of your emotions, vocal inflections, and movements. Below are some questions to help you create your scenes. Jot down notes.

     I. **WHAT** is the situation? Create a story. Are there obvious or subtle tensions in the scene? Try to find a conflict; your story will be more compelling.

     II. **WHO** are these people? What kinds of personalities do they have? What is their relationship? What does each of them WANT in the scene; what are their emotional states (angry, sad, joyful, etc?). A variety of emotions will make the scene more interesting.

     III. **WHERE** are they? DESIGN the Set-up of your space and any furniture you need (chairs, tables, cars, trains planes—remember chairs can represent anything you want.) **INCORPORATE** at least **ONE PROP or costume accessory**—In fact these may give you ideas as to your situation and characters.

     IV. Now that you've made some CHOICES, rehearse the scene. Determine the **BLOCKING** (when and where the actors move/gesture) and the emotions for the scene. (That is, how do you want the characters to say the lines relative to the situation?) You may use the parentheses to jot down these blocking and emotion notes for specific lines.

A: Hello. (                          )

B: Oh . . . hi . . . (                          )

A: What are you doing? (                          )

B. Nothing. (                          )

A: Nothing? (                          )

B: Yes, nothing? (                          )

A: Then what's that? (                          )

B: What's what? (                          )

A: That! (                          )

B: Oh . . . (                          )

A: Well?! (                          )

B: Uh . . . bye! (                          )

A: Wait! . . . oh forget it . . . (                          )

END.

# Class Activity
# Directing

## The Casting Process

**Your Name:** _____

### *Head-shots and Resumes:*

As you review the following head-shots, write down the actor's name and some notes about the actor's 'type', age-range and physical attributes. Consider the play (TBA) you are casting. Then check whether you will call that actor in for an audition.

1. Name: _____
   - Age Range:
   - Type (circle one or more):   Juvenile   Ingenue   Leading Man   Leading Lady   "Character" actor

   - Other Notes about Personality Qualities:

   - Call in for an Audition? ___ Yes      ___ No

2. Name: _____
   - Age Range:
   - Type (circle one or more):   Juvenile   Ingenue   Leading Man   Leading Lady   "Character" actor

   - Other Notes about Personality Qualities:

   - Call in for an Audition?        ___Yes ___ No

3. Name: _____
   - Age Range:
   - Type (circle one or more):   Juvenile   Ingenue   Leading Man   Leading Lady   "Character" actor

   - Other Notes about Personality Qualities:

   - Call in for an Audition?        ___ Yes        ___ No

4. Name: _____
   - Age Range:
   - Type (circle one or more):   Juvenile   Ingenue   Leading Man   Leading Lady   "Character" actor

   - Other Notes about Personality Qualities:

   - Call in for an Audition?        ___ Yes        ___ No

## THE AUDITIONS

As you watch the actor(s) present auditions, jot down a few notes about each actor's qualities, and decide whether you would "Hire" this actor based on this audition, "Call back" to keep the actor in consideration and see more of his/her work, or "Reject" this actor based on this audition. (The actors will not see this form!)

**1. The Actor's Name:**

_____

Names of audition pieces

1. _____

2. _____

**Notes:**

Voice work:

Physical work:

Personality traits:

Emotional qualities/Believability:

Stage presence?


**2. The Actor's Name:**

Names of audition pieces

1. _____

2. _____

**Notes:**

Voice work:

Physical work:

Personality traits:

Emotional qualities/Believability:

Stage presence?

# Class Activity
# Directors

## CREATING A CONCEPT

A young girl whose grandmother was very ill decided to make the dangerous journey through the woods to bring her some soup and some comforting words. While traveling through the dark forest, a large wolf leaped out of the darkness and growled, "I'm going to eat you up!" "Please spare me!" cried the girl, "for my grandmother is very ill and needs me to take care of her." The wolf, being a very sly fellow, feigned pity and said, "Where does your grandmother live? I will show you the quickest way." The girl told the wolf where her grandmother lived, and the wolf, in his cunning, sent her down the longer of the two paths in the woods. The girl thanked the wolf and went on her way. The wolf took the shorter of the two paths and arrived at the grandmother's house before the young girl, swallowed the grandmother up, dressed in the grandmother's bedclothes and pulled the covers up just as the young girl knocked on the door. "Come in!" cried the wolf in the grandmother's voice. The young girl came in and exclaimed, "Grandmother, what big ears you have!" "The better to hear you, my dear," replied the wolf. "And what big eyes you have!" said the girl. "Why, the better to see you with!" said the wolf, who started to grin. "And what big TEETH you have!" exclaimed the girl. "The better to EAT you with!" growled the wolf, who leaped from the bed with a snarl as the young girl screamed. Just then, a woodsman felling trees nearby heard the screams, and burst through the door just as the wolf was about to devour the young girl. With one swing of his axe, he cut the wolf in two, releasing the young girl's grandmother from the wolf's stomach. They both thanked the woodsman profusely, and later that night, skipped the soup in favor of wolf stew.

1. In one sentence, write your interpretation of the MORAL or MAIN IDEA of the story. (This is the genesis for your *concept*.)

2. Now join a group of 4 students. Introduce yourselves.
   1)                                          2)

   3)                                          4)

Share your morals/main ideas, and select one that you will all work on developing together. Now brainstorm: how could you stage this story to EMPHASIZE the moral or main idea? Together, choose the following:

3a. SETTING: Include place and time (for example, Philadelphia in 1776), and describe what's visible onstage.

3b. COSTUMES for at least 3 characters: Include period, style, and colors.

3c. MUSIC for your production: style, instruments and specific songs, if you know them.

4. Brainstorm: Cast your story with well-known actors in order to EMPHASIZE the moral or main idea. List the actors and their roles, and explain why they are the best actors for the roles:

5. How do your design and casting choices clarify or emphasize your interpretation (or concept) of the story?

# Class Activity
# Design and Production

## COSTUME DESIGN

### *Brainstorm*
- According to the scene given, use three words for each character to describe your impression of the characters. Put the words of your choice in order of importance.

Character #1 (name) _____; Three words _____

Character #2 (name) _____; Three words _____

### *Character Analysis*
- **Define the characters:**
  Fill out the form below.

| | _____<br>(character's name) | _____<br>(character's name) |
|---|---|---|
| **Age** | | |
| **Gender** | | |
| **Race** | | |
| **Physical appearance** | | |
| **Social/economic status** | | |
| **Educational background** | | |
| **Profession** | | |
| **Moral standards** | | |
| **Personality** | | |
| **Motivation** | | |

- **Identify the characters' relationship:**
  1. How are the two characters related to each other?
  2. How are they similar to and how do they differ from each other?
  3. Do their motivations conflict with each other?

- **Identify the situational context:**

| Locale | |
|---|---|
| Place | |
| Period | |
| Time | |
| Season and Weather | |
| Characters' relation to the space | |
| Occasion/situation for dressing | |

- **Identify the genre of the play:**
- **Bridge your idea of characters with visual images:**

  Use words that contain visual clues to describe the two characters. For example: sharp, transparent, soft, gloomy, iridescent, mossy, metallic, etc.

  Character #1 (name) _____

  Character #2 (name) _____

- **Make design choices:**

  Use Mannequin Plates in your design process. If lines are not enough to express your ideas, please feel free to use notes.

  In your design, you need to make choices for each of the following items:

  1. Costume items (from head to toe)
  2. Costume silhouette
  3. Fabric
  4. Cut
  5. Color
  6. Accessories
  7. Hair style
  8. Make-up

Have fun!

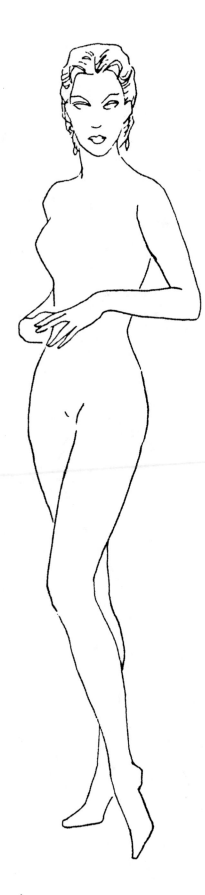

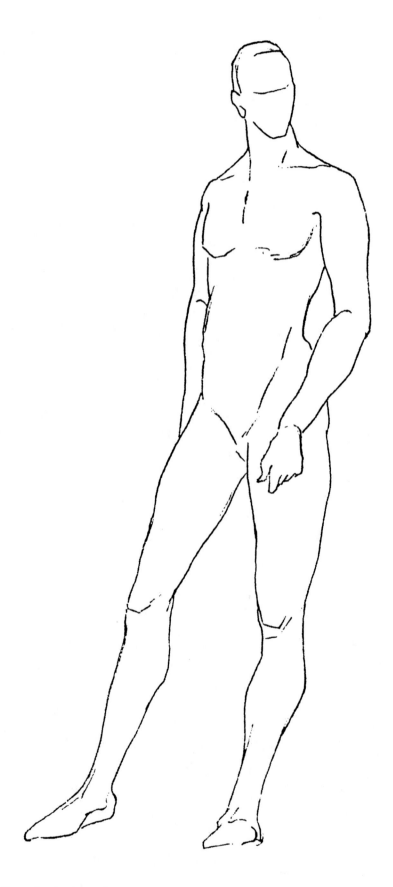

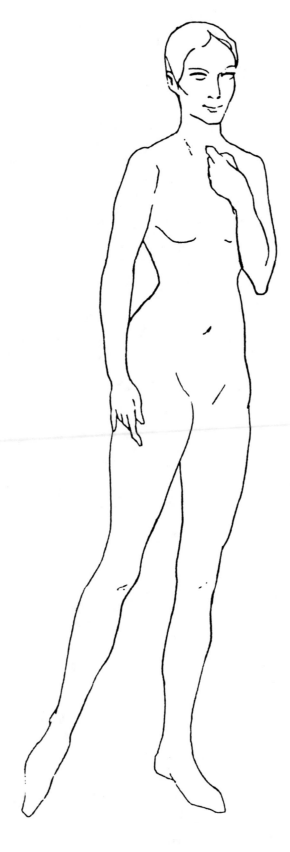

# Class Activity
## Designers

### CHARACTER AND SETTING

The place the character resides in reflects his/her social and economic status, taste, profession, trait, and hobbies etc. As you imagine the settings for the following characters, please take into consideration:

- The nature of the space (enclosed, open, cramped, many doors and windows, etc.)
- The kind of furniture and the arrangement of it (a bookcase by the desk, etc.)
- The set dressing (impressionistic painting on the wall or Braves baseball team banners, flags, and pictures of the players all over the room, etc.)
- The color scheme (black-white-red-gold or pastel colors, etc.)
- Light (neon light or isolated, practical light sources, etc.)

Try to imagine the settings for the following characters:

1. The study of an absent-minded professor of chemistry, who has worked at Georgia Tech for more than 10 years.
   Describe the setting:

2. A corner in the mansion of a drug dealer who has married an innocent wife and lives a double life.
   Describe the setting:

3. The drawing room of a wealthy miser.
   Describe the setting:

# Class Activity
# Designers

## CONVEYING THE MOOD WITH LIGHTING

You can create the mood or atmosphere for a scene through the assistance of light. As you conceive the lighting for the scenes described below, the properties of light are at your disposal.

- Source of light (sunlight, lamp, candlelight, etc.)
- Lighting direction and angle including the shadow (light from front, back, side, below, flat or with a steep angle, etc.)
- Lighting intensity (bright or dim, harsh or diffused, etc.)
- Color (blue, amber, purple, white, etc.)
- Area to be lit (spotlight, pool of light, flood-light or general light (all over), etc.)
- Motion (movement in light; for example, follow spot, changes in color or intensity, etc.)
- Shape or pattern (created by gobo, a patterned metal filter that the light shines through, or by image projector, etc.)

Now, let's try it.

Describe your lighting intentions for each of the following scenes:

Scene 1. At a bar, disco music is heard in the background. People are dressed in 60s clothes, dancing with the rhythm. Here, close up, Jason and May meet for the first time.

Lighting:

Scene 2. That night, Jane stayed at her deceased grandmother's country estate, the empty Lancaster castle. The old butler Lane had left home to be with his sick wife. It was quiet. In the middle of her dream, Jane was awakened by an unfamiliar voice calling her name. She grabbed the match, put on her nightgown, and followed the voice to the dark, narrow corridor, where she was immediately overwhelmed by a strong, strange smell that wasn't there during the day. She turned to her right and found the door to the dungeon was open. "Who is there?" she cried with a trembling voice.

Lighting:

Scene 3. Grace spreads the boldly patterned towel on the grass and starts to take out fruits and drinks from the basket. Suddenly, some movements at a short distance distract her. "Oh, look, Daddy—a blue jay!"

Lighting:

# Class Activity
# Design: Viewing Set Design

**Your Name:** _____

## Set Design:

Answer the following questions for each of the sets on the screen:

I. Name of show _____

   1. What is the most dominant **ELEMENT** of design in the scenery? Circle one.

      **Color**      **Line**      **Texture**      **Shape**      **Form**      **Space**

   2. What is the most dominant **PRINCIPLE** of design in the scenery? Circle one.

      **Unity**      **Variety**      **Balance**      **Emphasis/Focal Point**

             **Proportion/Scale**      **Rhythm**

   3. What geographical location and/or locale does the scenery convey?

   4. What time period does the scenery convey?

   5. What mood/atmosphere is created?

   6. What possible theme(s) are suggested?

II. Name of show _____

   1. What is the most dominant **ELEMENT** of design in the scenery? Circle one.

      **Color**      **Line**      **Texture**      **Shape**      **Form**      **Space**

   2. What is the most dominant **PRINCIPLE** of design in the scenery? Circle one.

      **Unity**      **Variety**      **Balance**      **Emphasis/Focal Point**

             **Proportion/Scale**      **Rhythm**

   3. What geographical location and/or locale does the scenery convey?

   4. What time period does the scenery convey?

   5. What mood/atmosphere is created?

   6. What possible theme(s) are suggested?

**III.** Name of show _____

    1. What is the most dominant ELEMENT of design in the scenery? Circle one.

        **Color**       **Line**       **Texture**      **Shape**      **Form**      **Space**

    2. What is the most dominant **PRINCIPLE** of design in the scenery? Circle one.

           **Unity**     **Variety**     **Balance**     **Emphasis/Focal Point**

                  **Proportion/Scale**     **Rhythm**

    3. What geographical location and/or locale does the scenery convey?

    4. What time period does the scenery convey?

    5. What mood/atmosphere is created?

    6. What possible theme(s) are suggested?

# Class Activity
# Design: Viewing Costume Design

**Your Name:** _____

## *Costume Design*

Answer the following questions for each of the costumes on the screen:

I. Name of show _____

   1. What is the most dominant **ELEMENT** of design in the costume? Circle one.

     **Color**       **Line**       **Texture**       **Shape** ("silhouette")

   2. What **occupation** does the costume suggest?

   3. What **two personality traits** does the costume convey?

   4. What social or economic status does the costume convey?

II. Name of Show _____

   1. What is the most dominant **ELEMENT** of design in the costume? Circle one.

     **Color**       **Line**       **Texture**       **Shape** ("silhouette")

   2. What **occupation** does the costume suggest?

   3. What **two personality traits** does the costume convey?

   4. What social or economic status does the costume convey?

**III.** Name of Show _____

    1. What is the most dominant **ELEMENT** of design in the costume? Circle one.

       **Color**        **Line**        **Texture**        **Shape** ("silhouette")

    2. What **occupation** does the costume suggest?

    3. What **two personality traits** does the costume convey?

    4. What social or economic status does the costume convey?

# Class Activity
## Design: Viewing Lighting Design

**Your Name:** _____

Answer the following lighting questions for each slide:

I. Name of Show _____

    1. What is the most dominant **"variable"** of lighting design in the slide? Circle one.

       **Color**        **Intensity**        **Direction/Angle**        **Form**        **Diffusion**

    2. What **mood** is created by the lighting?

    3. Is the effect **realistic** or **theatrical?** Explain your choice.

II. Name of Show _____

    1. What is the most dominant **"variable"** of lighting design in the slide? Circle one.

       **Color**        **Intensity**        **Direction/Angle**        **Form**        **Diffusion**

    2. What **mood** is created by the lighting?

    3. Is the effect **realistic** or **theatrical?** Explain your choice.

# Class Activity
## From Page to Stage: Creating a Theatrical Production

**Your Name:** _____

**Steps in the Theatrical Process:** (Do you have a clear understanding of each of the steps below?) Write down TWO questions about them.

1.

2.

Actor Coaching

Dress Rehearsal

Auditioning

Pacing the Play

Meeting and collaborating with Designers to develop designs

Play Analysis

Preview

Reading and re-reading the play

Blocking the Play

Opening Night

Casting the Show

Technical Rehearsals

'Read-through'

Choosing the Play

Standing Ovation (hopefully!)

Creating a Concept

**Using the List above, write down the step-by-step order of bringing a play from the "page to the stage."**

# Class Activity
## Artistic Director/Managing Director
## Non-profit Theater

### SELECTING A SEASON AND BALANCING THE BUDGET

Find a partner and tackle the problem of selecting a season of plays with an eye towards balancing the budget.

**Your Annual Budget: $1,000,000.00**

*Your Income:*

Insert figures according to the typical percentages discussed in lecture.

Earned Income: _____

Unearned Income: _____

Amount of Money you MUST earn in Ticket Sales: _____

### *Seven Plays Below. Pick Five:*

- *Hamlet* starring David Schwimmer from T.V.'s hit sit-com *Friends;* his quirky persona will make a terrific Melancholy Dane ($125,000 in projected ticket sales; thank you, David.)
- *A Christmas Carol,* a holiday classic everyone schedules into his/her holiday activities! (brings in $160,000)
- A favorite musical: *The Sound of Music* (It will bring in $150,000, but you'll have to add another $100,000 in expenses.)
- A Comedy: *Frasier, Live Onstage* (will bring in $75,000)
- *Treasure Island,* a family classic! ($65,000)
- A play called *Idioglossia,* our provocative world premiere; if we don't produce it we stand to lose our resident playwright whose world premiere works gather us significant prestige as a serious theater company (will only bring in $35,000)
- Compelling Drama! And an enduring American classic: *A Streetcar Named Desire* (Brings in $50,000; every year you get a $50,000 gift from a Southern lady who LOVES Tennessee Williams, and you want to keep receiving her gifts!)

### PICK YOUR SEASON AND BALANCE YOUR BUDGET!!!

IF YOU DON'T GET 2 OUT OF THE 3 SERIOUS PLAYS INTO THE SEASON YOUR SUBSCRIBER BASE (core audience) IS IN DANGER OF ERODING. YOU MIGHT MAKE IT UP IN SINGLE TICKET SALES, BUT THAT'S RISKY.

IF YOU DON'T BALANCE THE BUDGET YOU'RE FIRED. OR THE THEATER CLOSES.

# Class Activity
## The Audience

CONTEMPORARY THEATER: "IT'S SATURDAY NIGHT! LET'S TAKE IN A PLAY."

**I. First:** Please jot down what kind of experience YOU WANT out of an evening at the theater (for example: a good laugh? a good cry? grand spectacle? etc. Don't limit yourself to these examples):

**II. Viewing of video clips:**

A. Match the video clips on the LEFT column with the types of theater on the RIGHT. (Draw lines, or match letters to numbers.) More than one "type" may apply.

1. _____        A.  Musical (revival)

2. _____        B.  Solo Performance

3. _____        C.  New Musical

4. _____        D.  Intercultural Theater

5. _____        E.  Play (revival)

6. _____        F.  Ethnic Theater

7. _____        G.  Performance Art

8. _____        H.  Dance Theater

9. _____        I.  Gay or lesbian theater

**III.** A. NOW: You're in New York City, and you've got a wad of dough. Which of these shows would you go see?

*RANK THE CLIPS IN ORDER OF PREFERENCE,* #1 indicating your first choice, #2 your second, and so forth.

B. In one or two sentences give reasons for your first and last choices.

C. Discuss your preferences with someone else. How do your preferences correspond with your answer to #1?

# Class Activity
## Storytelling: Telling Your Story

**Your Name:** _____

1. Sit down next to a partner and introduce yourselves.

    Name of your partner _____

2. Tell each other your stories. Jot down your topic here.

3. Share comments about the stories. Jot down a comment or two that your partner made about your story below.

4. How can you tell the same story with more impact? Jot down some ideas.

5. Sit next to a new partner and tell the same story. (Try out some of your ideas from #4.)

    NAME of NEW PARTNER _____

6. After you have finished, make a few notes about how your second telling was different.

#  Terms

Below you will find definitions for terms which you are asked to utilize in your report forms:

*balance in visual art:* the visual effect of even distribution of weight in a work; symmetrical balance is achieved when two sides of a work are mirror images of one another; if this is not the case, the artist is using *asymmetrical balance.*

*blocking:* All of the actors' movements during the performance of a play. This includes entrances and exits on and off the stage as well as physical actions within the scenes. The blocking in a production is achieved through a collaborative effort by the playwright (by means of *stage directions* written in the script), the director, and the actors.

*book-writer:* the person who writes the dialogue for the spoken parts of a musical play.

*casting:* the process the director undergoes to select the most promising actor for each role in a play

*concept:* the theater director's central idea or interpretation of a playscript which informs all of the acting, blocking, and scenic, costume, lighting and sound design choices that are made for a particular *production* of that script.

*climax:* the maximum point of tension in a play. It often results in a turning point for the central character(s).

*composer:* the person who writes the music for an individual musical piece, or for an entire musical play, opera, operetta, etc.

*curtain call:* the series of bows taken by the actors after the performance of a play has ended.

*denouement:* the resolution of a play. French for "untying" the knot(s) or resolving the complications and conflicts within the plot of the play.

*empathy:* an audience member's feeling of mental and/or emotional identification with a character's emotions and/or problems in a play.

*fine art versus applied art:* In the visual arts, *fine art* is work which is created solely for visual, emotional and intellectual appreciation, whereas *applied art* is created for a utilitarian or commercial purpose.

*genre:* "kind" in French; this refers to the type or category of a particular play, such as tragedy, comedy, melodrama, musical, farce, etc.

*libretto:* the dialogue for the spoken parts of a musical play.

*lyricist:* the person who writes the lyrics or words to the songs in a musical play.

**plot:** series of compelling actions structured by the playwright to elicit suspense in the audience.

**production:** the particular version of a play-script which is brought to the stage by the collaborative efforts of the director, actors, and designers; the term is used to differentiate the *performance* of a play from the *script* or *text*.

**scenery:** the physical construction(s) onstage that are designed by a scenic designer after discussions with the director; scenery is a visual indication of location, time period, mood, and often theme for the play.

**set:** refers to the scenery for a play or one particular scene; plays which have different locations often have different sets which are changed as the play progresses.

**stage direction:** descriptions of setting, blocking, character emotions written by the playwright into the script. Often in parentheses and italicized.

**stage picture:** the visual compositions that a director creates using actor positions and gestures amidst the scenery. Lighting and costuming also play significant roles in stage pictures. The director uses these "pictures" to help illuminate the story and character relationships as well as create visual interest for the audience.

**staging format:** There are four basic staging formats: 1) *proscenium* (a rectangular theater where the audience sits on one side facing the stage on the other; 2) *thrust* (the audience sits on three sides of the stage); 3) *arena* or *"theater-in-the-round"* (the audience surrounds the stage on all sides); 4) *black box* (a bare room or open space where the audience seating can be set up in different ways for each production; the name comes from the fact that the space is usually painted black. Often used for more "experimental" theater.)

**suspension of disbelief:** an audience member's unspoken agreement to "believe" mentally and emotionally in the imaginary world of the play. The expression was coined by the 19th Century British poet Samuel Taylor Coleridge.

**theme:** central idea within a play; message or moral which the action and characters of a play convey.